# PRIVATIZATION IN TURKEY

# Studies in Critical Social Sciences Book Series

Haymarket Books is proud to be working with Brill Academic Publishers (www.brill.nl) to republish the *Studies in Critical Social Sciences* book series in paperback editions. This peer-reviewed book series offers insights into our current reality by exploring the content and consequences of power relationships under capitalism, and by considering the spaces of opposition and resistance to these changes that have been defining our new age. Our full catalog of *SCSS* volumes can be viewed at https://www.haymarketbooks.org/series_collections/4-studies-in-critical-social-sciences.

# PRIVATIZATION IN TURKEY

Power Bloc, Capital Accumulation and State

## AHMET ZAIFER

Haymarket Books
Chicago, IL

First published in 2022 by Brill Academic Publishers, The Netherlands
© 2022 Koninklijke Brill NV, Leiden, The Netherlands

Published in paperback in 2023 by
Haymarket Books
P.O. Box 180165
Chicago, IL 60618
773-583-7884
www.haymarketbooks.org

ISBN: 978-1-64259-924-4

Distributed to the trade in the US through Consortium Book Sales and
Distribution (www.cbsd.com) and internationally through Ingram Publisher
Services International (www.ingramcontent.com).

This book was published with the generous support of Lannan Foundation,
Wallace Action Fund, and the Marguerite Casey Foundation.

Special discounts are available for bulk purchases by organizations and
institutions. Please call 773-583-7884 or email info@haymarketbooks.org for more
information.

Cover design by Jamie Kerry and Ragina Johnson.

Printed in the United States.

Library of Congress Cataloging-in-Publication data is available.

# Contents

# Acknowledgements

There are many people who contributed to bringing this book to completion and in stimulating my ideas and thoughts on privatization and Turkey. I would particularly like to thank Thomas Marois, Şebnem Oğuz, Eren Düzgün, Fuat Ercan, Pınar Bedirhanoğlu, Galip Yalman, Zülküf Aydın, Gilbert Achcar, and Kate Bayliss who all read drafts or excerpts of this book at some point. I greatly appreciate the time these individuals gave to seriously engage and offer criticisms and comments. I would also like to thank the *New Scholarship in Political Economy* and *Studies in Critical Social Sciences* series editor David Fasenfest for his extremely helpful editorial input throughout the preparation of this book.

Many of the ideas in this book originate in my Ph.D. dissertation, completed in 2016 in the development studies department at SOAS, University of London. I thank all the faculty staff that made my time at SOAS such a pleasure and exciting learning experience. There are very few academic institutions that truly encourage critical thought in a contemporary university setting – the SOAS development studies department was one of these and it was a privilege to study and work alongside an exceptional group of faculty and graduate students. In particular, I would like to thank Thomas Marois, my dissertation supervisor. Thomas remained a wonderful intellectual mentor and friend who taught me an enormous amount about understanding the world and working to change it. This book would not have been possible without him.

While writing this book I spent six months in London carrying out research at the SOAS library and teaching at the Kaplan International College London (KİCL). Staff at KİCL were generous with their time and friendship. In particular, I would like to thank deeply Vjekoslav Butorac, Academic Director of KİCL. There are many other friends and relatives in London that also made my research possible. A special mention is needed for my aunt Pembe Balıkçıoğlu.

Finally, this book is dedicated to my wife, Şerife Komut, and my parents, Emine and Zafer Zaifer.

# Figures and Tables

## Figures

## Tables

# CHAPTER 1

# Introducing the Privatization in Turkey

Turkey is currently pursuing an aggressive and comprehensive privatization program, which involves different forms of privatization from divestiture to public-private partnership (PPP). Divestiture, known as classical privatization, occurs when all or some assets of a state in a state-owned enterprise (SOE) are transferred (or leased for long-term) to the private sector either through block sale or through public offering and capital markets. In 2013 and 2014, Turkey was the second-leading and third-leading non-EU privatizing country in terms of divestiture (Privatization Barometer 2015). PPP is a long-term contract (e.g., 20 and 30 years) between a private party and a state entity under which the private sector finances, builds, and operates major infrastructure projects from highways and airports to hospitals. Many PPPs involve new assets – often called greenfield projects (World Bank 2017). In conceptual terms, PPPs can be regarded as the present privatization of future state investments (Marois 2019). In 2017 and 2018, European PPP Expertise Centre counted Turkey as the largest PPP market in Europe in terms of value (EPEC 2019).

Yet privatization in Turkey has not always been that aggressive and comprehensive since its inception in 1984. For that purpose, the actual experience of privatization in Turkey can be categorized into two strikingly different phases. In the first phase, which corresponds to the period from 1984 to the economic crisis in 2001, privatization involved a slow pace and limited progress. As a reflection of the limited progress, first phase privatization value reached only about $19.7 billion, which averaged 0.69 per cent of the GDP per year. Just $7.5 billion of this value comes from divestiture while PPP amounts to $12.2 billion (see Table 1). The momentum of Turkey's privatization program, which continued today, gathered pace only in the aftermath of 2001 under a single-party AKP (*Adalet ve Kalkınma Partisi* – Justice and Development Party) government. The AKP came to power in November 2002 by forming one of Turkey's rare majority governments. The AKP had been established only in August 2001 from the remnants of the Islamist RP (*Refah Partisi* – Welfare Party), with the support of social and religious conservatives and representatives of Anatolian capital (Marois 2012, 177). The privatization program of the AKP first mostly opted for the full divestiture method in the 2000s, and then a mixture of divestiture and PPP methods during the 2010s. As a result, total privatization value of Turkey from 2002 to 2018 reached a record $190.1 billion ($62.7 billion divestiture and \$127.4 billion PPP), which averaged 1.61 per cent of the GDP per year (see Table 1).

Employing a Marxian-inspired analytical framework, this book seeks to explain the post-2001 acceleration of privatization in Turkey. From the onset, I challenge the dominant liberal-cum-institutionalist interpretations that have been given by many scholars during the 2000s. At the beginning, the liberal-cum-institutionalist interpretations mainly drew on legal and institutional framework to explain the success of privatization – the argument that what prevented privatization before 2001, and what enabled privatization after 2001, were institutions: the absence of strong institutions before 2001 and the presence of strong institutions after 2001 (which was achieved by the establishment of new Independent Regulatory Agencies, the strengthening of the Privatization Authority, the enactment of the FDI law).[1] Yet many of these accounts saw institutions as the final and determinant context. There was therefore a need to move beyond institutions, without jettisoning them, to understand the political struggles underpinning the formation of these institutions and the acceleration of privatization.

More recently, liberal-cum-institutionalist interpretations began drawing attention to the political struggles. They did this more out of necessity, and less out of choice. They had to do it because the AKP government not only curtailed the autonomy enjoyed by the regulatory and legal state institutions, but also concentrated most of the decision-making powers at the hands of the upper echelons of the party that quickly turned these legal and regulatory institutions into extensions of various ministries and the Presidency. It was, therefore, become impractical for these scholars to keep considering 'institutions' as the key explanatory variable of the privatization processes.

Under the new circumstances, some liberal-cum-institutionalist scholars developed analysis of government/business and/or state/capital relations in terms of "coalitions" and/or "networks" to explain the acceleration of privatization in Turkey.[2] For them, these networks were linking the government officials to the business actors, and thereby help the government to provide advantages to favourable (or selected) ones in privatization implementations (Buğra and Savaşkan 2014, 77). It has been argued that the AKP government has promoted privatization to support favourable business groups, while the

---

1    See Ertuna 1998; Fıçıcı 2001; Atiyas 2009; Güran 2011.
2    See Buğra and Savaşkan 2014; Özcan and Gündüz 2015; Gürakar 2016; Ocaklı 2018; Dorlach and Savaşkan 2018; Esen and Gümüşçü 2018.

TABLE 1    Privatization value in Turkey, 1984-2018 ($ billion)

|  | Divestiture value | PPP value | Total privatization value | Privatization value relative to GDP (%) |
|---|---|---|---|---|
| 1984–2001 | 7.5 | 12.2 | 19.7 | 0.69 |
| 2002–2018 | 62.7 | 127.4 | 190.1 | 1.61 |

SOURCE: CENTRAL BANK OF TURKEY; T.C. CUMHURBAŞKANLIĞI STRATEJI VE BÜTÇE BAŞKANLIĞI; WORLD BANK

preferences of these business groups have also shaped policy content on privatization much more profoundly than other socio-economic actors (Dorlach and Savaşkan 2018, 4; Gürakar 2016, 67).

Indeed, the main thrust of this argument is that favoritism in Turkey prevails within the atmosphere of the highly polarized business community (Buğra and Savaşkan 2014). In that regard, it is said that there are two rival business groups with wide disparity in privatization chances. The first group involves the TÜSİAD (Turkish Industry and Business Association) based secular entrepreneurs, which have tense relations with the AKP, and largely excluded from privatization tenders. The second group comprises MUSİAD (Independent Industrialists and Businessmen Association) based religious entrepreneurs and Anatolian capitalists, which are loyal to the AKP, and offered privileged access to privatization tenders. The liberal-cum-institutionalist literature characterizes this second group as 'favourable'; Turkey's privatization process is thus seen as part of rising favourable business groups (i.e., religious, Anatolian, and politically connected) and their evolving relationship with the AKP government within the context of the polarized business community.

As is to be expected, much attention of the liberal-cum-institutionalist scholars was devoted to identifying which favourable business groups have participated in the privatization tenders, and how these groups expanded in size and power as a result of the success in those tenders. For example, Buğra and Savaşkan (2014) identified ten business groups such Cengiz Holding, iç Holding, Çalık Holding, Kalyon Group, Ethem Sancak that have grown at a relatively high rate through privileged access to privatization and public procurement tenders.

These accounts gained widespread popularity after two conjunctural events happened in Turkey.[3] The 2013 corruption scandal that had reached the inner circle of the then Prime Minister Recep Tayyip Erdoğan brought politically connected nature of government/business relations as well as government's favourable treatment of particular business groups into the spotlight. Moreover, Turkey's mega projects that involved investment in infrastructure with the PPP model have sparked intense debate since the early 2010s concerning the selection of the above-mentioned business groups with close relations to the AKP as project companies that will construct the works (and then operate for certain period) and the state guarantees used in these projects.

There is no denying that the liberal-cum-institutionalist literature drew attention to political struggles and produced a convincing explanation of the acceleration of privatization in Turkey in the midst of these conjunctural events. The explanation appears compelling and deserves careful reading. However, it hides more than it reveals. First, the literature's strong focus on the struggles among fractions of capital and the privileged access of the favourable (religious-loyal) business groups to privatization tenders is allowed to obscure the fact that privatization, as a policy, consolidates the position of *Capital in General* in Turkey. Second, it is also striking that most contributors to this literature tend to disregard or simply ignore how the structural imperatives of global capitalism and domestic capital accumulation regime as well as the associated material demands of the Turkish economy actually condition the agency of actors that plan, make and participate Turkey's privatization strategy (Albo 2005, 79). For example, the AKP government's recent PPP program was not only designed to support favourable business groups, but also linked to the ways in which the government had to create new investment opportunities to revive economic growth, which also contributed directly and indirectly to the development of the so-called rival "secular TÜSİAD groups" (as is discussed in Chapter 5).

Marxian approaches could potentially help us to avoid these problems. Yet by elevating either external factors or political struggles (albeit in their class-oriented position) above all other explanatory factors of Turkish privatization process, Marxian approaches have narrowed their critical potential. One Marxian approach, which is clearly influenced by the David Harvey's

---

3  For coverage of the subject in popular press, see, for example, "Erdoğdu: Kamu Özel İşbirliği Projeleri Ülkeyi İpotek Altına Alıyor", *Dünya,* 4 March 2018; "Emre Deveci: Yandaşa 71 Milyar Dolarlık Dev Kıyak", *Cumhuriyet,* 10 January 2018; "Can Uğur: Yürü ya kulum denen 6 şirket", *Birgün,* 24 February 2016; "Bahadır Özgür: İşte Türkiye'yi Batıracak Tezgah", *Gazete Duvar,* 28 May 2018.

*accumulation by dispossession* (2003) and James Petras and Henry Veltmeyer's *outside-in account* (2001), appears to posit an "externally" imposed explanation of privatization in Turkey. According to this externally oriented approach, the shifting structural imperatives of global capitalism (e.g., financialization), global powers (e.g., the United States) and international financial institutions (e.g., the IMF, and the World Bank) imposed privatization "downwards" on Turkey's national and domestic political spaces.[4] This explanation seems problematic in two interrelated aspects. First, it leaves unexamined how other potentially active "internal" social factors contest, override, mediate, or shape the overstated external pressures towards privatization. Second, it is therefore far less concerned with the systematically uneven or variegated development of privatization – its acceleration, deceleration, breaks and hesitations within specific social formations – across geographical spaces. For example, even though privatization was thrust on Turkey by the structural dynamics, the IFIs and global capital, its implementation has been contested domestically in the 1980s and 1990s, which resulted in limited privatization compared with the privatization records of other similar emerging countries over the same period (Güran 2011, 23).

Another Marxian approach that is prevalent in the Turkish context is neo-Gramscian-inspired analyses.[5] These analyses analytically emphasize the importance of internal social forces and focus on the political dimensions of privatization. However, contrary to the liberal-cum-institutionalist literature, they integrate the concepts of social class and hegemony in their political analysis of why and how privatization accelerated in Turkey. Because of this, neo-Gramscian analyses are more capable of exposing the embedded nature of class power in the privatization process. By doing so, they demonstrate that privatization is a class-based policy that systematically privileges the interests of domestic and foreign capital over those of Turkey's laboring classes. In one example of these neo-Gramscian analyses, Merih Angın and Pınar Bedirhanoğlu (2012) locates the privatization processes in the political struggles, involving multi-level class conflicts that end up reproducing a particular "normality" in state-capital-labour relations at the expense of others, which in turn helps increasing the subordination of the state to capital.

Yet, these neo-Gramscian analyses still have one major weakness. Although they emphasize political struggles from class perspective, they seem to ignore

---

4 For the advocates of this approach in Turkey, see, for example, Ataay (2003); Yeldan (2005); Boratav (2010, 2011).
5 For neo-Gramscian analysis of Turkish privatization process, see, for example, Şahin (2010); Angın and Bedirhanoğlu (2012).

the impact that prevailing dynamics of domestic capital accumulation regime of Turkey (e.g., duty losses, state-debt financing, economic revival) also act back on the social class forces and reshape their strategies. This results in the "overpoliticization" of the privatization process. By overpoliticization, I mean reducing the privatization process to merely the political struggles that emanate from the rivalry of those who will actually buy the enterprises to be privatized (intra-capital struggle) as well as those struggles that will determine who will pay the expenses of privatization (class struggle between capital and labour) without detailed consideration of how the development of the domestic accumulation regime also acts back on the strategies of these class actors. For example, the unwillingness of the TÜSİAD-based big holdings to support privatization in Turkey in the 1980s and 1990s was not only reflected conflict with the interests of Anatolian capital fractions and foreign capital. It was also shaped by the dynamics of capital accumulation in Turkey at the time, which enabled big holdings to enjoy a comfortable relationship with SOEs (i.e., based on duty loss mechanisms) and provided prime opportunities for lucrative profit making through state-debt financing (as is discussed in Chapter 3).

Where does this leave us in terms of understanding the acceleration of privatization in Turkey? Indeed, much of the literature simply takes either institutions, or external dynamics, or political struggles as autonomous or determinant factors in themselves. This opens plenty of room for an alternative framework that emphasizes the complex interplay of four interrelated factors – contemporary capitalism (i.e., external dynamics), class agency of the power bloc (i.e., political struggles), domestic capital accumulation strategies, and state institutions. Unlike much of the literature, this framework will allow us to grasp the social reality of Turkish privatization process as a dynamic totality.

*Privatization in Turkey* aims to fill this gap. It will provide the first-single authored academic book written solely on privatization in Turkey in more than a decade. Through theoretically innovative, historically situated, and largely qualitative case study research, the book will tackle six overarching questions:
- Why has privatization accelerated in Turkey?
- What was the role of power bloc (i.e., fractions of capital) as a class actor in the context of the privatization processes of Turkey?
- Who benefited and harmed (e.g., capital, labour) from how privatization function in development processes of Turkey?
- How did privatization interact with the prevailing dynamics of domestic capital accumulation in Turkey?
- How has different social class forces struggled within the Turkish state to transform the state's capacity to implement privatization?

– What theoretical and practical lessons of the Turkish case can inform the
construction of a substantial alternative to privatization?

The book's central argument is that the acceleration of privatization in Turkey
in the post-2001 era was the result of a powerful combination of support from
the class agency of the power bloc, which has been achieved with a major subordination of labour. The power bloc and the subsequent AKP governments
saw previously unavailable advantages in supporting privatization within the
context of the post-2001 domestic accumulation regime and the wider world
market, and therefore acted collectively to strengthen the state's capacity to
implement privatization – first decentralization and depoliticization practices
in 2000s, and then centralization, politicization and personalization practices
in the 2010s. Contrary to the dominant liberal-cum-institutionalist argument,
Turkey's privatization program since 2001 has not only provided advantages
to (and supported by) favourable capital groups and the AKP elites, but also
consolidated the position of *Capital in General*. As such, the primary victims in
this situation are not the supposedly excluded TÜSİAD-based secular business
groups, but the laboring and popular classes and the natural environment of
the entire country.

## 1      Theoretical Approaches to Privatization

While many theoretical explanations have provided to interpret privatization
and its rise all over the world, comparative material that maps those theoretical explanations in a clear and accessible way remains in its infancy. By
unfolding the conceptual disagreements, different assumptions and prevailing
methodologies that exist in the privatization literature, we can divide the literature into three theoretical approaches – liberal, institutionalist, and Marxian.
This could be an appropriate way of developing a comparative review of the
theoretical approaches to privatization.

### 1.1      *Liberal Approaches*

The liberal orthodoxy is built around a core assumption that rational individuals respond best to market incentives and that market-based arrangements
are inherently more efficient than state sector arrangements. Privatization is
therefore defined as a technical policy of transferring ownership of state enterprises to the private sector in order to improve efficiency. As such, state failure
is seen as the norm, and the privatization is provided as a solution to such
failures (Megginson and Netter 2001; Shleifer and Vishny 1998). Liberal support
for privatization is unconditional.

The liberal orthodoxy came to this conclusion from different and complementary lines of argument. For example, property rights theory has attributed the superiority of private ownership to the fact that managers (agent) in the private sector face constant pressure from a competitive capital market (principal), where ownership is transferable and rights to profit are clearly defined, to achieve better performance (Alchian and Demsetz 1972; Crew and Parker 2008). By contrast, state managers (agent) have inferior incentives to allocate resources efficiently because taxpayer owners (principal) of state enterprises have low incentives to monitor the behavior of state managers (Tittenbrun 1996). The public choice theory, on the other hand, presented privatization as the solution because it helps saving the state from interest group capture and ending rent-seeking practices of politicians and bureaucrats (e.g., producing goods that consumers do not want, employing too many people, delivering output below the cost of production to favourable businesses) (Krueger 1990; Buchanan 1975; Boycko, Shleifer and Vishny 1996).

To support these theoretical claims with empirical research, liberal researchers feed data on dozens of countries and thousands of state-owned enterprises into large-scale regression models to identify positive gains in the efficiency of privatized firms (See Boardman and Vining 1989; Chong and De-Silanes 2003). In an important study, using a sample of 230 firms headquartered in 32 developing countries, Boubakri et al. (2008a) documented a significant increase in the post-privatization profitability, efficiency, and output. Megginson and Netter's (2001) empirical research also supported the proposition that privately owned firms are more efficient and more profitable than otherwise comparable state-owned firms.

It is important to note that some liberal researchers demonstrated awareness of the influence of interest-based political control over privatizations and deep ties between politicians, politically connected firms, and privatized firms in their analyses (Bortolotti and Faccio 2009; Boubakri et al. 2008b; Ramamurti 2000). They show that if there is business-politics connection involved in the process, privatizations may offer opportunities for new allocation mechanisms in favor of politically connected firms. As a result, businesses might get preferential access to a number of value enhancing resources and opportunities in privatization tenders through political favoritism, while politicians could collect rents and/or electoral support in return to stay in power. Such political interferences are seen as undesirable outcomes that can eliminate expected efficiency gains stemming from privatizations (Boubakri et al. 2008b).

The liberal orthodoxy has certainly provided some useful insights into privatization literature. However, there are two serious problems in the construction of its argumentation: universalist methodology and state-market dichotomy. First, universalist methodology ends up identifying individual as a 'thing' that possesses no contextual and historical values apart from pursuing its interest, which hold true for all times and places. In this approach, any historical changes or contextual specificity in capitalist accumulation strategies and the state are analytically firewalled (Marois 2012). Second, the state and market are presented as two social organizations that oppose each other in different ways, which is not necessarily valid. For example, what has been described as rent-seeking activity of state authorities by neoclassical and liberal studies sometimes corresponds with the necessities of market. Rather than seeking individual gain alone, state authorities are also use state enterprises and/or privatization process to complement market dynamics.

## 1.2    *Institutionalist Approaches*

Institutionalist literature offers more historically detailed and case study-oriented research that is critical of universal and dualistic state versus market views of privatization. This literature puts greater emphasis on context, institutions, and extra-market coordination in the explanation of privatization (Yarrow 1989; Gupta 2000). Contrary to liberal interpretations that provide unconditional support to privatization, institutionalist scholars tend to argue that privatization should only be implemented in settings with strong regulatory and institutional frameworks. This could not only provide a panacea to favoritism in the privatization process but also ensure that privatization implementations will produce more successful results in terms of expected efficiency and productivity gains (Vickers and Yarrow 1988; Parker and Saal 2003; Weizsacker et al. 2005).

Inspired by Polanyi, institutionalists contended that capitalist market sometimes generates social deficiencies (e.g., inequality, ethical fragmentation) that could not be remedied by its own mechanisms. This provides a sociological and economic rationale for extra-market coordination via state economic activity and therefore challenges market fetishism of liberal orthodoxy (Shonfield 1965; Crabtree and Thirlwall 1993). Institutionalists also observe that contextually specific circumstances have constitute effects on individual behaviors and implementation of economic policies (Veblen 1957; Shonfield 1965). This is in contrast with the liberal political economy, which makes the point that individuals (e.g., capitalists, state authorities) always pursue their self-interest in implementing economic policies.

It is important to be aware of the differences within institutionalist interpretations of privatization, emanating from relatively different applications of the theory. Scholars working within more classic premises of institutionalism tend to advocate a balance between the state ownership and privatization, between economic efficiency and social development (See Weizsacker et al. 2005; Gupta 2000; Parker and Saal 2003; Rowthorn and Chang 1993). For these scholars, the central issue is how countries effectively regulate a large number of possible institutional variations along the state-private continuum conducive to enhancing both economic efficiency and social development. However, the revised institutionalism (as per Managerial Perspective and New Institutional Economics) puts greater emphasis on the need for private ownership and privatization. The revised institutionalism is also more concerned with economic efficiency objectives rather than social development.[6]

The institutionalist approaches thus counter liberal individualism, market fetishism and universalism by pointing the importance of institutions, extra-market coordination and contextual-specific conditions. However, they tend to reveal other methodological and analytical issues, two of these are especially significant. Although a great deal of work has been devoted to understanding the constitute effects of contextually specific circumstances on the behaviors of individuals and the implementation of economic policies, this is proving to be limited and only to involve a small number of ideological and cultural factors. For example, the structural constraints to capitalist development are often left unexplored. As such, institutionalist analyses fail to explain why and how preferred policies (e.g., privatization) interact with the processes of accumulation, both at a national and global scale, and how this interaction has released forces that would render state ownership obsolete (Saad-Filho 2008). Another critical problem is that institutionalists see institutions as the final and formative analytical category and turn a blind eye to issues of power and class. But there is a need to analyze power and class struggles happening inside and outside of these institutions.

## 1.3    *Marxian Approaches*

Marxian approaches depart in a number of distinct ways from the methodological assumptions of both liberal and institutionalist approaches. One of these differences concerns the individual rationality. According to Marxism, the rationality of human mind always has some kind of social, historical and structural anchorage (Therborn 1976, 77). This means that individuals are endowed with consciousness and tend to act deliberately towards a goal, but their actions are subject to the structural logic of capitalism. When viewed from this angle, the presumption of liberal orthodoxy that individuals endlessly pursue self-interest – legitimately when performed through the market,

---

6    The Managerial Perspective includes influential scholars such as George Yarrow, John Vickers and Paul Cook. The New Institutional Economics includes scholars like Bernardo Bortolotti and Enrico Perotti.

but also illegitimately through the state as in rent seeking and corruption – is not always true.

Markets are also understood within broader pattern of capitalist economy by Marxian approaches (Therborn 1976, 108–113). As such, capitalist markets are not neutral mechanisms of voluntary exchange between equal participants because they reflect the underlying capitalist relations of power and production (Lapavitsas 2005, 64). On the one hand, the capitalist class controls the means of production, exploits labour power to put this capital into use, and realize the value of product through the circulation of commodities in the market. On the other hand, the working class only has available the sale of its labour power to earn its means of subsistence, and directly produces the social product (Albo 2005, 64). There exist, then, inherent conflicts between capitalist and working classes over the production process. Capitalist class seeks to optimize flexibility in employment and retain control over the production process, while the working class pursues appropriate income levels and attempts to exercise its own control in the production process (Albo 2009, 5). For Marxists, it is therefore misleading to speak about privatization as a simple market transaction, without bringing class character of privatization and its impact on the capital-labour relations into the analysis.

For Marxists, state-market dichotomy is also not compelling. This is because states have been complementing the capitalist markets (e.g., SOES), safeguarding their smooth expansion (e.g., bailouts) and serving class hegemony (e.g., social security) for a long time (Poulantzas 1978, 185). As such, the state is neither external to capitalist markets nor against them. This understanding provides a strong alternative to the liberal arguments that (i) state and market are two social organizations that oppose each other, (ii) and markets can work perfectly, unless their adjustment path is blocked by state interventions (Saad-Filho 2008, 338).

In line and based on above methodological grounds, Marxian approaches agree on the role of privatization in entailing the restructuring of social relationships of power between the state, capital, and labour substantially in favour of capital. For this reason, in contrast to the unconditional support of liberals and more balanced attitude of institutionalists, Marxists have often been highly critical of privatization and against of it. It has, however, to be noted that there is considerable variation and sometimes disagreement within Marxism about how to explain the acceleration of privatization processes. Much of the debate takes place with reference to the level of analysis (world market imperatives or specific localized conditions) and the agency (externally or internally driven).

As pointed out above, the dominant Marxian privatization literature on the spread of privatization in different parts of the world was mainly shaped by two important studies: David Harvey's (2003) accumulation by dispossession, and James Petras and Henry Veltmeyer's (2001) outside-in account. These two studies tend to subordinate the specific localized conditions to world market imperatives and the effects of internal factors to external factors.[7]

For Harvey, privatization is a means by which the capacity of capital to circulate is enhanced in order to overcome the structural problems of over-accumulation – a condition whereby surpluses of capital in the core economies lie idle with few profitable outlets in sight (Harvey 2003, 149–150; Harvey 2011, 28). This is because privatization entails "at very low or zero cost" of a set of assets formerly owned by the state that can be seized by over-accumulated private capital and used for profit. Those state assets that are subject to privatization include state utilities of all kinds (e.g., telecommunication, transportation), state manufacturing companies (e.g., iron and steel, petroleum refinery), social welfare provisions (e.g., public housing, health care), and state institutions (e.g., universities, prisons) (Harvey 2007, 35). Once in motion, this movement of accumulation by dispossession creates incredible pressures to find more and more arenas, in different parts of the world, where privatization might be achieved (Harvey 2003, 158). What is happening as a result of accumulation by dispossession is therefore not merely privatization of formerly state assets but their acquisition by over-accumulated capital from the core economies. In this way, Harvey's analysis emphasizes the tendency of over-accumulated capital from the core to move to the periphery and the processes of accumulation by dispossession (via privatization) taking place there, which was largely imposed on the periphery by external actors.

In a way consistent with and complementary to the Harvey's analysis, Petras and Veltmeyer's outside-in account emphasizes those external actors behind privatization. Petras and Veltmeyer argue that a range of international and foreign actors, known as the imperial centre, externally dictate and impose the time frame and scope of privatization in peripheral countries that occupy relatively subordinate positions within the hierarchy of states (Petras and Veltmeyer 2001, 93). The imperial centre, which initiates "downward" disciplinary imposition on developing countries to privatize, includes the US state, the EU, and multinational capital in the US and other core economies as well

---

7   As Greg Albo points out, "Although capital may be differentiated into national contexts (or into David Harvey's socio-spatial fixes), these institutional variations and class relations are increasingly subordinated to the structural imperatives of competition under neoliberalism …" (Albo 2005, 79).

as international financial institutions (IFIs) like the International Monetary Fund and the World Bank (Petras and Veltmeyer 2004, 21–23).

According to Petras and Veltmeyer, all this is done to pillage the resources of peripheral countries. Multinational companies that acquire state assets via privatization often send their earnings abroad (Petras and Veltmeyer 2007, 108). The peripheral states thus lose a strategic lever for shifting those earnings to new sectors of the economy, which could have positive impacts on employment and economic growth (Petras and Veltmeyer 2001, 101). Moreover, those multinational companies that are integrated in global production chains largely displace local small and medium producers in the process. The loss of local producers in turn further deepens peripheral countries' dependence on imports (Petras and Veltmeyer 2007, 46). In both instances, privatization leads to a huge transfer of wealth and resources from developing countries to the imperial center.

Harvey's and Petras and Veltmeyer's above interpretation of privatization has influenced the works of David Mansfield (2008), Susan Spronk and Jeffrey Webber (2007), Arundhati Roy (2001), Korkut Boratav (2010, 2011) and many others in contemporary Marxian privatization literature. Boratav, for example, described privatization in Turkey as a mechanism of surplus and wealth transfer to over-accumulated foreign and domestic capital. Boratav argued that the process was pushed by external actors such as the US and the IMF and occurred mainly through low pricing of state assets (Boratav 2010, 21–24; Boratav 2011, 197–206). Roy also argued with respect to the Indian case, that to snatch productive state assets away and sell them as stock to foreign companies is a process of barbaric dispossession (Roy 2001).

As we have seen, the dominant Marxian literature on privatization provides important insights into why and how external factors brought privatization policy to the fore. However, the same literature faces some difficulties especially when applied to variegated patterns of privatization in different parts of the world, two of which are briefly stated here. First, it is not very capable of explaining certain policy outcomes – why privatization has occurred, where it has or has not, and why at a different pace. This is because the privatization processes in peripheral countries were not only shaped by over-accumulation tendencies originated from advanced countries and were not just externally imposed from above by the imperial centre. These external pressures towards privatization are usually mediated and contested by domestic conditions of each national social formation before they can become institutionalized (Marois 2012, 169). What Harvey calls "accumulation by dispossession" in the global context acquires particular political meaning and variegated shape in different countries. Second, the primacy given to external factors diverts attention away from the material interests and actions of internal actors (e.g., local politicians, domestic bourgeoisie) within the privatization processes.

The criticisms that privatization may not be explained by external factors and/or at the most general level alone have slowly given rise to a body of alternative Marxian literature that attempts to bring internal factors (and variegation) back into the analysis of privatization.[8] This alternative Marxian literature pays special attention to the historically specific material, institutional and social dynamics of each country and sector within the context of contemporary capitalism. In this way, this literature attempts to address both the generality of contemporary capitalism and specific circumstances of a particular country and sector.

For example, Bayliss and Fine (2008) not only emphasize the importance of generic features of contemporary capitalism such as internationalization of production, financialization and loan conditionality of IFIs on privatization, but also pay significant attention to the specificity of different countries and sectors. Their take is to examine country-by-country, sector-by-sector, exactly what is involved in the privatization of state enterprises, whilst keeping within sight of the bigger picture. Fine and Hall (2012) take a similar position and argue that although the generic and exogenous factors are important, there is something different about water and housing, just as there is something different about South Africa and the UK. They put forward a multi-dimensional account that involves global, regional and national levels. At the global level, the key role is played by the IFIs like World Bank and their privatization conditionalities through many of their loans over the years. The regional development banks such as the African Development Bank and the Inter-American Development Bank have also actively promoted various forms of privatization in their regions; and the European Commission has promoted PPPs throughout Europe. At the national level; the political will of politicians, bureaucrats and regulators, the opposition emanating from the trade union movement, and the interest of domestic conglomerates to support privatization and invest in privatized companies are effective in influencing the fate of the national privatization process (see also Fine 1997).

The co-edited book by David McDonald and Greg Ruiters (2012) *Alternatives to Privatization* follows similar methodological and theoretical grounds. The book contains analyses backed up by comprehensive examination of privatization in over 50 countries in Latin America, Asia and Africa and in 3 sectors

---

8   See Bayliss and Fine (2008); Fine and Hall (2012); McDonald and Ruiters (2012); McDonald (2014); Zaifer (2018); Zaifer (2020).

(i.e., electricity, water, healthcare). A series of individual chapters focus on diverse actors, both internal and external, involved in historical processes of privatization and its alternatives. These actors include class based IFIs, external donors, organized labour unions, women's organizations and broad-based social movements. The chapters are organized along sectoral and regional categories to show how and why the implementation of universal privatization policy varies according to specific circumstances of sector and geographical location.

This book's theoretical analysis seeks to contribute to this alternative Marxian literature. The attempt here is to offer an analysis of privatization that consists of a complex interplay of three specific-internal factors of class agency of power bloc, domestic capital accumulation strategies, and state institutions under the competitive imperatives of contemporary capitalism at the global level. Let me now provide more details about my analytical framework that enables such a nuanced analysis.

## 2      An Analytical Framework for Understanding the Privatization Process

Privatization is a global phenomenon. Globality does not however mean uniformity: privatization processes are variegated and geographically uneven. Concretely this implies that privatization experiences take a wide variety of forms and pace in different countries and over time (Harris 2013, 126). There are therefore many domestic and national variations and temporalities within a contemporary capitalism context to be accounted for. But the explanation of these variations should not be limited to one or other factor – institutions or political struggles – given the complexity of privatization. More spadework must be done to investigate how those factors interact with one another and together provide the momentum for privatization. To be able to do this, I formulated an analytical framework based around four interrelated categories. These include: 1) contemporary capitalism, 2) state, 3) power bloc, and 4) domestic capital accumulation.

### 2.1     *Contemporary Capitalism Is the Context that Brought Privatization Policy to the Fore*
Capitalism strongly influences the lives of billions of people in every continent. One cannot fully understand what is going about economy, politics, international relations, ideology, and culture without analyzing the development of capitalism. The main characteristics inherent in capitalism are class

struggle and unending search for capital accumulation, which also lead to its continuous transformation: the emergence of new social patterns of capitalist reproduction (Burnham 1997; Albo 2012a). Capitalism should therefore be understood not ahistorically, but as a complex logic, able to transform the whole world around it, at the same time it is able to transform itself. In this regard, it can be said that contemporary capitalism (or neoliberalism) has emerged from the collapse of post-war state-led capitalism as a market-oriented class-based project to restore the profitability and power of capital in the 1980s (Marois 2012).

As Ben Fine and Alfredo Saad-Filho underlined (2017), contemporary capitalism (or neoliberalism) is the current phase, stage, or mode of existence of capitalism. It is characterized by such competitive imperatives as the internationalization of production and capital, financialization, and labour market flexibility that give structural context to privatization in general. In other words, these competitive imperatives of contemporary capitalism spread and universally favor privatization across the world market. Let me look in more detail how this happens.

One of the important features of the contemporary capitalism is the spatial dispersion of global production processes under the decisive domination of American capital. This is partly the outsourcing of specific tasks and services across borders, and the increasing organization of production and trade through international production networks. Developing countries, once mostly providers of raw materials and new markets for American and European finished goods, instead became manufacturing production nodes within what are known as 'international production networks' (Gereffi and Korzeniewicz 1994). These are networks of production processes resulting in a specific finished commodity, which cut across different countries or regions of the world. For example, leading electronics manufacturing multinational corporations (MNCs) such as Cisco, Apple, and Hewlett-Packard concentrate more on research and development, sales and marketing in their home markets, but outsource (or transfer to their foreign subsidiaries) production, assembly, and testing to low-cost manufacturing hubs in East and South Asia. This explains why the amount of foreign direct investment (FDI) and the number of MNCs have increased substantially over the last 40 years.

This internationalization of production enabled privatization in at least two ways. On the one hand, in the eyes of neoliberal state elites and the internationalizing domestic business groups, SOEs that were legally and administratively confined to domestic market where the state could dominate made it difficult to secure the country's participation in international production networks (Fine 1997). This generated pressures for the privatization of SOEs especially in the first shock phase of neoliberalism (i.e., from early 1980s to mid-1990s), in which the promotion of private capital and the international integration of domestic capital proceeded in country after country without regarding the consequences. To the surprise of those neoliberal state elites and the internationalizing domestic business groups, however, some surviving SOEs from emerging economies such as China, Brazil, India, Kuwait, UAE, Malaysia, Russia and Saudi Arabia, and from advanced economies such as France, Norway and South Korea, have recently extended their global reach.[9] On the other hand, the increasing organization of production and trade through international production networks was partly achieved through cross-border acquisitions of MNCs in multiple countries. Some of those acquisitions by MNCs realized through privatization of SOEs. For example, the British American Tobacco (BAT) acquired Tekel (Turkey's state-owned cigarette maker) in 2008 with $1.72 billion price. This was BAT's second major acquisition via privatization after it bought Italy's former state tobacco company in 2003.[10]

A second important feature of contemporary capitalism that promoted privatization is financialization. The term of financialization can be defined as an immense explosion in financial activities (Albo 2005, 76). The rise in financialization over the past 40 years resulted in the excessive expansion and proliferation of flows of financial capital that had to make itself busy by pursuit of privatization (Bayliss and Fine 2008, 14–17). Between 1980 and 2010, for example, private financial flows to emerging and developing countries have grown from about $15 billion to over $600 billion. State elites and domestic capitalists have led a corresponding shift to debt-led growth strategies. As a result, external debt increased nearly ten-fold or from nearly $570 billion in 1980 to nearly $5.5 trillion in 2010 (Marois 2015, 29). The problem was to find profitable uses for all that financial capital, and the privatization of state assets represented a massive frontier for investment and profit in water, energy, manufacturing, supply, telecommunication, transport systems, health services, pensions and so on.

The World Bank, the IMF and USAİD, often with the backing of domestic capitalists and neoliberal state elites, supported this process and promoted privatization in emerging and developing countries through structural adjustment programs, often as necessary conditions for loans. The subsequent rise of liberal orthodoxy also supported this process; it asserted that state-owned and – controlled enterprises were inefficient and bad for development and

9   *The Economist*, "Emerging-market multinationals: The rise of state capitalism", 21 January 2012.

10   *Independent*, "BAT wins auction for Turkey's state tobacco firm with $1.72bn bid", 23 February 2008.

that the only way to improve their performance is to pass them over to the private sector. The orthodoxy does not stand up to any detailed scrutiny. Some state-owned and – controlled enterprises are indeed inefficient, but some are not (Harvey 2011, 28). More importantly, state-owned and – controlled enterprises fare much better than their private counterparts in terms of other indicators such as resource sustainability, service delivery (e.g., providing access to marginalized groups and regions), commitment to societal objectives (e.g., community development) and the quality of the workplace (e.g., salary and benefits) (McDonald and Ruiters 2012). However, this comparison did not matter for the orthodoxy, which continuously argued that industries run by the state had to be opened up to private financial capital. Therefore, it can hardly come as a surprise that the aggregate global value of the privatization implementations reached nearly $3.63 trillion in 2016.

Third, the growing labour market flexibility, supposedly in order to increase employment and labour productivity, is another important aspect of contemporary capitalism. It includes the simplification of hiring-and-firing regulations, the sharp decline in permanent-secure contracts, the curtailment of labour union rights, the weakening of collective agreements, and the reduction of social security benefits (Standing 1997; Castel 2003). Robert B. Reich (2015) provides us important statistics to understand the implications of these transformations for workers in the United States. In 1980, more than 80 per cent of large and medium-sized American firms gave their workers defined-benefit pensions that guaranteed them a fixed amount of money every month after they retired. Now, the share is below one-third. Moreover, nearly one out of every five working Americans is in a part time job now. A growing number are temporary workers, freelancers, or consultants, whose incomes and work schedules vary from weak-to-weak or even day-to-day. Furthermore, when the General Motors was the largest employer in America fifty years ago, the typical GM worker, who had a strong union behind him that summoned the collective bargaining power of all autoworkers, earned $35 an hour in today's dollars. By 2014, America's largest employer was Walmart, and the average hourly wage of Walmart workers, who are on their own because they do not have a union to negotiate a better deal, was $11.

The imperative of labour flexibility has been intimately related to privatization (Fine 1997, 376). For example, privatization helped weaken the power of labour unions that were the main stumbling block for capital to ensure the implementation of labour market policies creating "flexibility" (Albo, Gindin and Panitch 2010, 90). It is important to note that SOEs had historically provided the most powerful base for labour in many countries. After privatization, the unionization of workers in many SOEs was weakened because the new private owners initiated massive lay-offs, encouraged some workers to accept early retirement, and employed new workers under flexible conditions and without union membership (Yücesan-Özdemir and Özdemir 2007, 467). This helped to paralyze labour class so that it failed to collectively oppose subordination of labour to flexibility imperative. Put it differently, privatization not only boosted a form of precarity in the former SOEs, but also denied these workers the capacity to struggle for their rights.

Three features of contemporary capitalism identified above explain the emergence of privatization in general all over the world, but the implementation and pace of privatization policy especially in the periphery was also shaped by the variations in the institutional materiality of the state, specific patterns of accumulation and political-class relations of each country (Albo 2005; Brenner, Peck and Theodore 2010). Is Turkey just another case of contemporary capitalism in practice, as Harvey (2003) and Petras and Veltmeyer (2001), among others, suggests? There is little doubt that ANAP (Motherland Party) and AKP (Justice and Development Party) governments in Turkey have pursued fairly orthodox policies from the beginning: their pursuit of privatization and embrace of openness to the world economy (e.g., financial and trade liberalizations). In certain respects, Turkey's privatization (and neoliberalization) process thus fits well with the general picture of contemporary capitalism. At the same time, the outcome of its privatization process is necessarily uneven, which requires explanation that captures both the generality of contemporary capitalism (as explained above) and the particularities of Turkey, which I address in the next three categories (Bernstein 2010, 182–183).

## 2.2    *The State Is an Integral Element of the Privatization Processes*
Despite its origins and evolution, and the stark realities of modern capitalism, the state needs not be treated as the exclusive instrument of capital, nor as a subject that holds power and makes use of it in an autonomous way. Instead, a Poulantzian understanding of the state may be described, which sees the state as a condensation of social class relations (Poulantzas 1978, 123). Nicos Poulantzas reminds us that capitalist states are relational formations; as such, they comprise and constitute historically specific material condensation and the institutionalization of politico-ideological relations that are malleable but also momentarily fixed and formative (Poulantzas 1978, 129).

The state is the heart of the exercise of political power. This means that the state apparatus, in relation to the conjunctural dynamics of class struggle and capital accumulation, is often involved in the formation not only of economic policies but also of the privatization policy specifically (Poulantzas 1978, 166–73). However, the state does not come automatically equipped with administrative, regulatory, and materially supportive units (i.e., an institutional-legal framework) for privatization (or with operational harmony on the question of privatization). The advocates of privatization within each state and society actively pursue changes (e.g., establishing executive organs such as a Privatization Authority, making legal reforms) that lead to the restructuring and strengthening of the state's capacity to implement privatization – that is, transforming the state's institutional materiality suitable for privatization (Brand and Heigl 2011, 255).

This is, however, not always a smooth process. It is subject to intra-state contradictions because privatization is a heavily contested issue. First, diverse fractions of capital could have different and conflicting interests over privatization. For example, the NP (National Party) government in South Africa in the early 1990s initiated a policy of wide-ranging privatization including SOEs such as ESKOM, TRANSNET and ISCOR. However, the South African conglomerates (i.e., big/monopoly capital) opposed to rapid privatization, as they were unwilling to invest in privatized utilities in politically uncertain conditions (Fine 1997, 403). This was indirectly reflected within the state apparatus (i.e., by way of the differentiations and dislocations between the various branches and apparatuses of the state, which reproduced the contradictions of the bourgeoisie). For instance, the Chair of the South African Competition Board unsurprisingly made a statement against privatization and instead called for the use of SOEs to support reconstruction and development of economy (Hentz 2000, 213).

Second, although the dominant classes by and large structurally and strategically dominate the state, the popular classes also exist in the state apparatus (e.g., parliaments, the judiciary, the police, the armed forces, higher education) essentially in the form of centres of opposition to privatization efforts of dominant classes (Brand and Heigl 2011, 248). For instance, the environmental groups, labour unions and opposition political party (Frente Amplio – Broad Front Party) in Uruguay established a strategic alliance and created a massive national campaign against water privatization. The campaign then succeeded in gaining enough signatures to force a popular referendum on whether water administration should be exclusively the jurisdiction of the state or permitted to be outsourced to multinational firms. The successful referendum in 2004 resulted in a constitutional amendment creating a human right to water (Almeida 2010). Another referendum was held in Uruguay in 2004 over whether to repeal or ratify a law paving the way for privatization of the state oil company, ANCAP. The vote to reject prevailed by a wide margin – 62.02% of the vote (Harnecker 2016a, 23). It is, however, important to remember that the referendum system in Uruguay provides a major institutional avenue for popular classes to channel their grievances, unlike in most other Latin American countries.

Third, there is the constitutive role of the state itself. The state is not reducible to a relationship of forces; state/government authorities may exhibit a relative autonomy and interest of their own, albeit within limits (Poulantzas 1978, 130–42). The relative autonomy of the state/government authorities from the classes and fractions increases under exceptional state forms – absolutism, Bonapartism, military dictatorship, and fascism (Poulantzas 1970, 59). The appearance and rise of these exceptional state forms often correspond to the political crises in the society: the sharpening of the internal contradictions between the dominant class fractions, the inability of dominant class fraction to impose its leadership on the other fractions of the power bloc, a crisis in dominant ideology, the deepening contradictions between the dominant classes and the dominated classes (Poulantzas 1970, 16, 71–86).

Hence the increased relative autonomy of the state does not necessarily imply a coherent and rational will on the parts of the agents of the state (e.g. political party, governing class, the head of state), as an intrinsic entity; it largely exists as the resultant of the balance of forces which is condensed in the state (i.e. effect of the struggle of the dominated classes, the contradictions of the power bloc itself, and the needs of capital accumulation) (Poulantzas 1974, 164). Therefore, the various state policies (e.g., privatization) under exceptional state form, seemingly corresponding to the interests of agents of the state (and/or specific fraction of capital that is close to those agents), are thus concerned with the extended reproduction of capital (i.e., of the whole social capital).

Therefore, contrary to the liberal-cum-institutionalist interpretations, it is inadequate from this point of view to say that the agents of the state are solely pursuing their interest, or the state is in the exclusive service of specific fraction of capital (e.g., religious, loyal and politically connected capital groups in the Turkish context). But there is more to it than that. The state's economic interventions (e.g. privatization implementations) in favour of 'specific fraction of capital' are not simply technical or corrupt interventions deriving from the requirements of 'specific fraction of capital', but they are political interventions to mediate a re-stabilization of political domination and position of the dominant class (i.e. the general political interest of the power bloc as a whole) as well as to address the needs of capital accumulation by virtue of state's relative autonomy (Poulantzas 1974, 160).

## 2.3    *A Power Bloc Is the Key Class Agent behind Privatization*

Inter-relations between the dominant classes, as related to the institutions of the capitalist state, happen within a specific political unity of the power bloc.

A power bloc is composed of sometimes competing, often interrelated, bourgeoisie class fractions (for the bourgeoisie is divided into class fractions) but organized within the state to create an unstable alliance of unity and compromises generally under the hegemony or leadership of one fraction – the fraction whose specific interests are prioritized by the policies of the state to the detriment of the interests of other fractions. It is through the power bloc that fractions of capital, which have formal and informal representation within the state apparatus, are organized to rule (Poulantzas 1978, 126–127). As such, power bloc, as a concept, takes into consideration both the general interest of the bourgeoisie class in safeguarding capitalism, and the specific interests of its fractions (Boito 2010, 190).

As a result of the internationalization of capital and production, the power bloc cannot be located any more on a purely national level. The increasing amount of FDI and number of MNCs meant the penetration of foreign capital (e.g., American, European and Japanese), as a transformative force, within each national (host) formation and its power bloc (Poulantzas 1974, 72). However, these foreign capitals do not directly participate in each of the power blocs involved in order to assert their interest; the American bourgeoisie or the German bourgeoisie are not directly present as such, for example, in the Turkish or Brazilian power bloc. Their presence in the Turkish or Brazilian power bloc is rather ensured by certain fractions of Turkish or Brazilian bourgeoisie and the state (Poulantzas 1974, 75).

The notion of power bloc is also related to the relationship between the bourgeoisie and popular classes (e.g., the peasantry, the middle class, the workers). It is difficult to talk about the strength and interest of power bloc without saying something about its relation of force with the popular classes (Poulantzas 1970, 81). As discussed above, power bloc constitutes a political unity on the part of the bourgeoisie so as to establish its hegemony over the politically unorganized popular classes. In the case of privatization, the power bloc attempts to disperse and divide popular classes, and thus prevents the emergence of an organized reflex of popular class movement against the accelerated privatization both within and outside of the formal state (Yalman and Topal 2017). Although a large part of the popular classes resist privatization, some segments may ally themselves with bourgeoisie fractions in the power bloc, and others may be a part of a support class motivated by complex ideological illusions (e.g., paternalism, religious networks, politics of identity), which help to sustain privatization policies even though they injured by it (Boito 2010, 194).

It is important to emphasize that the organization and composition of power bloc fractions is not homogenous in every country. The power bloc is present in each country in a specific form, depending on national relations of forces, traditions, and history. In many countries, the power bloc fractions reflect the typical classification of capital according to functions: the industrial bourgeoi-sie, banking bourgeoisie, commercial bourgeoisie, and agrarian bourgeoisie (Poulantzas 1974, 92). For instance, as Drahokoupil points out, industrial bour-geoisie constituted the core of the power bloc while banking bourgeoisie were marginalized and subordinated in Slovakia in the 1990s (Drahokoupil 2009, 110) In some countries, the power bloc fractions are categorized according to the size of capital (large and small) or market orientation (export-oriented and domestic market-oriented) or a mixture of all.

In the particular context of Turkey, the composition of power bloc fractions can be specifically classified as such: big capital (holdings), which is an early participant in the accumulation process, brought together the industrial, bank-ing and commercial functions of capital, concentrated around Istanbul, has secularist orientation, and represented by TÜSİAD; Islamic-influenced capital (varying in terms of size from large trading and construction firms to medium-scale manufacturing firms), which is a late participant in the accumulation process, geographically diffused, often organized around Muslim business principles, and represented by different business associations such as MUSİAD, TUSKON (Confederation of Businessmen and Industrialists of Turkey) and ASKON (Anatolian Lions Businessmen's Association), with MUSİAD being the leading one; and foreign capital (mostly European and Middle Eastern), which is constituting partnerships and joint ventures with local capital groups and direct investments that reached a record level in mid-2000s, and repre-sented by YASED (International Investors Association of Turkey) (Marois 2012; Bekmen 2013). The leadership of the power bloc in Turkey has historically come from TÜSİAD-based big capital (although seemed increasingly unable to impose its leadership after the global crisis of 2008), which is known to have important connections with foreign capital.

The inter-relations and class compromises between the fractions of capital within the power bloc are important material forces in shaping privatization processes. Two questions are crucial in investigating this phenomenon. First, how willing are fractions of the power bloc to integrate privatization into state policy as a priority? The limited extent of privatization may result from the unwillingness of the power bloc to make privatization the priority option for a variety of economic and political reasons. When fractions of power bloc refuse to invest in privatized companies (e.g., South Africa in 1990s) or engage in an ideological strategy of 'nationalism' with the aim of equating privatization with 'foreignisation' (e.g., Turkey in late 1980s), the attempt at privatization is less likely to succeed.

Second, are different fractions able to combine their interests and achieve a contradictory unity of compromises when it comes to privatization policy? The creation of an overall consensus (on privatization) within the power bloc is often problematic because there may be conflicts between the different fractions of domestic capital or between domestic and foreign capital. For example, Samson (1994) has pointed out that companies that purchase state-owned enterprises via privatization are empowered, while those companies that are excluded from privatization implementations or former private beneficiaries of state provision that has been cut are weakened economically and politically. The Brazilian case is illustrative of this. Privatization has not been broadly supported in Brazil because it has marginalized small and medium-sized capital in order to privilege large domestic corporations and foreign capital. During the privatization tenders under the Collor, Itamar and Cardoso governments, it was mainly large domestic corporations in banking, industry, and construction sectors as well as foreign capital (Portuguese and Spanish capital has been most prominent) that tended to take over the SOEs (Boito 2010, 191).

## 2.4 Privatization Is a Constitutive Element of Domestic Accumulation Strategies

The totality of the capital accumulation process has three constituent dimensions – production (including the extraction of surplus value), realization (the transformation of commodities into money by an act of exchange), and revalorization (the allocation of surplus value to new production) (Ercan and Oğuz 2015, 115). Domestic accumulation strategies characterize the totality of the capital accumulation process within a specific geography and within a certain period of time (Saad-Filho 2003, 7). The logic and strategies of domestic capital accumulation thus mediate agents' choices over privatization. In other words, the prevailing dynamics of domestic capital accumulation act back on the power bloc fractions and state authorities and decrease (or increase) their support for privatization.

For example, in the inward-oriented capital accumulation strategy, the alliance between state and domestic capital is of paramount importance for domestic capital accumulation (Saad-Filho 1998, 194). In this model, SOEs are providing subsidized industrial inputs and investment capital to the domestic capital, which is transforming itself into manufacturers of previously imported consumer durables. The willingness of the power bloc fractions to support privatization of such effective SOEs is therefore fragile. In contrast, the outward-oriented capital accumulation strategy is more dependent on international competitiveness of domestic capital and its alliance with foreign capital. In the new model, the state is no longer supporting industry with subsidized inputs (e.g., cheap electricity or steel). Instead, it is ready to surrender important areas of the economy (e.g., electricity generation and distribution, steel making, telecommunications, petroleum refinery) to private accumulation (both domestic and foreign) (Saad-Filho 1998, 194). This, of course, increases the power bloc fractions' support for privatization.

In many core countries where domestic capital accumulation regimes gained outward orientation after the 1980s in the wake of revalorization problems, power bloc fractions supported privatization so as to seize on new economic fields, sectors, land, or natural resources (Harvey 2003, 147). By contrast, when a domestic accumulation regime was still inward-oriented and enabled domestic private corporations to enjoy a comfortable relationship with the state-owned enterprises, as happened in South Africa in the 1990s, power bloc fractions were unwilling to support privatization (Fine 1997, 403).

In the case of Turkey, where the domestic accumulation regime started to gain an outward-orientation and to center on production capacity (including expanding surplus value for the enhancement of competitiveness) of large firms so as to compete for commodity exports in the world market during the early 2000s, for the determined entrepreneurs and state authorities, privatization may have become a measure of competitiveness. This is because the promotion of privatization was instrumental in paving the ground for the subordination SOE workers to competitive and productivity imperatives by increasing both absolute surplus value (paying workers less or making them work longer hours) and relative surplus value (increasing the amount of work the workers had to handle in a given time). These examples show how significant privatization is for the functioning of domestic accumulation strategies – a significance far greater than the struggle over the buying and selling off state assets.

Failure to link privatization with an evolving domestic accumulation regime amid global neo-liberalization results in the "overpoliticization" of the privatization process. By overpoliticization, I mean reducing the privatization process to merely the political struggles that emanate from the rivalry of those who will actually buy the enterprises to be privatized, without consideration of how the development of the domestic accumulation regime also acts back on the strategies of social actors.

## 3    Understanding Privatization in Turkey – the Structure of the Book

With these initial analytical and theoretical perspectives established, it is now possible to summarize the basic structure of this book. The first point to note is the division of Turkish privatization process into three historical phases (Chapters 3, 4, and 5). The first phase (1984–2001) involved a slow pace and limited progress, despite the structural pressures of contemporary capitalism. During the second phase (2002–2010), privatization accelerated with divestiture method. This acceleration was accompanied by unified power bloc fractions, decentralized and depoliticized state practices, and competitiveness based domestic capital accumulation regime. In the third phase (2011–2019), there has been continued acceleration in the privatization via divestiture and newly expanding PPP method. However, there have been significant changes in the background factors that together provided the momentum for privatization: the sharpening of the internal contradictions between fractions of power bloc, the increased relative autonomy of state that led to centralized, politicized and personalized state practices, and consumption-construction based domestic capital accumulation regime.

It should also be noted that because this book is concerned with the acceleration of privatization, which is understood as the outcome of a complex interplay between contemporary capitalism, state, power bloc, and domestic accumulation, the evidence base mixes both qualitative and quantitative sources. Much of the data is collected by a review of articles from national newspapers and face-to-face interviews with key informant groups (capitalists, labour unions, state authorities). The annual reports of the leading TUSİAD members and Islamic-influenced capital groups are also examined in detail to produce comparative data about their participation in privatization implementations and overall business development from 2002 to 2018. Quantitative data and empirical trends are drawn from electronic databases available through the World Bank, the IMF, the EPEC, Turkish Presidential Budget and Strategy Directorate, Turkish Privatization Administration, and Turkish Ministry of Development. This data is used in such a way as to be accessible to all social sciences scholars. The book's appendices provide more information about these data collection methods.

Chapter 2 explores the development of the SOEs in Turkey from the establishment of the Turkish Republic in 1923 to the beginning of neoliberal era in the early 1980s, with a view to identifying historical legacies that have shaped the Turkish privatization process in the following decades. It concretely traces the successive expansion of SOEs through this period, focusing in particular on how state policies on SOEs were a reflection of the demands coming from clashing social classes (e.g. capital, labour as well as the constitutive role of state authorities) and shifting needs of capital accumulation dynamics (e.g. capitalist consolidation in the 1930s, capitalist expansion in 1950s, capitalist expansion with duty losses in 1960s and 1970s) of the country. As we will see, relations between SOEs and the social classes were internal and complementary, rather than external and antagonistic. The SOEs were providing the bulk of industrial inputs and investment capital to the power bloc fractions within the context of an inward-oriented pattern of domestic capital accumulation. The SOEs were also benefiting the laboring classes in terms of employment opportunities and higher wages. These specific historical legacies would influence the shape of the privatization experiment to come in Turkey in the following decades.

Utilizing this understanding of the SOEs, Chapter 3 presents a detailed examination of privatization process in Turkey between 1984 and 2001. The chapter argues that, despite government efforts and IFI pressures, the implementation of privatization largely failed to materialize during this period. It particularly focuses on the interventions of the power bloc, which remained unwilling to support privatization within the constitutive context of the prevailing strategies of domestic capital accumulation at the time. It then discusses some of the reasons for this: (1) the comfortable relationship (e.g. subsidized inputs) that the power bloc had enjoyed with the SOEs as a result of the duty loss mechanism, (2) the intra-capital conflicts between TUSİAD-based big holding groups and Islamic-influenced capital groups, (3) the reluctance of big holdings to commit large-scale finance to privatization when other accumulation opportunities (e.g. state debt financing) were available in the financial markets, and (4) the lack of operational harmony within the state institutional apparatus on the question of privatization.

Chapter 4 examines the acceleration of privatization in Turkey in the post-2001 period. The chapter argues that, unlike the 1984–2001 period, the complex interplay of those stated interrelated factors (i.e., state, power bloc, capital accumulation) worked in the opposite direction and enabled the acceleration of the privatization. Each of the interrelated factors is then explored in detail. First, there was a shift in the fractions of the power bloc that had previously been unwilling and incapable of supporting privatization. Second, the privatization of SOEs constituted a central strategy, for the power bloc as a whole, in which domestic accumulation strategies were internally restructured to respond to the new imperatives of international competitiveness in the aftermath of the 2001 economic crisis. Third, a single party AKP government, in line with the pressures of the accumulation strategies and the interests of the power bloc, undertook a series of neo-liberal institutional reforms to facilitate privatization and weaken the resistance of labour. Such an interpretation goes well beyond the dominant liberal-cum-institutionalist literature on the acceleration of privatization in Turkey, which has confined its scope of analysis to networks between the government and favourable business groups.

Chapter 5 explores the latest phase of Turkish privatization process characterized by the expansion of public-private-partnerships (PPPs). Between 2010 and 2018, Turkey has implemented over $100 billion worth of PPP projects. The first part of the chapter conceptualizes the PPP phenomenon in such a way that it allows for an interpretation of PPP as a highly complex arrangement that can bring together multiple stakeholders: not just the public contracting authority and private project company, but also lenders, engineering-design contractors, input suppliers, and community in the form of users and workers. The second part of the chapter provides broad contours of PPP implementations in Turkey during 2010s, which expanded through more than 100 PPP contracts that made Turkey one of the top countries using PPPs among the European and the developing countries. The third part of the chapter then discusses the complex background to this expansion of PPPs in Turkey: (1) although the Turkish power bloc is not unified anymore as the internal contradictions between fractions of capital sharpened, the capitalist class' support for privatization and PPP remained strong, (2) as Turkey failed to increase relative surplus production and international competitiveness during the 2010s, PPP projects became increasingly important to create new financial resources (e.g., opening up state land to profit imperatives and creating extra demand through state guaranteed infrastructure contracts) to postpone crisis dynamics, (3) the exceptional state formed under the AKP government during 2010s has increasingly managed to bypass legal and institutional checks and balances that enabled the implementation PPP projects without delays. The chapter ends with a brief explanation of the six showcase PPP projects to provide concrete and specific details.

Chapter 6, the final contribution, briefly examines the implicationsof the Turkish case for privatization processes in different geographies and times. The chapter then looks at alternatives to privatization, which I call state ownership, corporatization, and democratic control; these will be studied in several historical settings, including Turkey, the UK, and several Latin American countries. Working squarely within the view that the experience of contesting capitalist power within capitalist societies is crucial for building the capacity to transcend capitalism as such, the chapter calls for a sophisticated, non-binary approach to combining various arenas (inside the state; outside the state) in which democratic control may be built. The construction of a substantial alternative to privatization based on democratic control would therefore promote the welfare and development of the popular and laboring classes.

# CHAPTER 2

# The Development of SOEs in Turkey in Historical Perspective

In the wake of the establishment of the republican regime in 1923, the SOEs began to play an active role within Turkish society and the economy. In the 1930s, the SOEs emerged in textile, agriculture and mining sectors. Within a couple more decades the SOEs expanded in manufacturing, energy, transport and communications and banking sectors. The aggregate value added of the SOEs reached 11.5 per cent of the Turkish GDP prior to the official announcement of Turkey's SOE privatization program in the early 1980s (World Bank 1993). This was higher than the developing countries average, which was less than 10 per cent at the time (Shirley 1983).

Why has Turkey developed such a significant SOE presence? Many analysts, who share the similar theoretical foundations that can be found in liberal-cum-institutionalist studies discussed in Chapter 1, interpreted this as a strategy of the Turkish state to maintain its domination over society.[1] It has been argued that the development of SOEs had enabled the state and state bureaucrats to control and manipulate elements of the Turkish society (Keyder 1987, 98–99; Heper 1985, 92; Insel 1995, 48). Contrary to this interpretation that see state and society as externally related entities of which the former is dominating the latter, this chapter concretely traces the development of SOEs in Turkey from 1923 to the early 1980s, focusing in particular on how state policies on SOEs were a reflection of the demands coming from different social classes and shifting needs of capital accumulation. As we will see, the relations between SOEs and the social classes were internal and complementary, rather than external and antagonistic. The SOEs were often established in such sectors where the private sector was unable to enter because of the vast outlay of capital involved, or unwilling, because the venture was not sufficiently profitable, but was indispensable to overall consolidation of capitalism in the country. The SOEs were providing the bulk of industrial inputs and investment capital to the power bloc fractions within the context of an inward-oriented pattern of domestic capital accumulation. At the same time, SOEs were benefiting the laboring classes in terms of employment opportunities and higher wages. These specific

---

1    See Heper 1985; Keyder 1987; Buğra 1994; Insel 1995.

historical legacies would influence the shape of the privatization experiment to come in Turkey in the following decades.

## 1    SOEs and Consolidation of Capitalism in Turkey: 1923–1945

The 1919–22 national liberation struggles against foreign occupation culminated in the founding of the Republic of Turkey in 1923. Mustafa Kemal (Atatürk) assumed the first presidency and helped centralize political power within the CHP (Republican People's Party – *Cumhuriyet Halk Partisi*). At the time, the capacity of the state administration was modest, and the domestic economy was largely subsistence-based agriculture organized around small villages. The relatively large part of the population lived outside of any generalized money relations and formal wage labour. Only a few small agrarian companies grew export commodities like unprocessed tobacco leaves, cotton, grapes and wheat. Local manufacturing did not have capacity to compete with European companies because techniques were traditional. Foreign capital invested in Turkey, but mostly in large ventures such as railroads, mining and ports. Turkey's economy was dependent on imports for most manufactured goods and capital flows (Marois 2012, 47).

The 1923 Izmir Economic Congress, which had a thousand of participants from CHP, state administration, the class of big landowners, commercial and industrial capital, aimed to initiate an industrialization process to overcome conditions of underdevelopment noted above. The participants agreed upon an active state apparatus that would support private sector development by offering public tenders, public-private partnerships, investment incentives, subsidized credits, and technical advice. The policy preference was thus for state-supported private-sector-led model of development over state-led model of development. The main reasons for this preference were the modest capacities of the state apparatus, restrictions imposed by the Great Powers on international trade (i.e frozen tariff rates at the 1916 rates that obliged the government to maintain a relatively open market), and the political aspiration of the new Turkish state to demonstrate its commitment to private-sector-led capitalist world (as opposed to state ownership of economic activity in socialist bloc).

To support private sector and ensure capitalist development, the Kemalist CHP cadres of the state helped domestic capital to establish a private domestic bank – Türkiye İş Bank – in 1924. Atatürk himself in collaboration with his father-in-law (i.e., prominent İzmir businessmen) subscribed an initial paid-up capital of the bank. The task of organizing and managing the bank was given to Celal Bayar, who had the total confidence of the entire business

community (Ahmad 1993, 96). İş Bank took the lead in financing infrastructure investments to stimulate domestic markets and mass consumption, while
allowing private sector to generate profits. İş Bank also initiated a series of participations in several sectors of the economy such as sugar and glass industries.
Iş Bank thus represented a class compromise between Kemalist-CHP cadres
and fractions of the power bloc that provided a route for capital accumulation
precisely at the time it was most needed.

The government then passed the 1927 Law for the Encouragement of
Industry (*Teşvik-i Sanayii Kanunu*). The objective was to provide all necessary
incentives (e.g., discounted transport on railways, free land for investment) for
nascent industrialists to profit handsomely that they would gain power and
make further industrial investments. This policy partly worked, and industrialists made huge fortunes within a short period of time. However, rather than
using these fortunes to make further industrial investments, they tended to
import and hoard foreign goods.

Although the CHP government's preferred policy was the private-sector-led
model of development, it had to establish some SOEs in order to take over
factories inherited from the Ottoman Empire as well as foreign companies.
For example, the Turkey Industry and Mining Bank (*Türkiye Sanayii ve Maadin
Bankası*) opened in 1925 as the first development bank to take over the textile miles inherited from the Ottoman Empire. To nationalize foreign-owned
railway lines and operate it under state ownership, the government created
the General Directorate of Railways (GDR) in 1927. By 1930, the GDR spent
almost 15 per cent of the state budget to nationalize 3,000km of foreign-owned
railway line, construct 800km of new railway line, and establish an iron-steel
plant (i.e., Kırıkkale) for producing rail bars (Hale 1981, 40–41). The goal was to
integrate Anatolian cities into a national market. When the line from Ankara
to Sivas was completed in 1930, daily *Cumhuriyet* newspaper wrote: "We are
knitting a web of steel around our territories" (Ahmad 1993, 90).

The impact of the Great Depression in 1929 led policymakers to recognize
that capitalist development would require more direct state investment. The
Great Depression caused disruption in international trade and prevented
Turkey from accessing vital imported items for consumption and production.
The power bloc and its hegemonic fraction (i.e., commercial capital) proved
to be ineffective in embarking upon significant investments, which would not
only substitute some industrial imported items for domestic ones, but also
bring real material benefits to the country that people could be grateful for.
Additionally, the trade restrictions that were imposed by the Lausanne Treaty
in 1923 came to an end at the beginning of 1929 and Turkey newly acquired
the freedom to increase tariffs to protect its infant industries. As a result, a

form of state-led model of development (*Etatisme*) took hold in the 1930s. The state assumed major responsibility for rapidly establishing SOEs, which undertook an import substitution strategy (ISI) to process domestically available raw materials mainly in the textile, paper, glass, and chemical industries (Boratav 2011, 59–80). State investments doubled from TL10 million annually during the period 1927–1930 to TL20 million during the 1930s (Tezel 1999, 79).

The establishment of SOEs was not, however, detrimental to the development of the bourgeoisie. As we will see below, the state established SOEs in sectors where the bourgeoisie was unable to enter at the time because of the vast outlay of capital involved, or unwilling, because the venture was not sufficiently profitable, but was indispensable to overall industrialization of the country (Yalman 2009, 163). The government did all it could with SOEs to enhance the prospects for private accumulation and encourage the growth of a bourgeoisie. The relations between SOEs and bourgeoisie were therefore complementary rather than antagonistic. The establishment of SOEs was also vital for mediating tensions between the wealth producing classes (the popular masses including the workers and the peasantry) and the wealth appropriating classes (the state elite and bourgeoisie) to ensure the stability of capitalist development in such early years of the Turkish Republic (Yalman 2002, 26–27).

It is important to say that the bourgeoisie was influential in affecting key decisions regarding the SOE program. For example, different elements of the Turkish business community pressured the CHP government to replace arbitrary-behaving and statist-minded Mustafa Şeref (Minister of Economy) with more business-friendly-liberal Celal Bayar, who had become responsible for orchestrating the state-led development program and thus establishing several SOEs between 1932 and 1939 (Ahmad 1993, 64). Korkut Boratav describes this important incident of the Turkish political economy history as the "Yalova Operation" (Boratav 1974, 258–259).

The various bourgeoisie fractions of the power bloc thus influenced the establishment process of SOEs and benefited from them. The commercial capitalists (e.g., İş Bank, Koç, Yaşar, Akkök and Borusan groups) had gained benefits by buying and selling SOE products in the domestic market and bidding for state investment tenders throughout the decade. For example, Koç Group was selling products of SOEs like Karabuk Iron and Steel. The large landowners and agricultural capitalists (e.g., Çukurova and Sabancı Groups) had benefited by selling their agricultural products to SOEs, when export markets were in crisis due to Great Depression. For example, Sabancı Group was selling cotton and wool to state textile factories above world market prices (Başkaya 2012). Industrial capital was also gaining in power, although not enough to have a strong representation within the power bloc and the state. More than 200 private industrial establishments came into operation between 1936 and 1938 (Tezel 1999, 80).

Although the ordinary wage earners had taken the brunt of taxation, as the level of taxation on industrialists and merchants was relatively much lower (Yalman 2019, 26), the working and popular classes were integrated into the SOE program in three ways. First, the state provided support to the agricultural sector, which was employing a large bulk of labour force, through SOEs. Second, newly established SOEs were providing secure employment opportunities for the popular masses. Third, the state established some state institutions to prevent price fluctuations in agricultural crops negatively influencing the daily lives of popular masses. In 1936, the CHP established the Office of Soil Products (TMO) to buy and sell wheat and build grain silos in order to even out the fluctuations in crop prices and output from year to year. The government also converted the Ziraat Bank (Agricultural Bank) into a state-owned bank and increased its capital base in order to subsidize crop prices and meet the financing needs of small farmers and agricultural co-operatives (Marois 2012, 48). It is important to remember that the agriculture sector as a whole was vital for the functioning of the state-led SOE program during the 1930s because it was providing inputs to newly established state-production units such as textile factories.

The establishment of SOEs had found ideological and policy expression in the first five-year industrialization plan (1934–1938) of the country. The plan suggested that Turkey should undertake an import substitution strategy based on state enterprises that process domestically available raw materials. This strategy aimed at protecting agricultural and mining sectors from falling prices in the world market and reducing Turkey's import needs for basic consumption goods.

The CHP government created two development banks – Sümerbank and Etibank – to organize and finance the implementation of the plan. Both entities acted as state-owned holding companies with minor banking functions, rather than state-owned banks as their titles might have suggested. Sümerbank was set up in 1933 and took over the responsibility of the majority of the new textile and paper plants established under the plan. Etibank was created in 1935 with primary responsibility for the state enterprises operating in the mining and chemicals industries.

Thus, the first five-year industrialization plan focused on establishing SOEs in five main industrial categories: textile, mining, paper, glass, and chemicals. The priority was primarily on the textile. Nearly half of the investment budget was spent on four new textile factories that Sümerbank established in different parts of Anatolia to manufacture cotton clothes and wool fabrics (Inan 1972).

One of the largest textile factories was opened in central Anatolian city of Kayseri in 1935. It boasted 33,000 spindles, 1,082 looms, a dyeing plant, and had become a showpiece of Turkish industry. The machinery was supplied by the Soviet Union, while winding apparatus from the United States (Ahmad 1993, 98). Other three textile factories were opened in Konya, Nazilli, and Malatya.

Besides textile, one-quarter of the planned investment went into mining, 12 per cent to paper industry, and 5 percent each for the glass and chemicals industry (Birtek 1985). In the mining industry, the Karabük Iron and Steel Plant as Turkey's first integrated plant was the biggest investment. The plant used domestically extracted iron ore and coal to produce 175,000 tons of iron and steel to meet Turkey's needs. In the paper industry, the most important new SOE was the Izmit Cellulose & Paper Factory, which was established by Sümerbank in 1936. In the glass industry, Sümerbank and the Is Bank joined together to build the Paşabahçe glass factory as a new SOE in Istanbul, where raw materials such as glass sand and lime powder were available in abundance. In the chemicals industry, Etibank established several small-scale superphosphate and chlorine factories in 1938 (Inan 1972).

Concurrently, the CHP government nationalized some of the foreign-owned mines (e.g., coal, iron ore, copper, sulphur) to support newly created SOEs. The government believed that these mines, which were expected to provide inputs to SOEs, had engaged in speculative activities around selling mining licenses and thus worked with low capacity. In addition to mines, the government nationalized most of the remaining foreign-owned railway lines with the aim of using them to move inputs from mines and farms to SOEs with subsidized prices. For example, Adana railway line in southern Turkey was strategically important to move cotton from the fertile lands of Çukurova region to state-owned textile factories of Sümerbank.

Although the CHP government was criticized by foreign capital and advanced capitalist states for its tendency to nationalize foreign-owned mines and railways, it mitigated those criticisms through a series of announcements that such nationalizations did not mean systematic opposition to foreign capital, but only represented a tactical behavior to improve economic efficiency (Boratav 1974). In fact, the CHP's positive attitude towards foreign capital was expressed most concretely in its agreement with the British state to allow British companies such as H. A. Brassert to involve in Karabük iron and steel investment mentioned above.

Overall, the implementation of the first five-year industrialization plan was successful. At the close of the plan in the late 1930s, nearly all the targets were fulfilled and dozens of new SOEs were established to consolidate capitalism. The process of industrialization set in motion and Turkey was already producing some of the goods she had previously imported. However, the Second World War interrupted the continuation of these efforts. Although the CHP government adopted the second five-year industrialization plan in 1939, the plan had to be abandoned as military expenditures stemming from war preparations dominated the state budget.[2]

The Second World War not only prevented the implementation of the plan but also caused high inflation, black marketing and speculative activities as the prices of food products and raw materials increased significantly. This led to growing tensions between the capitalist classes and popular-working classes. On the one hand, Turkey's popular and working classes felt the direct impact of wartime conditions through a public wage freeze, food price increases and great deprivation. The government was forced to ration even bread, that is the staple of the Turkish diet. On the other hand, the commercial and agricultural capitalists, who controlled the production, distribution and export/import of food and consumer products, accumulated a lot of money capital during the Second World War. They then used that money capital to establish new banks such as Yapı Kredi Bank, Garanti Bank, Akbank, and insurance companies like Doğan Insurance and Halk Insurance (Öztürk 2010, 61).

The Turkish state played a crucial role in actively mediating those tensions building between popular-working classes and domestic capitalists. The intro-duction of a new range of legal and economic measures was an important part of this process. Many of these measures were designed to prevent inflationist pressures and wartime profiteering exceeding the toleration level of popular-working classes. For example, the National Defense Law (*Milli Korunma Kanunu*) of 1940 gave the government extensive emergency powers to control prices and the supply of goods in the market (e.g., forced collection of farm produce), to sequestrate property and private establishments temporarily, and to enforce compulsory labour especially in the mines (Hale 1981, 59–60).[3]

Another example of these measures was the Wealth Tax (*Varlık Vergisi*) of 1942, which in theory had the aim of soaking up part of the vast profits gained by speculative activities in the inflationary wartime conditions and was to be applied on a non-repetitive basis to wealthy segments of the population. In practice, however, local evaluation committees had made wealth assessments based on arbitrary criteria. As such, these committees had discriminated

---

2   The military expenditures constituted 60 per cent of the state budget during the Second World War.

3   Important examples of these property and business sequestrations include Ankara Cement Factory, Zeytinburnu Cement Factory, and Tuzla Brick Factory. Examples of compulsory labour happened in Zonguldak coalfield, and Soma, Değirmisaz, Tavşanlı lignite mines.

against the minority groups and foreign investors in big cities like Istanbul, which paid nearly 65 per cent of the total amount of tax collected (Hale 1981, 70–71). The Wealth Tax thus helped to divert the increasing discontent of popular-working classes from the state to minority groups and foreign investors (Ahmad 1993, 71). It also indirectly strengthened national-Anatolian capitalists as Vehbi Koç and Hacı Ömer Sabancı, who accumulated significant amount of capital by trading agricultural products and basic consumer goods since the outbreak of war and were ready to use the space that just opened up to head towards Istanbul.

By 1945, a shaky Turkish economy was radically transformed from a largely non-capitalist subsistence production basis, depending on the foreign markets for even non-durable basic consumer goods, to a relatively stable capitalist society defined by emerging national bourgeoisie and effective SOEs geared towards national capitalist development. Capitalist social relations assumed an undeniably important influence over everyone's lives and society's natural development trajectory.

## 2      SOEs and Post-war Expansion of Capitalism in Turkey: 1946–1960

During the war years high inflation, black marketing, speculative activities, and severe restrictions on social, economic and political freedoms created hardships that led to resentment among pro-market political elites, landlords, small farmers, rural residents and students. The desire for change was also expressed by the Istanbul Merchant Association (*Istanbul Tüccar Derneği*), which comprised commercial capitalists and would-be industrialists (Yalman 2009, 185). Building on this discontent the newly formed Democratic Party (DP – *Demokrat Parti*) broke with the CHP leadership in 1946 and established links to those groups. Four of the founding fathers of the DP were the businessman-banker Celal Bayar, the bureaucrat Refik Koraltan, the historian Professor Fuad Köprülü, and the cotton-growing landlord Adnan Menderes (Ahmad 1993, 103). In May 1950, the DP won the general election with 53 per cent of the vote.

As the basic outlines of the postwar international order were emerging, the DP government and the Turkish bourgeoisie seemed to be confronted with an important question: how to reorganize the fields of activity between the private sector and expanded state sector so as to achieve capitalist industrialization-expansion while also integrating Turkey into the liberalizing world economy (Yalman 2019, 31). After few years of liberalization and anti-state discourse during which the DP leadership pushed for liberalized foreign trade and a retreat of the state in the realm of economic activity under the influence of the

Truman Doctrine and the Marshall Plan, the DP shifted back towards a strategy of ISI with restrictive import regime and an expansion of the state sector in the mid-1950s.

There was, however, a new development to accompany the old processes. For the first time, the emerging national bourgeoisie were ready and willing to turn themselves into manufacturers of previously imported and traded consumer durables on a mass scale (Savran 2011, 162–63). As Galip Yalman has put it, "the newly established Istanbul Chamber of Industry had been making clear that the DP government's decision to implement a restrictive import regime had been taken in consultation with them and had their full support as a necessary policy to develop national industry" (Yalman 2009, 204). The aforementioned Vehbi Koç and Hacı Ömer Sabancı were two good examples of these would-be industrialists. Koç founded Arçelik and Türk Demirdöküm in 1955 to manufacture household appliances such as radiators, boilers, washing machines and refrigerators. Koç also founded Otosan automobile factory in 1959, which transformed him from being a distributor to assembler-manufacturer of Ford automobiles in Turkey (Koç 1983, 77–85). Likewise, Sabancı established Bossa to produce textiles (Öztürk 2010, 61).

Within this context, the representatives of the private sector had begun to collectively articulate and organize for more effective state, especially in the area of intermediate goods production and infrastructure investment that would support not only of new industrialists but also the expansion of capitalism in Turkey in general. Unsurprisingly, the government supported the demand of the private sector for more intermediate goods production and infrastructure investment. So, the establishment of SOEs in those areas took major steps forward.

Let me now look at new investments in intermediate goods production in more detail. First, the DP government established the Turkish Cement Industry (TCI) as a state-owned enterprise in 1953 to build cement plants and participate in private cement plant investments. Due to efforts of the TCI, the cement production of Turkey rose from 0.9 million tons in 1956 to 2 million tons in 1960 (Sönmez 1978, 73).

Second, the Turkish Petroleum Corporation (TPAO) was established in 1954 as a vertically integrated state-owned petroleum company to operate across the entire supply chain, from production to refinery and distribution of petroleum products. As one of its first projects, the TPAO built the Batman Refinery, Turkey's first modern crude oil refinery, with annual capacity of 330,000 tons. It was the American Parsons Corporation that designed, engineered and provided construction oversight for the refinery project. Parsons Corporation also trained hundreds of Turkish workers in various crafts to operate the refinery. The scale of the Batman Refinery project becomes more apparent when considering that Turkey had only two more refineries with annual capacities of 3,000 and 70,000 tons respectively at the time. It should be remembered that the Batman Refinery project was vital to satisfy domestic petroleum consumption demand that increased eightfold, or from about 205,000 tons to about 1,594,000 tons from 1945 to 1960 (Neyzi 1963, 124–125).

Third, the government founded the Turkish Iron and Steel Enterprise (TDCİ) in 1955 to take over the ownership of Karabük Iron and Steel plant and several iron ore fields to create a major state company specializing in iron and steel production. This was a necessary step to increase production that would respond to increasing demands of new industrial establishments for iron and steel products. To support funding all these investments in intermediate goods sectors, new state-owned banks such as Deniz Bank and Vakıf Bank were established in 1952 and 1954, respectively. The missions of these banks were to set as contributing to increasing savings rate and utilizing them for financing new investments.

In addition to making investments in intermediate goods production, the state became active in the infrastructure sectors. For example, Etibank, a state-owned holding company, made significant efforts to improve electricity infrastructure of major industrial hubs like Istanbul, Izmir and Adana. As a result, total electricity production of country rose threefold in a period of ten years between 1950 and 1960 (Sönmez 1978, 67–68). What was also noticeable state investment in the infrastructure sectors was the considerable expansion of the road network of the country that opened up the villages of Anatolia for the first time. Supported by the financial and technical assistance of the United States, hard surface roads capable of carrying heavy vehicles from automobiles to heavy trucks increased from 1,642 km in 1950 to 7,049 km in 1960 (Ahmad 1993, 115). Such road network provided the basis for the Turkish automobile industry, which was beginning to set up in the late 1950s. It also connected people in small villages to the lifestyle of towns and cities, which led to growing demand for household appliances provided by new industrialists.

In this period, foreign capital significantly contributed Turkey's efforts to turn to industry on a mass scale and achieve capitalist expansion. There were two interrelated dynamics at work here. Domestically, the DP government relaxed controls on foreign capital by the enactment of the Law for the Encouragement of Foreign Capital in 1954. Globally, the productive capital of industrialized countries entered the process of international expansion and had begun searching for direct industrial investments in the industrializing countries like Turkey. One example of this was the Ford Motor Company's partnership with Turkey's Koç Group to establish Ford Otosan automobile factory. Another example of this was the German industrial conglomerate Mannesmann's collaboration with Turkey's Sümerbank to establish a steel tube-pipe manufacturing factory (Şeni 1978, 48–49).

The World Bank also involved in the process; it helped to establish the TSKB (Industrial Development Bank of Turkey; *Türkiye Sinai Kalkınma Bankası*) as the first private investment and development bank of the country. TSKB was the only organization handling cash sales of foreign currencies released under the Marshall Plan in the 1950s. TSKB played a critical role in the development of import-substituting industrialization by providing credit support for a wide range of manufacturing projects (Yalman 2019, 33). Examples of these projects include Aksu Textile of Akkök Group, Bossa Textile of Sabancı Group, Demirdöküm of Koç Group, and DYO of Yaşar Group (Öztürk 2010, 72).

Overall, postwar capitalist expansion had meant more infrastructure investment and industrial production, greater domestic market, and a larger population. According to one survey, 40 per cent of the private sector firms which were in operation at the end of 1960s had been established during the 1950s (Yalman 2009, 211). The number of automobiles and trucks significantly increased from 8,012 to 37,616 over a period of just a decade.

Yet the deepening foreign exchange crisis, gaping budget deficit, and rising polarization of society in the late 1950s demonstrated that the situation was not sustainable. The DP government, under the increasing influence of large landowners and merchants, found it increasingly difficult to put industry (over agriculture and commerce) and planning (over arbitrary governing) at the top of its list of policy priorities. In this context, new but well-organized modernizing fractions of industrial capital slowly dissociated themselves from the class alliance represented by the DP. The urban intellectuals, student movements and strengthening industrial workers also became discontented with different aspects of DP rule, such as the alleged violation of secular foundations of the state and increasing resorts to repressive measures following the emergence of economic hardships (Taylan 1984, 13). The turbulence culminated in the 27 May 1960 military coup that was ended the DP rule and deposed its leaders.

## 3 SOEs, Duty Losses and Class Compromises: 1961–1980

Out of the 1960 military coup emerged the 1961 Constitution that introduced and institutionalized development planning and social justice dimensions within the state apparatus and its regulatory and distributive framework.

The development-planning dimension included new mechanisms that mitigated the fears of the industrial capital. One of these mechanisms was the introduction of five-year development plans (FYDPs) and the creation the State Planning Organization (SPO) as a specialized economic unit charged with a duty of managing the FYDPs. Another new mechanism that mitigated the fears of the industrial capital was the introduction of a system of controls on party politics to restrict the powers of the rurally based majority in parliament through various checks and balances such as a Constitutional Court and a High Administrative Court with extended powers (Taylan 1984).

The social justice dimension, on the other hand, provided the legal framework for the working classes to establish their own economic and political organizations. This included the rights to form trade unions, to engage in collective bargaining and to strike, which were largely absent until this point in time. Perhaps as important as the worker rights were the explicit guarantees of freedom of thought, expression, association and publication as well as other civil liberties, contained in the new constitution. Indeed, it could be argued that the authors of the 1961 Constitution strived to realize both planned economic development and social justice, thereby creating the conditions for a new political consensus on a lasting basis.

The development plans had been the backbone of that strategy. The first five-year development plan lasted from 1963 to 1967, the second from 1968 to 1972, and the third from 1973 to 1977. It is important to note, however, that these three development plans were substantially different from the industrialization plans of the 1930s discussed above. The earlier plans were 1) based on domestic inputs, 2) depended heavily on the state sector to undertake industrial investments, and 3) oriented to the production of basic consumer goods for mass market with little participation of foreign capital. The latter plans were 1) based on both domestic and imported inputs, 2) depended on the private sector to undertake industrial investments, wherein state sector served the private sector interest by producing intermediate goods and providing investment capital within the mixed-economic framework, and 3) oriented to the production of durable consumer goods for a relatively high-income market with significant participation of foreign capital.

During the 1960s and 1970s, the state and SOEs were entrusted with important duties in the development plans of mixed-economic framework. These ranged from producing intermediate goods, accelerating infrastructure investments and providing investment capital for capitalists to providing employment opportunities for workers.First, state turned more and more to those industries that produced intermediate goods and established SOEs to satisfy growing demand for iron and steel products, cement, aluminum, and petroleum products.[4] A particularly important example of this was the establishment of Erdemir (Ereğli Iron and Steel Enterprise) as a state-owned enterprise. Construction and installation work of Erdemir started in 1961 with a USAİD (United States Agency for International Development) loan of $130 million and only after four years, it started production in 1965 with a production capacity of 470,000 tons of flat steel (Szyliowicz 1991). Indeed, Erdemir might be considered as one of the major investment projects realized after the declaration of the Turkish Republic. The founding shareholders of Erdemir included Turkish state, Iş Bank and Koppers Associate (i.e., a consortium of three US companies – Koppers, Blaw Know and Westinghouse International) (iBRD 1972). Although Karabük Iron and Steel factory had been producing long steel products since the late 1930s, Erdemir became the first and only domestic producer of flat steel products such as hot roll, cold roll and tinplate that were used as basic inputs in newly emerging automotive, white goods, pipes and tube, electronics, mechanical engineering, heating equipment and packaging industries. Some of the recently established private companies that were using Erdemir's flat steel included Arçelik (consumer electronics), Otoyol (trucks and tractors) and Tofaş (automobiles) of Koç Group; Oyak Renault (automobiles) of Oyak Group; BMC Turkey (bus and truck) and Çelik Montaj (motorcycles) of Anadolu Group.

The establishment of Petkim (Petkim Petrochemical Complex) in 1965 was another important example of state activity in intermediate goods industries. Petkim produced a wide range of petro-chemical products that were needed by private industrialists (e.g., Çukurova, Eczacıbaşı, Sabancı and Dinçkök Groups) working in chemical, pharmaceutical and textile industries. Other relatively smaller state investments in intermediate good industries included the establishment of three mineral processing plants (e.g., Seydişehir Aluminum, Bandırma Boric Acid and Karadeniz Copper) as part of the state-owned Etibank as well as the formation of four more cement plants in various parts of Turkey under the structure of the state-owned TCI. It is important to remember that the state took the initiative to invest in these intermediate good industries because they required great capital, large organization, and high risk taking where Turkish private sector did not and could not satisfy at the time.

Second, the state accelerated its infrastructure investments through SOEs and other state institutions in the post-1960 period. One priority area was electricity production. On the one hand, the DSI (State Water Works – *Devlet Su*

---

4    Approximately 35 per cent of the total state budget in Turkey was spent on the intermediate
     goods industries throughout 1960s and 1970s (Öztürk 2010, 83–84).

*İşleri*) invested in dams and hydroelectric power plants (HEPs). In 1967, Sarıyar HEP was established as Turkey's first large-scale hydroelectric power plant near the capital city Ankara. In 1971, Doğan Kent and Kovada HEPs were put into operation with 74 million and 200 million kilowatt-hour yearly energy production capacity respectively. In 1975, Turkey's largest dam and HEP, Keban, was established on the Euphrates in Eastern Turkey with a capacity of 5.5 billion kilowatt-hour energy.

On the other hand, Etibank and TEK (Turkish Electricity Administration – Türkiye Elektrik Kurumu) significantly expanded the number of thermal power plants (TPPs). In 1973, Seyitömer TPP was established in Kütahya province with engineering and technical support of French firms (Sofrelec and Stein) to produce 1.8 billion kilowatt-hour energies. The plant burned lignite that mined locally and supplied electricity to rapidly industrializing and urbanizing northwestern region of Turkey. In the same year, Hopa TPP was put into operation in the Northeastern Anatolian region with a capacity of 300 million kilowatt-hour energy. Afşin-Elbistan TPP, one of the largest TPP in the country, was built by the TEK in Mediterranean region of Turkey. This plant, which supplied by the local Afşin-Elbistan lignite mines, had a capacity to produce 600 million kilowatt-hour energies. All these investments were made possible by the large resources dedicated to the Ministry of Energy at the time. On average, the investments of the Ministry of Energy accounted for the 35 per cent of total public investments over the late 1960s and 1970s.[5]

Third, the SOEs supported private capital formation through the "participation" (*iştirak*) mechanism, which enabled SOEs to participate in the establishment of industrial enterprises in the private sector. More specifically, SOEs acquired 15 to 49 per cent of shares of new industrial enterprises of private companies and became their minority partners. Given the lack of capital market as a source of funds necessary for new investments, such mechanism of support was mainly aimed to encourage private companies to take a more aggressive role in direct investments into manufacturing sectors. It was a successful attempt. The number of SOE-private companies participations rose from 72 in 1962 to 281 in 1984 (Sönmez 1987, 120). Due to their dominant positions in the manufacturing sectors, Koç, OYAK, and İş Bank groups were particularly benefited from the participation mechanism. Koç Group founded Türk Traktör (tractor producer) with 45 per cent participation of state-owned Ziraat Bank, and Tofaş (automobile producer) with 23 per cent participation of state-owned

---

5    This information about HEPs, TPPs and Ministry of Energy is drawn from the minutes of the Senate of the Republic, which was the upper house of Turkish Parliament between 1961 and 1980.

MKEK (Mechanical and Chemical Industry Institution). OYAK group entered into cement sector with participation of the state-owned TCI. İş Bank group participated with the state-owned Turkish Electricity Institution to operate in the electricity generation sector (Sönmez 1987, 122–125).

It was the duty loss (görev zararı) mechanism that institutionalized and made all these state and SOE supports to private sector possible. Duty losses are mandated financial losses officially assigned to SOEs that should be compensated for by government transfers (Marois and Güngen 2016, 11). For example, if a SOE product was sold to industrialists as an input below the cost of production, the difference was considered as a duty loss and was paid by the government to the SOE budget. In 1976, Petkim sold PVC products to industrialists for a price of TL 12.5 thousand, when the cost of production was TL 14 thousand. Similarly, Etibank sold copper 12 per cent below the production cost, while Seydişehir Aluminium factory sold products 28 per cent below the production cost (Sönmez 1987, 120). As such, duty loss mechanism enabled SOEs to channel resources into the industrialists, whether in the form of subsidized inputs, favourable equity participations, or cheap credits.

Duty losses also benefited the laboring classes in terms of employment opportunities, higher wages and cheap credits. Although SOEs were suffering large financial problems and waning profitability in the post 1961 period, SOE workers did not experience job losses. Instead, the number of total SOE workforce increased from 321,000 in 1967 to 550,000 in 1977. Moreover, a growing and organized SOE workers had 95 per cent real wage gains in the same period, much higher than private sector workers (Kepenek 1990, 95–100). Furthermore, state-owned banks such as Ziraat Bank provided loan write-offs for struggling Turkish farmers in the rural areas (Marois 2012, 118). It is critical to remember that a concept of duty loss was very compatible with the

TABLE 2     Duty losses in Turkey

| Year | Share of state budget (%) |
| --- | --- |
| 1940s | 1,0 |
| 1950s | 0,9 |
| 1960s | 1,3 |
| 1970s | 5,9 |
| 1980s | 5,6 |

SOURCE: KEPENEK (1990)

development planning and social justice dimensions of the mixed-economic framework discussed above. In this way, SOE duty loss mechanism represented a post-1960 class compromise between capital, labour and state to facilitate stable capitalist development in Turkey (see Table 2).

This compromise was far from perfect. A small number of capital groups – especially the large ones – took the greatest advantage of the state support via duty losses and acquired a position of oligopolistic production power. For example, four capital groups acquired a third of pharmaceutical sector, six capital groups secured half of the motor land vehicles sector, and two capital groups controlled much of the consumer appliance sector (Sönmez 1987, 45–62). Such centralization and concentration of capital encouraged the development of individuals and family-based groups into large conglomerates known as holdings. While there were only two holdings during the early 1960s, more than fifty new holdings were formed between 1963 and 1976 (Öztürk 2010, 92). Some of the leading ones were Koç Holding (1963), Sabancı Holding (1967), Yaşar Holding (1968), Anadolu Holding (1969), Eczacıbaşı Holding (1970), Tekfen Holding (1972), Alarko Holding (1973), Borusan Holding (1973), Çukurova Holding (1973), and Enka Holding (1973).

Three key characteristics of these holdings need to be highlighted. First, these holdings had economic activities that stretch across all moments of the circuit of capital: production of commodities, the sale of commodities, and eventually financial accumulation. Over the last decade, the holdings made a special effort to gain control over money capital through ownership of banks. The number of holdings with bank ownership reached 11 by the end of 1970s (Yalman 2019, 39). For instance, Koç Holding became a majority partner of Garanti Bank, Sabancı Holding established Akbank, and Çukurova Holding acquired Yapı Kredi Bank (Oğuz 2008). Second, in terms of geographical distribution, most of the holdings concentrated around two biggest western cities of Turkey – İstanbul and İzmir (Çokgezen 2000, 530–531). Third, the activities of these holdings were buttressed by – and connected with – accumulation structures of large foreign capital, either through acquiring licenses or establishing partnerships and joint ventures with foreign industry giants. For instance, Koç Holding, the largest Turkish conglomerate at the time, collaborated with Ford Motors in its automobile production journey.

However, the expanded presence of İstanbul/İzmir based large holdings within the Turkish economy clashed more and more frequently with the interests of Anatolian-based Small and Medium Enterprises (SMEs). The main points of conflicts and divisions between the two bourgeoisie fractions were about the access to SOE inputs, the use of participation mechanism, the distribution of state credits and import quotas (Marois 2012, 58). Those who represented the Anatolian SMEs in the business community and political scene began to say that SMEs were increasingly failing to survive competition with large holdings that were supported by the state and SOEs (Ahmad 1993, 143).

These conflicts and divisions were initially reflected in the TOBB (Union of Chambers and Commodity Exchanges of Turkey; *Türkiye Odalar ve Borsalar Birliği*) election in 1969. Since its establishment in 1950, TOBB had historically served as the only official representative body of the Turkish business community – encompassing all businesses across different sectors, sizes and geographical locations. In 1969, with the support of the delegates from Anatolia, Professor Necmettin Erbakan defeated the large holdings' candidate in the election for the presidency of the TOBB. This result was partly due to the TOBB's representation mechanism that entitled each local/city chamber to have at least one delegate/vote, but no more than ten (Çokgezen 2000, 530). Such an institutional mechanism prevented local chambers around large cities like İstanbul and İzmir that had large holdings in their membership from influencing the outcome of election.

Of course, the victory of Necmettin Erbakan, who represented the interests of Anatolian SMEs, led to discontent of large holdings. As a result, holdings decided to further their interests through their own exclusive organization. They eventually split from TOBB and formed the TUSİAD (Turkish Industry and Business Association; *Türk Sanayicileri ve İş İnsanları Derneği*) in 1971. Since then, TUSİAD had become known as the main representative body of big holdings headquartered around İstanbul and İzmir. TOBB, on the other hand, increasingly turned toward being a representative body of SMEs located in Anatolian cities (Çokgezen 2000, 531).

The conflicts and divisions between two bourgeoisie fractions were reflected in the political scene as well. As the ruling AP (Justice Party; *Adalet Partisi*) under the leadership of Süleyman Demirel rejected to accept Erbakan's application to be a party candidate in the 1969 general elections, Erbakan and his supporters founded a new political party known as the MNP (National Order Party; *Milli Selamet Partisi*) in 1970. The party programme of the MNP combined Islamic and nationalist rhetoric with references to a glorified Ottoman past. Unsurprisingly, the party expressed anti-Western sentiments and directly challenged close relations with the European Economic Community. This was in contrast with the political project of holding groups supporting Turkey's integration with Europe and Western capital. This signaled a polarization of the political scene. The holdings acquired dominance within the AP and favoured Turkey's close relations with the West, while the Anatolian SMEs developed strong ties with the Erbakan's MNP (Taylan 1984, 26).

Class conflict also appeared between Turkish capitalists and workers. The breaking point came with the 1967 split of three unions from the non-political, pro-government trade union confederation Türk-İş (Confederation of Turkish Trade Unions; *Türkiye İşçi Sendikaları Konfederasyonu*), which along with other independent unions formed the DİSK (Confederation of Revolutionary Trade Unions of Turkey; *Türkiye Devrimci İşçi Sendikaları Konfederasyonu*). Unlike Türk-İş, the DİSK adopted what is called a "class and mass based militant unionism" (Akkaya 2002). Through the 1970s, the DİSK had been the main actor leading the class-based politics in Turkey and supported the socialist Turkish Labour Party (TIP), some of whose founding members were DİSK leaders.

Collective bargaining negotiations between 1974 and 1976 and metal industry strikes between 1977 and 1978 showed how effective the working class could be against capital. While the trade unions became increasingly effective in defending their members' interests, the Turkish bourgeoisie had started to see the rising class-consciousness of the working class as a threat to the existing social order (Yalman 2019, 43). For example, Koç Holding Chairman, Vehbi Koç, writes in his memoirs: "For me, the mid- and late-1970s was a nightmare" (Koç 1987, 60). His daughter and board member of Koç Holding, Suna Kıraç, adds: "We do not have any more power left to endure another 8.5 months long strike" (Kıraç 2006, 101).

In addition to deepening class conflicts, the economic conditions of the ISI regime were worsening. Industrialists were struggling to buy necessary inputs to keep ISI regime continuing. This was partly due to the destabilization of the public finance records. SOEs such as Sümerbank and Etibank that were providing subsidized inputs to industrialists accumulated significant amount of duty losses and found it financially unsustainable to maintain their roles as input providers. At the same time, growing foreign exchange shortages had made it increasingly difficult for the Turkey to import energy-generating commodities such as oil and gas, which were vital inputs for manufacturing and other businesses.

It is in this context of worsening economic conditions and deepening class conflicts that a wide range of policymakers and different social forces began to raise their voices against the post-1960 mixed-economic framework that was based on development planning, social justice and duty loss mechanisms. This eventually led to the military coup of 1980, which ended the mixed-economic framework and brought the neoliberal SOE privatization efforts to the fore.

## 4        Conclusion

Turkey had experienced a capitalist consolidation and expansion processes since the establishment of the republican regime in 1923. Contrary to statist studies that interpret state and SOEs as entities against market/social forces, the state and SOEs played indispensable roles in the capitalist consolidation and expansion processes in Turkey. As such, the relations between SOEs and the social classes were internal and complementary, rather than external and antagonistic. The SOEs were often established in such sectors where the private sector was unable to enter because of the vast outlay of capital involved, or unwilling, because the venture was not sufficiently profitable, but was indispensable to overall consolidation and expansion of capitalism in the country. State policies on SOEs should therefore be seen as a reflection of demands coming from different social classes and shifting needs of capital accumulation dynamics. Between 1923 and 1945, the SOEs played a system-supporting role, nurturing and sustaining conditions that enabled the initial development of private sector and the consolidation of capitalism. The period after World War Two saw a phenomenal growth of SOEs that were providing the bulk of industrial inputs, infrastructure services and investment capital to expanding private companies within the mixed-economic framework, while intra-capital conflicts over access to those SOE benefits began escalating in the late 1970s. In both periods, SOEs were also benefiting the popular and laboring classes in terms of employment opportunities, higher wages, cheap credits and consumption, which had greatly facilitated the stability of capitalist development in Turkey.

These specific historical legacies would influence the shape of the privatization experiment to come in Turkey in the following decades. First, the neoliberal privatization efforts would have to face the challenge of transforming the age-old relationship between SOEs and the private companies. Second, intra-capital conflicts would weaken the capacity of neoliberal advocates to create unity inside the power bloc and the state in their efforts to privatize the SOEs.

# CHAPTER 3

# To Privatize or Not to Privatize? Interventions to Privatization Process: 1984–2001

Turkey's neoliberal transformation was initiated by the launch of the stabilization program on 24 January 1980. The program signified a radical change both in the mode of articulation of the Turkish economy within the global economy and in the role that the state used to assume in the conduct of economic policy for most of the time since the establishment of the Turkish Republic in the early 1920s. Regarding the mode of articulation, it was officially announced that import-substitution industrialization that created balance of payment difficulties and macro economic instabilities would be scrapped and replaced with an export-oriented trade and development strategy. In relation to the nature of state-economy relationship, it was proposed that the dominance of the state in key industries and services would be removed with privatization, and the state's intervention with the pricing and resource allocation processes of the market economy would be minimized. Yet it was the 12 September 1980 military coup's violent suppression of all social opposition – the organized working class and leftist intelligentsia being the primary target – that facilitated the neoliberal transformation (Yalman 2019, 51–52).

As one of the key aspects of neoliberal transformation, privatization was therefore placed on the Turkish policy agenda in 1984. In fact, Turkey was among the first developing countries to announce a comprehensive privatization program. However, the implementation of the program largely failed to materialize between 1984 and 2001. In this period, Turkey generated only around $19 billion of value from the process. About $7 billion of this came from divestitures. More than half of all divestiture revenues came from sales of SOE participations in private companies, or from the sale of minority shares in large-scale SOEs. The full divestiture (over 51%) was realized only in a few sectors such as cement and banking, where the privatized SOEs were small and medium-sized. The remaining $12 billion came from PPPs – the majority of which were realized only in the second half of the 1990s. The limited size of privatization in Turkey between 1984 and 2001 could be starkly illustrated by the comparison with other countries. While the privatization revenue/GDP ratio were 25% in Portugal, 18% in Australia, 10% in Malaysia, 9% in Italy, 7%

in Greece and 6% in Mexico, it was only 2% in Turkey.[1] Moreover, Turkey's ratio was less than both the developed countries average and developing countries average (See Bortolotti, Fantini and Siniscalco 2003, 321; Belke et al. 2007, 225).

Although the competitive imperatives of contemporary capitalism (or neo-liberalism) and the structural adjustment programs of the World Bank and the IMF placed significant pressure on Turkish government and state elites to implement privatization during the 1980s and 1990s, the implementation of privatization has been contested inside and outside of the state apparatus by the Turkish power bloc (i.e., fractions of capital) within the constitutive context of the prevailing strategies of the domestic capital accumulation regime of Turkey at the time. More specifically, power bloc's intervention to prevent complete privatization of SOEs was driven by a variety of factors: (1) the comfortable relationship that the power bloc had enjoyed with the SOEs as a result of the duty loss mechanism described in the previous chapter, (2) the reluctance of the TUSİAD-based big holdings to commit large-scale finance to privatization when other accumulation opportunities (e.g. state debt financing) were available in the financial markets, (3) the intra-capital conflict between the TUSİAD-based big holdings and Anatolian capital fractions, and (4) the lack of operational harmony within the state institutional apparatus on the question of privatization.

1     The World Bank and Foreignization Campaign of the Power
      Bloc: 1984–1993

Following the military coup, Turgut Özal, who had close ties to financial circles in the West (especially the IMF and the World Bank), emerged as the key political figure behind Turkey's neoliberal transformation and privatization program. Özal first served as the Deputy Prime Minister in the military government between 1980 and 1983, then as the Prime Minister and the leader of ANAP (Motherland Party – Anavatan Partisi) from 1983 to 1989, and the President of Turkey from 1989 to 1993.

The Özal ANAP (Motherland Party – Anavatan Partisi) administration officially started the SOE privatization program in 1984. The World Bank had a crucial influence on the initiation of the program through provision of five structural adjustment loans (SALs), a record number between 1980 and 1984.

---

1  Privatization revenue/GDP is the ratio of total privatization revenues (excluding PPPs) cumulated in the period (i.e., 1977–1999) to 1999 GDP. It is important to note that the PPP revenues in those countries show similar trends too.

Under the conditions of those SALs, Turkey had to diminish the size of the state sector and push through legal and institutional changes enabling the privatization of the SOEs.

In line with the conditions of SALs, in May 1984, the Özal government passed a new law (2983) that created an extra-budgetary fund agency (Mass Housing and Public Participation Agency; *Toplu Konut ve Kamu Ortaklığı İdaresi – TKKOI*) responsible for privatization. Then in June the government passed another law (233) to define a new organizational framework for SOEs that would facilitate privatization. The new framework introduced the category of contract worker that could be employed under a temporary-individual contract (as opposed to long-term secure employment of traditional SOE worker) and excluded from a collective agreement. More importantly, the new framework divided large SOEs into several small units to make their privatization easier. For example, an integrated state petroleum company TPAO, mentioned in Chapter 2, divided into six units: TPAO (deals with drilling and production), BOTAŞ (involves pipeline transportation and storage), DİTAŞ (deals with oil-tanker transportation), TÜPRAŞ (responsible for refining of petroleum crude oil), PETKİM (deals with manufacturing of petro-chemical products), and POAŞ (deals with marketing and distribution of products derived from crude oil). The enactment of Laws 2983 and 233 was thus important for the Özal government, not only to keep promises to the World Bank but also to make necessary legal and structural arrangements for privatization.

The World Bank continued to exert pressure on the Özal government and provided technical-financial assistance to help find foreign consulting firms that could prepare reports (i.e., roadmap) on Turkish privatization.[2] After contracted by the government and the World Bank, the American management-consulting firm, Boston Consulting Group, prepared the first report in 1985 on textile sector. The report recommended the immediate privatization of Sümerbank that owned and controlled Turkey's largest textile plants. It concluded that the machineries in Sümerbank's plants are all between 6 and 50 years old and the cost of modernizing the factories is so high that Sümerbank could not finance it within its current means. It also identified 22 American and 28 European firms as potential buyers of Sümerbank.[3] Moreover, a French firm, Sema-Metra Conseil (SC) prepared another report on the cement sector, which suggested that the government should privatize the cement plants in the Western part of Turkey and restructure the plants in the East before being

---

2  See "KİT'lerin yeni yapısı belirleniyor" [New structure of SOEs are being determined], *Cumhuriyet,* 15 July 1986.
3  See "Sümerbank'ı hemen satın" [Sell Sümerbank immediately], *Cumhuriyet,* 25 November 1985.

sold (Saygılı and Taymaz 2001, 585). Furthermore, American consulting firm, Arthur D. Little, worked on the fertilizer sector and prepared a report that suggested the privatization of fertilizer plants in time.[4]

The Morgan Guaranty Bank (J. P. Morgan) – along with Turkish Industrial Development Bank, State Planning Organization and World Bank experts – drew up a more detailed Master Plan for privatization in all sectors in 1986. The Master Plan, which was financed by the World Bank, suggested that Turkey should privatize SOEs to increase economic efficiency, generate growth and enhance development of capital markets. It studied 32 SOEs that represent about 40% of industrial production and 60% of fixed capital in Turkey and classified them into groups according to their prospects for privatization. The top priority has been given to 5 SOEs, of which two operating in transportation (USAŞ, THY), one in tourism (TURBAN), one in animal feed industry (YEMSAN) and one in cement sector (ÇİTOSAN). At the next stage two communication SOE, namely TELETAŞ and NETAŞ, were envisaged to be privatized (Tecer 1992, 136–138). In ways similar to the previously mentioned sector-specific reports, the Master Plan identified foreign investors as the principal candidates for taking over SOEs.

All the sector-specific reports, and particularly the Morgan Guaranty Master Plan, received positive reactions from the Özal government.[5] The government even appointed a committed neoliberal, Cengiz İsrafil, Morgan Guaranty Bank vice president and the former World Bank expert, as the head of recently established TKKOİ to implement privatization in Turkey.[6] In information exchange meetings conducted with leading international investors in 1987 and 1988, İsrafil along with other senior government officials reiterated the government's commitment to privatization and invited international capital to participate in Turkey's privatizations.[7]

The first major SOE sell-offs came in 1988 with the sale of Teletaş, a telephone firm, and Ansan-Meda, a soft drink bottling company, to foreign companies. In 1989, the French company SCF (Societe des Ciments Francais) acquired 90% shares of five cement plants (Afyon, Ankara, Balıkesir, Pınarhisar, Söke) owned

---

4  See "Gübrede özelleştirme planı" [Privatization plan in fertilizer sector], *Cumhuriyet,* 5 December 1985.
5  See "İlhan Selçuk: Morgan + ANAP Co.", *Cumhuriyet,* 2 July 1986.
6  See personal profile of Cengiz İsrafil: http://www.akintekstil.com.tr/wp-content/uploads/pdf/cengizisrafil.pdf.
7  See "Londra Borsası Başkanı Sir Nicholas Goodison: Özelleştirme Avrupalıyı çeker" [Head of London Stock Exchange Sir Nicholas Goodison: Privatization attracts Europeans], *Cumhuriyet,* 29 June 1988.

by ÇİTOSAN in return for $105 million. As part of the deal, the SCF agreed to undertake investments of $60 million over the next three years in order to modernize the plants (Kjellstrom 1990, 30). As noted above, it was the Sema-Metra Conseil, another French firm that prepared privatization report for Turkish government on the cement sector and suggested the privatization of cement plants. The same year, the Scandinavian Airlines Service Partner (SAS) purchased 70% shares of the aircraft catering company USAŞ for $14 million.

A significant development came with the introduction of the Decree Law 32 of August 1989 under the Law of Protection of the Value of the Turkish Lira (TL), which completed the liberalization of capital account and foreign exchange operations. The government lifted the limits on the amount of foreign assets that could be owned domestically and the limits on foreign borrowing by Turkish banks. Furthermore, foreign capital was allowed to openly trade in corporate stocks and government securities in the İstanbul Stock Exchange (ISE). This law augmented the capacity of foreign capital to enter and purchase SOEs in Turkey.

Soon after the privatization of the cement plants and USAŞ through block sales to foreigners and the enactment of Decree Law 32, senior government officials announced a shortlist of major input-producing SOEs (including Petkim petro-chemicals, Tüpraş petroleum refineries, and Erdemir iron and steel) for privatization with foreign investors emerging as the principal purchasing candidates.[8] Unsurprisingly, the US and the EU leaders, international financial institutions like World Bank and the IMF, and financial capital have enthusiastically welcomed this announcement. Foreign companies announced one after another that the purchase of Turkey's major SOEs was in their corporate expansion plans. For example, the American multinational corporation, Exxon Mobil, expressed an interest in buying Tüpraş as soon as the government would transfer the company to the privatization portfolio.[9] Moreover, multinational chemical companies such as Exxon Chemical, Mitsubishi Chemical, Shell, and Dow Chemical stated their desire to purchase Petkim.[10]

In this context, as one high level bureaucrat in the Turkish Privatization Authority stated in an anonymous interview, the Turkish power bloc faced an immediate dilemma: either to compete with foreign companies to bid for shortlisted SOEs and, ultimately, sacrifice the comfortable relationship (i.e. subsidized inputs based on duty losses) enjoyed with those SOEs, or to freeze

8    See "Özelleştirmede güz atılımı" [Fall progress in privatization], *Cumhuriyet*, 13 August 1989.
9    See "Exxon, Tüpraş'a talip oldu" [Exxon wants to buy Tüpraş], *Cumhuriyet*, 9 June 1989.
10   See "Ve Petkim de pazara çıktı" [And Petkim is also on the market], *Cumhuriyet*, 8 September 1989.

privatization plans until a more favourable context emerged that would prevent foreign investors from acquiring the SOEs in the short term.[11] A review of
the national newspapers and business associations' reports at the time reveals
that fractions of the power bloc opted for the second option.

The powerful TÜSİAD, as the main representative body of big holdings, had
seemed dissatisfied with the ways in which the government is handled with privatization.[12] Specifically, TÜSİAD complained that government worked closely
with foreign consultancy firms (e.g., Morgan Guaranty Bank) and excluded the
domestic private sector from any involvement in preparation for privatization
(TÜSİAD 1992, 114, 117). TÜSİAD criticized government in three areas. First,
privatization program should be gradually implemented and the privatization
of those SOEs that produce vital inputs to industry could wait for some time.
Instead, SOEs that produce basic consumption goods and/or services could be
a good starting point for privatization (TÜSİAD 1986, 63; TÜSİAD 1992, 113–115).
Second, the government should give priority to SOE workers, local population
and domestic investors when selling SOEs; the foreign investors could be welcomed, but only as the fourth option (TÜSİAD 1992, 139). Third, even if government decides to sell SOEs to foreign investors, it should prefer limited share
sale to block sale method (TÜSİAD 1992, 118). In short, according to TÜSİAD,
the sale of the major input producing SOEs to foreign investors through block
sale method would lead to undesirable outcomes for Turkish economy.

Moreover, the TOBB (Union of Chambers and Commodity Exchanges of
Turkey), as a representative body of SMEs located mostly in Anatolia, criticized the government's privatization strategy on the same grounds. TOBB
viewed major input-producing SOEs as strategic assets of the Turkish economy
and opposed their block sale to foreign investors, after negotiations that were
not particularly transparent (TOBB 1993, 44, 151).[13] The ISO (İstanbul Chamber
of Industry) also stated that, if the government sold the major SOEs to foreign
capital, it would have devastating effect on Turkish industrialists, as they would
not be able to readily and conveniently access intermediate goods.[14] For example, a private company – DenizlerKinteks – was complaining that the price
of cement increased from 2200TL to 4600TL soon after the sale of ÇİTOSAN's
cement plants to the French SCF.[15] In this way, different fractions of the power

---

11    Interview with high-level state bureaucrat, Privatization Authority, 18 October 2012.
12    See "Özelleştirmede TÜSİAD'ın tavrı" [TÜSİAD's attitude for privatization], *Cumhuriyet*,
      14 November 1989.
13    See "Petkim için bu telaş niye" [Why this hurry for Petkim], *Cumhuriyet*, 14 September 1989.
14    See "Yabancı sermaye kuşkusu" [Doubt on foreign capital], *Cumhuriyet*, 15 May 1989.
15    See "Satışa bir dava daha" [One more lawsuit against the sale], *Cumhuriyet*, 4
      November 1989.

bloc exercised unity and organized a major "foreignization" campaign in the media to impose a freeze on the privatization plans.

The campaign by the power bloc was successful in generating popular opposition to privatization plans, and led many people, particularly the labour unions and SOE workers wishing to protect their secure jobs, to equate privatization with "foreignization". Popular opposition then prompted the opposition parties in Parliament to start legal proceedings through the state institutions to block the process.[16] For instance, the parliamentarians from the DYP (True Path Party – Doğru Yol Partisi) filed a suit against the TKKOİ (i.e., state institution responsible for privatization) for the ÇİTOSAN and USAŞ sales. The Ankara 1st Administrative Court ruled in 1990 that the sale of those SOEs to foreign investors via block sales had contravened the previous decisions of the TKKOİ on sales methods and target groups. A World Bank expert, Sven B. Kjellstrom, described the implications of this succinctly: "The implications are potentially far-reaching. Privatization through block sales to foreigners has been ruled out by the courts. Moreover, the whole privatization process has become politically contested" (Kjellstrom 1990, 32).

In a desperate move, the government turned away from block sales to foreigners and toward share sales to locals. To begin with, between 1990 and 1991 the government sold state shares in some large-scale SOEs through public offerings for about $400 million. Only a small portion of the total state shares in those SOEs was sold under the scheme, ranging from 2 per cent for Tüpraş petroleum refinery and 3 per cent for Erdemir steel plant, 4 per cent Poaş petroleum distribution to 8 per cent for Petkim petro-chemical facility (Kilci 1994, 35). Second, the state had large amounts of shares in some companies that were in majority privately owned and controlled (formed as part of the participation mechanism described in the previous chapter). From 1990 to 1993, the state participation shares in these private companies were sold mostly to the existing majority shareholders without undue difficulty (see Table 3).

These sales, however, have had little real efficacy and have not substantially altered structure of the SOE sector. The authorities could do little to sell heavyweight SOEs and accelerate the privatization process. Despite extensive involvement and heavy pressures from the World Bank and foreign consultancy firms, the complex interplay of such three factors as the class agency

16   See "Muhalefet, özelleştirmeyi frenlemek için harekete geçti" [Opposition mobilized to stop privatization], *Cumhuriyet,* 27 September 1989; "Yabancılaştırma yargıç huzurunda" [Foreignization is in the presence of the judge], *Cumhuriyet,* 5 October 1989.

TABLE 3     Sale of state participation shares in private companies (selected list)

| Private company | Government shares sold (%) | Buyer | Price ($) million |
|---|---|---|---|
| Çukurova Electricity | 11 | Rumeli Holding | 81 |
| İpragaz | 49 | French Primagaz | 64 |
| Kepez Electricity | 25 | Rumeli Holding | 33 |
| Netaş Telecommunication | 20 | Northern Telecom | 28 |
| Ray Insurance | 49 | Doğan Holding | 10 |
| Türk Tractor | 34 | Koç Holding | 8 |
| Tat Canned Goods | 17 | Koç Holding | 8 |
| Polinas Plastic | 30 | Ülker Holding | 7 |

SOURCE: KILCI (1994) PP. 32, 50–53

of the power bloc, capital accumulation based on subsidized inputs via duty losses, and state institutions like courts and parliament halted Turkey's privatization program.

## 2       The IMF Programs, Intra-capital and Intra-state Conflicts: 1994–2001

The 1989 financial liberalization measure triggered an initial upturn in economic activity by drawing international flows of capital into Turkey that also attempted to purchase Turkish SOEs as discussed above, but the consequences of financial liberalization would be fatal for the Turkish economy. It had accelerated the internalization of foreign currency and encouraged Turkish Lira (TL) substitution. This caused the shrinking of money resources in TL terms, which pushed up domestic interest rates and shortened the maturity structure of credit. A series of credit downgrades and the erosion of financial market access worsened the situation (Marois 2012, 107). In 1993 capital flight reached nearly 2.15 per cent of Turkish GDP and the financing need of the Central Government (PSBR) rose to nearly 12 per cent of GDP, which forced Turkish state agencies to rollover public debt at extremely high costs.

Under these circumstances, the economy drifted towards the 1994 economic crisis, as chronic fiscal deficits coupled with high real interest rates led to unsustainable debt dynamics (Yalman 2019, 75). The 1994 crisis started when Standard and Poor's and Moody's reduced Turkey's credit rating. In the aftermath of the crisis, the Turkish economy contracted by 6 per cent, the highest level of annual output loss since the establishment of the Turkish Republic. Moreover, the TL was devalued more than 50 per cent against foreign currencies, the Central Bank lost half of its reserves, and the interest and inflation rates reached three-digit levels (Celasun 1999, 2).

The Turkish government responded with the April 1994 IMF-crafted stabilization program, which involved a 14-month stand-by arrangement that totaled nearly $1 billion (FESSUD 2013, 325). The stabilization program was built around a large and front-loaded fiscal adjustment that included, among other things, price increases in SOE products, a public wage freeze, deep cuts to public spending (followed by a six-month freeze), and, of course, privatization of SOEs (Barth and Hemphill 2000, 13–15). It is important to point out that privatization occupied a central place inside the program.

Under the influence of the IMF-crafted stabilization program, the then Prime Minister, Tansu Çiller of DYP (True Path Party – Doğru Yol Partisi), envisaged privatization as a possible solution to the ever soaring public deficit and took the attitude that privatization was necessary, no matter the effort.[17] Çiller even came to the point that she had to threaten her junior coalition partner SHP (Social Democratic Populist Party – Sosyal Demokrat Halkçı Parti) that no step would be taken in other policy areas of the government agenda before the privatization program started.[18] Çiller has in particular aimed to privatize Türk Telekom – the only fixed line communications company in Turkey – which, according to her, would end domestic indebtedness of Turkey at the time.[19]

Having maneuvered the SHP leader, Murat Karayalçın, into finally accepting the start of the privatization program, the Çiller government moved to better institutionalize the legal bases of privatization in Turkey. The outcome was the Privatization Law No. 4046 of November 1994, which remains in force today with amendments (FESSUD 2013, 325). First, the said law specifically determined all the principles and procedures with regards to the privatization. Some of these procedures focus on privatization methods, value assessment

---

17   See "Çiller, özelleştirmeye destek istiyor" [Çiller demands support for privatization], *Zaman*, 30 September 1994.
18   See "Çiller'den ortağına sitem" [Çiller reproached her coalition partner], *Zaman*, 5 October 1994; "Çiller: Dengeler yeniden bozulabilir" [Çiller: The balances could be unsettled], *Zaman*, 9 October 1994.
19   See, "Fikret Bila, PTT'nin T'siyken satsaydık makus talihimizi yenerdik" [Fikret Bila, If we were sold Türk Telekom, we would avoid our ill-fated future], *Milliyet*, 4 July 2005.

of SOEs, formation of tender commissions and tendering methods, and the protection of strategic sectors. Second, the Law 1994 created the Privatization High Council (PHC – *Özelleştirme Yüksek Kurulu*) as the main decision body. The PHC is chaired by the Prime Minister (PM) and is composed of members such as the Deputy Prime Minister (in case of coalition of more than one party), a PM-designated Minister, the Minister responsible for the privatization portfolio, the Minister of Finance, and the Minister of Industry and Commerce.[20] The PHC decides all key SOE privatization matters. The PHC can add SOEs in the privatization portfolio, determine the time periods for their privatization, decide on the method of privatization, and approve the final sale. Third, the 1994 Law established the Privatization Administration (PA – *Özelleştirme İdaresi Başkanlığı*) as a centralized implementation authority. The PA is responsible for executing decisions of the council, implementing all necessary procedures in preparation for privatization, managing the privatization fund, and conducting activities such as advertisement, promotion and public relations to enhance the salability of SOEs. Fourth, the Law 1994 addressed redundancy payments and labour adjustment issues for the first time and enabled the transfer of public employees to other state entities if the Privatization Administration believed the labour force needed to be relocated. Finally, the said law established the Privatization Fund to help smooth privatization process by helping pay for severance and retirement payments for redundant employees, cover debt of privatized SOEs, and/or improve the financial position of SOEs in preparation for sale by increasing their capital and so on (FESSUD 2013, 326).

Moreover, the Çiller government wanted to experiment with new forms of privatization, notably public-private partnerships (PPP). In 1994, the government introduced a new and more widespread Built-Operate-Transfer (BOT) Law (No. 3996) to increase investment in infrastructure, especially in areas such as electricity and airline transportation.[21] The BOT Law was intended to open these areas to the private sector participation and private accumulation opportunities (Marois 2019, 127). To encourage private sector participation, it provided tax exemptions and authorized the Treasury to grant guarantees.

Indeed, the enactment of such detailed Privatization Law (4046) and BOT Law (3996) within a short period signaled that the Çiller government was

---

20    Following the system change (from Parliamentary to Presidential) in 2018 and through the Presidency Circular numbered 2018/3, crucial powers of the PHC were transferred to the President.

21    Law No. 3996 is titled as 'Law for Certain Investments and Services to be Carried Out under the Build-Operate-Transfer Model'.

strongly committed to accelerating privatization in line with the IMF-crafted stabilization program. However, any progress in privatization would have to face serious obstacles. Since 1994, as a result of those obstacles discussed below, privatization in Turkey has been a stop and go process.

### 2.1   TÜSİAD-based Holdings and Privatization

The reluctance of the TÜSİAD-based big holdings to fully support privatization constituted one of the biggest obstacles. As a senior bureaucrat of Privatization Administration commented, holdings did not seem very enthusiastic about privatization during the 1990s (Interview with Ali Güner Tekin, Head of Project Group, 8 February 2013). A higher-level manager of one of TÜSİAD's holdings added specific details to explain why:

> Big holdings desired to keep large-scale input-producing SOEs (e.g., Erdemir, Petkim, Tüpraş) under state ownership and control because they had established favorable connections with the politicians to purchase the commodities produced in those SOEs at a discount. Moreover, those SOEs were very large entities with massive annual turnovers and operations, which exceeded the funding capacity of the Turkish private sector at the time.
>
> Interview, SERDAR KOÇTÜRK, 6 February 2013

Therefore, holdings tended to be very selective about privatization, pressuring state officials to concentrate on particular sectors (e.g., banking, infrastructure), but not on the others. In particular, holdings were more interested in participating PPP tenders in electricity generation and transportation sectors. Between 1994 and 2000 the holdings agreed to construct five power plants and two international passenger terminal buildings on a build-operate-transfer (BOT) basis. Prominent Turkish holdings including Enka, Gama, Oyak and Akfen in partnership with foreign capital invested more than $6 billion in those BOT-based PPP projects (see Table 4). The government agreed to provide sovereign repayment guarantees that proved to be useful in convincing foreign investors to participate the projects, which expanded the availability of funding sources for Turkish holdings. Under BOT contracts, above-mentioned holdings acquired concessions to operate power plants and/or terminals for a period (from 7 to 20 years) before handover to the state. Power plant contracts had also purchase agreements between the holdings and government utility TEAŞ (Turkish Electricity Generation and Transmission Corporation – Türkiye Elektrik Üretim ve İletim A.ş.) that included take-or-pay clauses that committed the TEAŞ to purchase a specified amount of electricity at pre-specified

TABLE 4    BOT-based PPP projects: 1994–2000

| Project | Investment value | Holdings participated | Foreign partner | Contract period |
|---|---|---|---|---|
| Gebze-Adapazarı-İzmir Natural Gas Power Plants | $2.2 billion | Enka | InterGen (USA) | 20 years |
| Birecik Hydo Power Plant | $1.59 billion | Gama | Philipp Holzman (Germany) | 15 years |
| İsken Coal-Fired Power Plant | $1.37 billion | Oyak | RAG Beteiligungs-Group (Germany) | 20 years |
| Trakya Natural Gas Power Plant | $604 million | Enka | Inter RAO UES (Russia) | 20 years |
| Esenyurt Natural Gas Power Plant | $170 million | Doğa Enerji | Edison International (USA) | 20 years |
| Atatürk Airport New International Terminal | $305 million | Akfen-Bilkent (TAV) | Airport Consulting Vienna (Austria) | 7 years |
| Antalya Airport International Terminal | $85 million | Bayındır | Fraport AG (Germany) | 10 years |

SOURCE: WORLD BANK, HTTPS://PPI.WORLDBANK.ORG/EN/SNAPSHOTS/COUNTRY/TUR KEY, ACCESSED 12 MAY 2020

prices during the contract period. For example, the electricity generated in the Gebze-Adapazarı-İzmir plants of Enka and InterGen sold with an average tariff of 4.2 US cents for the 20-year period (Enka Annual Report 2004, 35). All these factors explain why holdings turned their attention to BOT-based PPP projects.

Moreover, holdings indicated wide interests in the privatization of state banks. They paid over $1 billion to acquire state bank shares that comprised 37% of Turkey's divestiture revenue between 1994 and 1998. This included the sales of Sümerbank, Etibank, Denizbank, and Anadolubank. Minority state participation in private banks also liquidated, including a substantial sale of the state's 12.3% share in İş Bank for $651 million (see Table 5). The very same holdings, on the other hand, expressed the view that it was probably not possible to private the major SOEs in all sectors within a relatively short period

TABLE 5      Privatization of state banks (1994–1998)

| Bank | Year | Price ($) million | Buyer |
|------|------|-------------------|-------|
| Sümerbank | 1995 | 103 | Garipoğlu Holding |
| Anadolubank | 1997 | 70 | Habaş Holding |
| Denizbank | 1997 | 66 | Zorlu Holding |
| Etibank | 1998 | 155 | İpek Holding |
| İş Bank (12.3%) | 1998 | 632 | Several Institutional Investors |

SOURCE: TÜRK 2011

(TÜSİAD 1995, 131–134). The special interest of the holdings in bank privatizations was related to the fact that, during the 1990s, bank ownership provided prime opportunities for lucrative profit making through state debt financing (e.g., trading government securities) and/or so called 'connected lending' opportunities within the capital groups concerned (Gültekin-Karakaş 2009, 97; Yalman 2019, 70–72). The head of Financial Markets Department of the Turkish Ministry of Development, Alper Bakdur, stated in an interview: "In the 1990s, the state borrowed heavily from holding banks with high interest rates. Those banks have therefore sought to capture more domestic savings to help feed the lucrative business of supplying state debt. As a result, those banks were unwilling to offer loans to consumers and investors".[22] According to one estimate, the annual interest revenue of banks earned through trading government securities increased from $450 million in 1989 to $5 billion in 1997 (Öztürk 2010, 148).

## 2.2    *Intra-capital Conflicts and Privatization*
Intra-capital conflicts between the TÜSİAD-based big holdings and Anatolian capital fractions acted as the next significant obstacle to privatization. Let me look in more detail. As the significant share of world manufacturing activities had been relocated to developing countries including Turkey through the global re-organization of production, Anatolian firms grew rapidly in the

---

22    Interview with Alper Bakdur, Head of Financial Markets Department at the Ministry of Development, 16 October 2012.

1980s by entering into subcontracting agreements in the area of textiles, garments and automobile auxiliary products with larger domestic and foreign firms (Gülalp 2001, 437). Anatolian firms, especially starting from mid-1980s onwards, increasingly searched for new sources of finance to grow further. However, TÜSİAD-based holding banks refrained from lending to Anatolian firms in order to avoid increasing default risk in the private sector, as they found a secure alternative in the form of government securities and 'connected lending' opportunities within their own holding structures (Öztürk 2010, 161–162). Whatever credits the holding groups made available to the remaining private sector including Anatolian firms, after they had lent to the state and spent in other productive and commercial activities of their own holdings, often proved to be too expensive to be of any use and primarily lent to people with whom they were acquainted or with whom they shared related activities (Marois 2012, 110–111). Unsurprisingly, this exacerbated intra-capital tensions between TÜSİAD-based holdings that owned banks and Anatolian firms that did not.

Having felt excluded from the holdings-dominated Turkish banking system, Anatolian firms collectively turned towards Islamic capital from the Gulf countries and religious orders (or sects). Some relied on special finance houses such as Faisal Finance House, Al Baraka Turkish Finance House, Kuwait Turkish Evkaf Finance House, Anadolu Finance House, and Asya Finance House that were connected to Gulf capital and Islamic sects.[23] Some relied on the transfer of remittances by the migrant workers as an alternative source of finance, which led to the formation of Islamic-influenced holdings such as Yimpaş, İttifak, and Kombassan with multiple shareholders (Oğuz 2008, 132–134). For example, Kombassan had nearly 30,000 shareholders and possessed companies in Turkey, Germany and the United States (Hoşgör 2011, 347). As a result, the injection of Islamic capital into the Turkish economy accelerated the *Islamification* process of socially conservative and religious Anatolian

---

23　The enactment of the 'Special Finance Houses' decree of 1983, with the intention of attracting capital from Arab Gulf countries, paved the way for Islamic banking segment in Turkey. Faisal Finance House of Turkey was established in 1985. The majority shareholder was the Saudi prince Mohamed Al Faysal Saud. Al Baraka Turkish Finance House was established in 1985 as an affiliated institution of the Saudi conglomerate, the Dallah Al Baraka Group. Kuwait Turkish Evkaf Finance House was established as the subsidiary of Kuwait Finance House, which is currently the second-largest bank in Kuwait, the eight-largest in the Arab world and 43 per cent owned by the government. All these three Islamic finance houses were either from Saudi Arabia or Kuwait. Yet, in the 1990s, three special finance houses were founded by domestic investors: Anadolu Finance House (1991), İhlas Finance House (1995) and Asya Finance House (1996).

firms, which turned many of them into what I describe as "Islamic-influenced Anatolian firms".

The foundation of MÜSİAD (Independent Industrialists' Businessmen's Association – *Müstakil Sanayici ve İşadamları Derneği*) was the real break-through for Islamic-influenced Anatolian firms. Although MÜSİAD was founded by five businessmen in 1990, its membership significantly expanded to include 2,700 firms in 1997. Unlike TÜSİAD affiliated holdings, more than two third of these firms were established after 1980. In contrast to big holdings of TÜSİAD that are geographically concentrated in major cities such as İstanbul and İzmir (and surrounding industrial zones), MÜSİAD members included mostly small and medium enterprises (i.e., employing less than 50 workers) from Anatolian cities (Çokgezen 2000, 537). Despite this, there are few notable exceptions – big holding companies employing thousands of workers such as Ülker, Çalık, Kombassan and İttifak. Moreover, in contrast to TÜSİAD's positive attitude towards European integration and its adherence to liberal values, MÜSİAD members were explicitly against Turkey's European Union (EU) membership and adopted conservative religious mores. Instead, MÜSİAD aimed to forge closer links with the Islamic world (e.g., Middle Eastern countries, the emerging states of post-Soviet Central Asia, and newly industrializing countries with predominantly Islamic population such as Malaysia and Indonesia) and supported the establishment of an Islamic Common Market (Hoşgör 2011, 351).

MÜSİAD also interpreted the significant power of the TÜSİAD-based holdings in the domestic markets and in politics as a threat to the survival and development of the group it represents. In the interviews I have conducted, and also in their press announcements, the representatives of MÜSİAD stated that the Turkish economy was controlled by the 15–20 big holdings of TÜSİAD, which were protected and strengthened by doing business with the state.[24] As such, MÜSİAD members believed that they had not benefited from the existing socio-economic structures as much as TÜSİAD members because they were distant from the sources of state power (Çokgezen 2000, 538).

Therefore, MÜSİAD members became the major social force behind the Islamist RP (Welfare Party – *Refah Partisi*) of Erbakan in expectation of increasing their presence within the state, which would enable them to access state resources. The RP, with the support of strengthening MÜSİAD, first managed to stage a meteoric rise to take hold of municipalities of most big cities such as

---

24    Interview with Mustafa Albayrak, Head of Energy and Environment Sectoral Committee
      of MÜSİAD, 1 February 2013.

İstanbul and Ankara in the local elections of 1994.[25] The RP then won 1995 general elections with 21.13 per cent of the votes and came to power through a coalition government in 1996.[26] During the period when the RP was in local and central government, there was significant increase in the presence of MÜSİAD. For example, the number of MÜSİAD members increased significantly, those members received preferential treatment in receiving municipal contracts and some of them had a chance to receive credits from the government (Çokgezen 2000, 539).

The strengthened MÜSİAD members also began to search for privatization opportunities, albeit with little success. One concrete example is the privatization of Petlas – a state owned tyre-producing company. Kombassan, an Islamic-influenced Anatolian company, won the privatization tender of Petlas in 1996 with a $36 million bid. However, the TÜSİAD-based holding groups such as Sabancı Holding were not happy with Islamic-Anatolian companies winning such major privatizations.[27] A Privatization Administration (PA) official said in his interview that Sabancı Holding saw Kombassan as a potential competitor and led a sustained lobbying effort to stop the sale of Petlas to Kombassan.[28] Other TÜSİAD-based holding groups also supported Sabancı's lobbying effort and pressured state authorities to prevent Kombassan from acquiring Petlas in a variety of ways, including: delaying Privatization High Council's (PHC) approval, placing extra conditions on the sale agreement, and labeling Kombassan a threat as it was an agent of fundamentalist Islam (Oğuz 2008, 136–137). An influential MÜSİAD member and the chairman of the Kombassan Holding administrative board, Haşim Bayram, expressed his opinions:

> Some monopolies and [TÜSİAD-based] holdings in Turkey do not want Kombassan to control Petlas. We had to wait 63 days to get PHC's approval. The PA then added extra conditions on the sale agreement,

---

25    The core of the AKP was later formed from the elected mayors of the 1994 local elections and some of high-ranking officials that they appointed to municipalities: Recep Tayyip Erdoğan (Mayor of İstanbul-Leader of AKP), Melih Gökçek (Mayor of Ankara-Member of AKP), Veysel Eroğlu (Head of İstanbul Municipality Water and Sewerage Administration-Minister of AKP), Hilmi Güler (Head of İstanbul Municipality Gas Administration-Founding Member of AKP), İdris Naim Şahin (Deputy Secretary General of the İstanbul Municipality-Founding Member of the AKP).

26    The then main opposition Motherland Party won 19.66 per cent of the votes, while the Prime Minister Tansu Çiller's True Path Party acquired 19.37 per cent.

27    Sabancı Holding owned the Lassa Tyres, which is one of the largest tyre-manufacturing companies in Turkey.

28    Interview with Ali Güner Tekin, Head of Project Group, 8 February 2013.

which were initially not in there. [TÜSİAD-based] holdings, which owned most of the banks in the country, were also not eager to give us letter of guarantee for Petlas purchase, even though we were meeting all of their requirements.[29]

Another concrete example is the privatization of TEDAŞ – Turkish Electricity Distribution Company. In 1997, MÜSİAD encouraged its members to contribute to the creation of a new entity called 'the Investment Partnership Fund' to pool together the money resources and bid for TEDAŞ.[30] For instance, Ömer Cihat Akay, the then Chairman of the İzmir Branch of MÜSİAD, publicly announced MÜSİAD's strategy as follows: "Our Partnership Fund will participate in THY, Sümer Holding, İşdemir, TEDAŞ and Petkim privatizations. We are particularly interested in the TEDAŞ privatization".[31] The unexpected competition emanating from MÜSİAD posed a threat to the interests of the TÜSİAD-based holding groups such as Doğan Holding, which had been hoping to acquire TEDAŞ and other SOEs themselves.[32] The discomfort of the holding groups found expression in a Turkish National Security Council briefing (known as the 28 February post-modern military coup in Turkey), which emphasized that the government should not give priority to MÜSİAD-based Islamic-influenced companies in the privatization tenders, particularly in strategic sectors like energy (Silverman 2014, 140–141). As a result, the 28 February intervention seriously curbed the organizational and financial power of the MÜSİAD members. State authorities adopted a wide range of methods and strategies against MÜSİAD members, which involved legal actions, use of police force, financial investigations, systematic public display of unlawful acts by Islamic-influenced companies, boycotts and campaigns supported via TÜSİAD controlled media. The membership of MÜSİAD has fallen by about 30 per cent (Hoşgör 2011, 352). It is also important to mention that the 28 February intervention initiated the process that precipitated the resignation of Islamist Prime Minister Necmettin Erbakan of the Welfare Party, and the end of his coalition government.

29 See "Bayram: Petlas'ı bu hafta devralacağız" [We will take over Petlas during this week], *Zaman,* 5 May 1997.
30 See "MÜSİAD'dan 1 Milyar Dolarlık Elektrik Havuzu" [$1 billion electricity investment pool from MÜSİAD], *Milliyet,* 16 January 1997.
31 See "MÜSİAD tüm özelleştirmelere katılacak" [MÜSİAD will participate all privatizations], *Milliyet,* 03 March 1997.
32 See "MÜSİAD and Doğan Media Group head for hard competition", *Hürriyet Daily News,* 21 March 1997. See also "Media bosses press on to get energy projects", *Hürriyet Daily News,* 13 November 1997.

These interventions, as we saw in the concrete examples of Petlas and
TEDAŞ, limited Islamic-influenced Anatolian capital's chance of participating
and winning privatization tenders. Feeling excluded from privatization, those
capital groups, MÜSİAD, and their representatives on the political scene (i.e.,
RP – Welfare Party, and its successor FP – Virtue Party) increasingly opposed
Turkish privatization efforts. For example, two sectoral committee chairs of
MÜSİAD stated in personal interviews that: "Because the TÜSİAD-based holding groups attempted to prevent us participating on equal terms in privatization tenders, we fought hard to slow down Turkey's privatization program. We
could not put nation's privatization program into the hands of TÜSİAD's corrupt system".[33]

### 2.3    Intra-state Conflicts and Privatization

Another obstacle to the progress of privatization was the intra-state conflicts
within the state institutional apparatus.

The international impact of the 1997 Asian crisis caused capital inflows
from advanced capitalist states into Turkey to slow dramatically, which in turn
led to the collapse of growth by up to 3 per cent by 1998. The 1998 Russian crisis
only worsened matters (Marois 2012, 118–119). At the same time, Turkey has
also suffered from chronically high inflation and large budget deficits. By the
end of the 1990s, all these factors that undermined the economy forced Turkey
to once again come under the supervision of the IMF, first with a monitoring
agreement in 1998 soon to be followed by a three-year stand-by agreement at
the end of 1999. As part of these agreements, the IMF was increasing its pressure on the government to urgently accelerate Turkish privatization program.
As such, the financial support of the IMF was made conditional on Turkish
government selling SOEs, which IMF framed as vital to reducing distortions,
improving resource allocation and a major source of budgetary financing (IMF
1997). In the Memorandum of Economic Policies to the IMF, the government
stated its commitment to privatization and outlined an action plan. This is
worth quoting at length:

Before the end of this year [1998], we plan to sell share holdings in POAŞ,
Turkish Airlines, Erdemir, and a number of other companies, with substantial additional sales scheduled in 1999. The Council of Ministers
has given approval for the sale of 49 per cent of Türk Telekom, a

---

33    Interview with Bekir Erkuş, Chair of Machinery Sector Committee, 30 January 2013; and
      Interview with Mustafa Albayrak, Chair of Energy Sector Committee, 1 February 2013.

> transaction that will be completed in 1999. Once the approval of the High Administrative Court (Danıştay) has been secured, it will be possible to move quickly in finalizing the transfer of operating rights for the generation and transmission of electric power [plants]... and the first 15 of the eventual 20 distribution districts ... The aim is to generate receipts of at least $3 billion this year [1998], and at least a further $3.6 billion (and very possibly well over $5 billion) in 1999.
>
> IMF 1998

Turkey had made, however, little progress by the end of 1999. Key privatization initiatives were either suspended or postponed, and the privatization of Türk Telekom and electric power generation/distribution remained stalled by legal difficulties and intra-state conflicts within the state institutional apparatus. Although the program targeted the generation of privatization proceeds of $6.6 billion in two years (1998–1999) from divestitures, only about $1 billion was realized. These intra-state conflicts were especially evident in Türk Telekom's privatization, which became an important item in the reform agenda immediately after the Turkish economy went under the supervision of the IMF. Before moving on to the discussion of privatization of Türk Telekom, it is worth explaining the history of the PTT – the precursor to the Türk Telekom.

The Turkish state established the PTT (State Postal, Telephone and Telegraph Administration) in 1924 as a state enterprise with a monopoly over post, telegraph and telephone services. Between 1924 and 1980, the development of the PTT by and large remained slow because state authorities directed financial resources into priority economic sectors such as manufacturing. The little interest shown on the part of the state in the PTT led to some negative outcomes, especially in telephone services. There were nearly as many people waiting for telephone lines as there were lines and more than 72 per cent of Turkey's 40,000 villages had no access to telephone services in the late 1970s. As such, the telephone line density had grown to only 2.5 lines per 100 inhabitants (Wolcott and Çağıltay 2001). Other developing countries such as Argentina with 7 lines per 100, Greece with 24 lines per 100, and Mexico with 4 lines per 100 were doing much better (World Development Indicators 1980). As Walter Weiker, a specialist in Turkish politics and history, puts it: "There are few things about which there are more complaints than the telephone system in Turkey. Estimates of projected demand far exceed foreseeable supply (1981, 202)".

The neoliberal adjustment program crafted by the Turgut Özal signaled a turning point for PTT because the program placed a high value on its

TABLE 6     PTT investments, 1983–1993 ($ million)

| Year | Investment | Investment/GNP (%) |
|------|-----------|---------------------|
| 1983 | 288 | 0.56 |
| 1985 | 459 | 0.85 |
| 1987 | 876 | 1.28 |
| 1989 | 402 | 0.50 |
| 1991 | 852 | 0.80 |
| 1993 | 770 | 0.71 |

SOURCE: WORLD BANK (1993); ÇAKAL (1996)

expansion. From the 1983 onwards, then, the Ministry of Transport[34] and the PTT embarked on a sustained investment program with the financial resources made available by the shift away from manufacturing investments and the World Bank's structural adjustment loans. As a result, PTT's investments increased from $288 million in 1983 to $770 million in 1993, with a peak of $876 million in 1985 (World Bank 1993, 124). As Table 6 shows, the PTT investments/GNP ratio stayed around 0.83 per cent average in the period between 1983 and 1993. This ratio was higher than any other OECD country. The effects of the investment program on the telephone network soon became evident. For instance, the number of subscribers rose from 1.6 million to 6.8 million, the number of villages without access to telephone line decreased to zero, and the waiting list reduced to nearly one sixth of the existing subscribers (World Bank 1992, 12; DPT 1990, 278).

In 1994, the parliament passed a law that split the expanded and modernized PTT into two separate companies; one would be responsible for the post and telegraph services, while the other would be responsible for telephone services. This led to the creation of Türk Telekom, as a state-owned enterprise whose shares are 100 per cent owned by the state to provide telephone services. All of the personnel, assets and obligations of the PTT pertaining to telephone services were transferred to Türk Telekom, which has since become a national monopoly with exclusive rights to all fixed-line voice operations and all telecommunications infrastructure (Akdemir, Başcı and Togan 2007, 1116). In this year, the government began an effort to privatize Türk Telekom.

---

34     At the time, the Ministry of Transport was responsible for the communication sector in general and the PTT in particular.

As mentioned above, the most significant obstacle to the realization of Türk Telekom privatization was the intra-state conflicts within the state institutional apparatus. One form of intra-state conflict was created by the popular classes – academics, labour unions, and social democratic politicians. Under the leadership of the SHP deputy and law professor Mümtaz Soysal, these popular classes worked together to establish KİGEM (The Centre for the Development of Public Management – *Kamu İşletmeciliğini Geliştirme Merkezi*).[35] KİGEM turned out to be enthusiastic opponent of Türk Telekom privatization on the grounds that the sale of such profitable and strategic state enterprise would be detrimental to the public and national interest. KİGEM believed the idea that the Türk Telekom could be operated efficiently and reform could be accomplished without giving up state ownership (Soysal 2005, 60). Following the appeal of KİGEM the Constitutional Court blocked Türk Telekom's privatization several times between 1993 and 1999. The former lawyer of the Petrol-İş, Gökhan Candoğan, stated in a personal interview, 'most of the Constitutional Court judges at the time embraced the principles of public ownership and public interest (as opposed to privatization and private interest) and had close ideological relationship with the KİGEM members'.[36] Following the application of KİGEM, those judges frequently made reference to the public interest and public ownership principles in the constitution and generally ruled against privatizing Türk Telekom.[37]

KİGEM lost some of its capacity to struggle against privatization through legal means in September 1999 when the DSP (Democratic Left Party – *Demokratik Sol Parti*) coalition government of Bülent Ecevit brought through Parliament an important amendment to the Turkish Constitution. The Parliamentary decision incorporated the concept of privatization into the Constitution by changing the title of the Article 47 from 'Nationalization' to 'Nationalization and Privatization' (Oğuz 2008, 178). The Minister responsible for the privatization portfolio at the time, Yüksel Yalova, stated in 2012 that: "This new arrangement, for the first time, gave constitutional ground for the privatization of Türk Telekom" (Personal Interview).[38]

---

35   Interview with Ayfer Eğilmez, Former Head of Petrol-İş Union's Research Unit and KİGEM Activist, 1 February 2013.
36   Interview with Gökhan Candoğan, Petrol-İş Union's Lawyer, 22 October 2012.
37   Interview with İzzettin Önder, Professor of Economics and İstanbul Representative of KİGEM, 5 February 2013.
38   Interview with Yüksel Yalova, State Minister responsible for privatization (1999–2002), 16 October 2012.

At the very moment when KİGEM and its legal challenges over Türk Telekom seemed sidelined after the constitutional amendment in 1999, another form of intra-state conflict arose between Enis Öksüz, Transport Minister from MHP (Nationalist Action Party – *Milliyetçi Hareket Partisi*), and his partners in the coalition government over key aspects of Türk Telekom privatization. In particular, there was increasing disagreement on the proportion of saleable shares and control rights. Öksüz was unwilling to sell more than 20 per cent of Türk Telekom shares that would transfer Türk Telekom's control rights from state to private investors, while Yüksel Yalova, State Minister responsible for privatization, insisted that no one would buy Türk Telekom unless 33.5 or 51 per cent of shares with strong control rights tendered for sale. Kemal Derviş, a capable neoliberal technocrat appointed as the Minister of Economy to spearhead reforms, also stepped in to warn Öksüz that granting 33.5 or 51 per cent of shares with strong control rights to buyer was among the commitment made to the IMF (Kıyan and Yüksel 2011, 57). In a 2013 interview, a senior government official in the PA of Turkey summarized how the demands of Öksüz made it difficult to privatize Türk Telekom:

> When you offer 20 or 33.5 per cent of shares without strong control rights, the buyer would be dependent on public procurement law, would have to employ public employees, and would have to ask for permission of the State Planning Organization before making any significant investment. Convincing investors to bid for Türk Telekom under these conditions was always going to be difficult task.[39]

The next issue of considerable dispute between Öksüz and other government ministers was the shares that could be sold to foreign investors. Öksüz aimed to limit the amount of Türk Telekom shares that could be sold to foreign companies on the grounds of national security, but Derviş rejected any legal barriers to the participation of foreign capital in the Türk Telekom privatization process.[40] The Turkish military also became a party to the dispute and expressed its concerns over the security implications of the Türk Telekom privatization. These concerns of the military were even reflected by the journalists Murat Belge and İsmet Berkan who commented in their columns, "... the Turkish military openly stepped into Telekom disputes ... and raised serious doubts about

---

39    Interview with Günden Çınar, Head of Türk Telekom Privatization Project at the PA (2004–2006), 12 February 2013.

40    "Türk Telekom wrestles with privatization", *EuroAsianet.Org,* 26 March 2001.

the sale of Türk Telekom".[41] The military was especially concerned about the potential problems with foreign ownership and control of the fifty thousand fiber-optic cables and satellite components it was using together with Türk Telekom.[42]

Two state ministers, Derviş and Öksüz, also clashed over the Telecommunications Law 4673. While Derviş was willing to include a special article into that law that would transfer licensing authority to the new regulatory institution (i.e. Telecommunication Authority), Öksüz vehemently insisted that the Ministry of Transport should retain licensing authority (Oğuz 2008, 172). Moreover, the Deputy General Manager of the Türk Telekom at the time, Zafer Tekbudak, noted that even though Öksüz attempted to appoint elected politicians and state bureaucrats like him to work on the Türk Telekom board, Derviş's choices were professionals and sector leaders.[43]

As these different conflicts within the state apparatus delayed the conclusion of Türk Telekom privatization, the IMF increased its pressure on the Turkish government and emphasized that privatization of Türk Telekom is an essential element of the program (IMF 2001). Unsurprisingly, the IMF directors announced that if the expected changes did not occur in line with the agreed stand-by agreements and letter of intents, the next part of the loan might not be released.[44] The World Bank, which was also expected to release loans to the Turkish government, made the same announcement that the Türk Telekom privatization constituted a significant part of the government's promises to external funders (Oğuz 2008, 172). This sounded a wake-up call. The leader of the MHP and Deputy Prime Minister Devlet Bahçeli asked Öksüz to take a step back (Kıyan and Yüksel 2011, 57). Bahçeli told Öksüz that, "As leaders of coalition parties we signed IMF's letter of intent. The austerity conditions of Turkey are making this [privatization of Türk Telekom] compulsory. Let's close this matter".[45]

It should however be noted that these intra-state conflicts within the state apparatus (e.g., KİGEM's legal battle, Öksüz vs. Yalova/Derviş clashes) were not fully independent from the influence of the power bloc. The RP (and its

41    "Murat Belge: Telekom savaşının savaşçıları" [Murat Belge: The warriors of the Telecom war], *Radikal*, 5 May 2001; "İsmet Berkan: Telekom" [İsmet Berkan: Telecom], *Radikal*, 5 May 2001.

42    "Telekom yasası nihayet" [Finally, Telecom law], *Radikal*, 6 May 2001.

43    Zafer Tekbudak, Deputy General Manager of Türk Telekom (2000–2001), 18 October 2012.

44    "Turkey Signals Compromise with IMF", *AP News*, 9 July 2001; "Privatization of Turk Telekom Hit Snag, Sending Stock Lower", *The Wall Street Journal*, 29 June 2001.

45    "Öksüz, böyle teslim olmuş" [Öksüz surrendered like this], *Radikal*, 11 May 2001.

successor FP – Virtue Party) and MÜSİAD members frequently provided political support in parliamentary votes, which enabled KİGEM to file constitutional reviews for legislation proposing the privatization of Türk Telekom (there need to be at least 90 signatures from parliamentary deputies to file a constitutional review); while the Turkish military and some domestic holdings indirectly supported the case of Öksüz by presenting their concerns over the relationship between privatization, the nation's security, and foreign control of the economy.[46]

Overall, despite IMF pressures and programs, the extent and pace of privatization in Turkey remained limited in the late 1990s. Turkish governments failed to complete large-scale privatizations like Türk Telekom. Yet there are two notable exceptions – Tüpraş and POAŞ – in 2000 that signaled that Turkey's arguable "lost two decades" was about to come to an end. First, the PA sold 30.66 per cent of Tüpraş (state petroleum refinery complex) shares on the İstanbul and London Stock Exchange for $1.1 billion in April 2000. Tüpraş's shares attracted considerable demand because the world market oil prices were increasing at the time – nearly doubled from $15 per barrel in 1999 to $27 per barrel in 2000. Small domestic investors acquired most of the shares as the PA offered up to 15 per cent discount for them, possibly to increase public support to privatization program. The only investor that acquired more than 5 per cent of shares was the UK based Franklin Templeton Investment Management Limited (Borsa İstanbul 2000a; Borsa İstanbul 2000b). Second, the PA sold 51 per cent of the shares of POAŞ (state petroleum distribution company) to the Turkish conglomerate, Doğan Holding, in July 2000 in return for only $1.2 billion (Angın and Bedirhanoğlu 2012).

## 3    Conclusion

Although Turkey was among the first developing countries to announce a comprehensive privatization program in 1984, the implementation of the program largely failed to materialize over the next seventeen years. Indeed, in this period the competitive imperatives of contemporary capitalism (or neoliberalism), and the structural adjustment programs of the World Bank and the IMF placed significant pressure on Turkish government and state elites to implement privatization. As we have seen, and quite contrary to the expectations of

---

[46]    "Genelkurmaya güvence verildi" [Guarantees were given to military high command], *Radikal,* 4 May 2001.

external funders and state elites, the Turkish power bloc (i.e., fractions of capital) had actively contested privatization within the constitutive context of the prevailing strategies of the domestic capital accumulation regime of Turkey at the time (i.e., duty losses, state debt financing). More specifically, the power bloc's intervention to prevent acceleration of privatization was driven by a variety of factors, including: (1) the comfortable relationship that the power bloc had enjoyed with the SOEs as a result of the duty loss mechanism, (2) the reluctance of the TUSİAD-based big holdings to commit large-scale finance to privatization when other accumulation opportunities were available in the financial markets, (3) the intra-capital conflict between the TUSİAD-based big holdings and Anatolian capital fractions, and (4) the lack of operational harmony within the state institutional apparatus on the question of privatization.

In the changed environment of the post-2001 era, however, the complex interplay of those factors – class agency of the power bloc, domestic capital accumulation strategies, and state institutions – worked in the opposite direction and enabled the acceleration of Turkish privatization processes. The following chapter explores this story in detail.

# CHAPTER 4

# The Acceleration of Privatization in the Post-2001 Era: 2002 to 2009

While developing since the mid-1980s, it was not until after Turkey's massive 2001 crisis that the privatization accelerated decidedly both in the form of divestiture and PPP. In the first phase of the post-2001 era (from 2002 to 2009), the bulk of the shares in the large-scale SOEs, including Tüpraş ($4.1 billion), Türk Telekom ($6.55 billion), Erdemir ($2.77 billion), and Petkim ($2.0 billion), were divested by block sale to domestic and foreign investors. During the same time period, many large-scale projects, including the Atatürk Airport Expansion ($2.5 billion), Antalya Airport Expansion ($1.7 billion), İstanbul Sabiha Gökçen International Airport Expansion ($1.3 billion) Enerjisa Hydro Plants ($1.5 billion), and Zonguldak Coal Fired Power Plant ($1.5 billion), were completed with the implementation of the PPP model. As a result, the total privatization value, which had been $19 billion between 1984 and 2001, reached $70 billion at the end of 2009.[1] The figure is even more impressive when we consider that the privatization value realized only within 8 years was reached nearly three times that of the preceding 18 years. The former Turkish Finance Minister (2002–2009) and the head of the Privatization Administration (2003–2009), Kemal Unakıtan, tried to demonstrate the defining motto and operating credo for the privatization policy of the newly elected AKP government at the time, which is well expressed in his famous statement: "We will sell whatever we want ... He who pays the piper calls the tune".[2]

The chapter argues that, unlike the 1980s and 1990s, the complex interplay of those previously stated interrelated factors (i.e., power bloc, capital accumulation, state) worked in the opposite direction and enabled the acceleration of Turkish privatization in the first decade of the post-2001 era (2002–2009). First, the privatisation of the SOEs constituted a central strategy, for the power bloc as a whole, in which domestic accumulation strategies were internally restructured to respond to the new imperatives of international competitiveness in the aftermath of the 2001 economic crisis. Second, there was a shift

---

1  Between 2002 and 2009, Turkey realized $51 billion worth of privatization. Nearly $32 billion of this value comes from divestiture while PPP amounts to approximately $19 billion.

2  "Babalar gibi satacağız" [We will sell whatever we want], *Yeni Şafak*, 13 April 2003; "Parayı veren düdüğü çalar" [He who pays the piper calls the tune], *Hürriyet*, 21 July 2005.

in the fractions of the power bloc that had previously been unwilling and incapable of supporting privatisation. Third, a newly elected single party AKP government, partly in line with the pressures of the domestic accumulation strategies and the interests of the power bloc, undertook a series of neo-liberal institutional reforms to facilitate privatisation and weaken the resistance of labour and judiciary. Such an interpretation goes well beyond the dominant literature on the acceleration of privatization in Turkey, which has confined its scope of analysis to coalitions and/or networks between the government and favourable business groups. Let me look at these three factors in detail in the following four sections.

## 1  Privatization and Internal Restructuring of Accumulation Strategies

The need for an internal restructuring of the accumulation strategies to enhance competitiveness and export capacity of Turkish firms started to be voiced with the Customs Union agreement with the EU in 1996 and gained pace from December 1999 onwards with the signing of three-year stand-by agreement with the IMF, and the granting by the EU at its Helsinki summit of candidate status to Turkey (Bedirhanoğlu and Yalman 2010, 120). For example, the TÜSİAD prepared the *Competition Strategy Series* in 1998 and 1999 and conducted surveys with prominent industrialists in key industrial sector such as automobile, electronics, domestic appliances and cement to identify best practices in each sector as well as prepare action plans for adjusting these sectors to competitive world markets (TÜSİAD 1998; TÜSİAD 1999).

Nonetheless, most fractions of capital including TÜSİAD in Turkey were not ready to escape from their comfortable habit of relying on short-term capital flows, state-lending practices and duty losses to make profit and accumulate capital. It was the very depth of the February 2001 crisis that exposed the accumulation of bad banking debts, both public and private, and convinced state elites and fractions of capital (i.e., power bloc) that a systemic and fundamental structural change is needed. In response, the coalition government introduced the neoliberal-inspired 'Transition to Strong Economy' (TSE) recovery program in April (Marois 2019, 110).

The TSE program gave rise to the 2001 Banking Sector Restructuring Program (BSRP), a key moment in Turkey's neoliberal transformation. The BSRP focused on the reconfiguration of the relations between banking and industry. In this way, it intended to shift money-capital from state debts (and duty losses) into fixed capital investments through comprehensive banking and regulatory reforms (Ercan and Oğuz 2015, 121). Kemal Derviş, Minister of the Economy, characterized the BSRP as an institutionalized means of "creating a competitive industry by stopping the struggle for rent" (Gültekin-Karakaş 2009, 120). Institutionally, the government gave the Bank Regulation and Supervision Agency (BRSA; created just before the outbreak of crisis in 2000) new powers and charged the institution with resolving the current crisis and for building state capacity to manage future financial risks within Turkey's borders (Marois 2019, 110).

The TSE program also initiated the Reform Program for the Improvement of the Investment Environment (RPiiE) in 2001. The RPiiE aimed at improving the business environment for the private sector and encouraging the inflows of foreign direct investment into Turkey (Cebeci 2012). The RPiiE covers a wide range of reform activities, including: gradual removal of the legal-institutional barriers to private domestic and foreign investment; enactment of reforms for establishing new and variegated control mechanisms over labour to increase productivity; development of new industrial policies for the purpose of improving international competitiveness of Turkish firms through a shift in the sectoral composition of investments from labour-intensive and low-value added to capital-intensive and high-value added areas. The top priorities of the RPiiE program were thus foreign direct investment, productivity, and international competitiveness.

The TSE program has acquired a new momentum after AKP's coming to power in the 2002 general elections, a development that was arguably the outcome of the extraordinary post-2001 atmosphere. As a result, the post-2001 accumulation strategies in Turkey were characterized by a transformation in which the fractions of capital (i.e., power bloc) moved away to some degree from their unsustainable reliance on inflows of finance, state-lending practices, and duty losses to dealing with increased production and integration into world markets through augmented competitiveness and commodity exports (Ercan and Oğuz 2015, 117; Taymaz and Voyvoda 2009, 151). This, however, by no means suggests that the dependence of the capital accumulation on financial flows has disappeared in Turkey. What was new in the post-2001 era was the fact that the financial flows had also become a channel for the acceleration of productive capital formation and commodity exports (Gültekin-Karakaş and Ercan 2013). In that sense, it differed from the previous era during which financial flows tended to finance state debt. Financial flows in the post-2001 era began to be used more and more to finance the needs of production, infrastructure and commodity exports (Ercan 2012). These needs mostly included the import of capital goods, intermediate goods, and energy as well as national investment in infrastructure (airports, roads, ports) and both renewable and nonrenewable national energy resources, including coal, petroleum, wind, hydro, and even nuclear energy.

In this altered atmosphere, the entire power bloc and the policymakers became enthusiastic supporters of economics policies that would enhance the international competitiveness of Turkish firms in particular and the Turkish economy in general (Ercan and Oğuz 2015, 120–121). In fact, the restructuring of the SOE and public provision system was an important part of the broader goal of enhancing international competitiveness. This meant that the post-1945 internal relationship between the SOEs and the social classes, which had been based on duty losses and resource transfers, had to be reestablished around competitive imperatives. For example, duty losses in non-financial enterprises have decreased from 1.5% of GDP in 1999 to 0.4% of GDP in 2001 to 0.1% of GDP in 2006, and the level of subsidized bank lending has declined from 0.2% in 2001 to 0.1% of GDP in 2005 (Kraan, Bergvall and Hawkesworth 2007, 52; IMF 2000). In this way, the power bloc began promoting privatization to restructure the entire productive apparatus – SOEs and public provisions – to its advantage (through cost reduction, productivity gains, new investment opportunities with state guarantees) and to the detriment of the laboring classes (through employment losses, de-unionization, socialization of investment risks). This referred what is indispensable to the power bloc as a whole.

First, the power bloc promoted privatization to treat the SOE workers as highly malleable factors in the enhancement of competitiveness and profitability. During the 2001–12 period, about fifty thousand SOE workers were laid off by the new private owners. The State Pension Fund (*Devlet Emeklilik Fonu*) and the Privatization Fund (*Özelleştirme Fonu*) paid over $150 million worth of 'special job loss compensation' to those laid-off workers in order to ease the process and mitigate social resistance (Doğan 2012, 60). Moreover, more than ten thousand SOE workers were encouraged to accept early retirement by the PA that offered them 30 per cent extra retirement payments (worth about $40 million in total) from the Privatization Fund. Furthermore, the State Personnel Department (*Devlet Personel Başkanlığı*) forced over 28,500 workers, which had made redundant as part of the privatization of SOEs, to move elsewhere in the state apparatus (Doğan 2012, 59). This would, in turn, inflate the category of state employees with no job security that came to be known as 4-C employees.[3] 4-C status meant a precarity in the public sector, as these people

---

3  4-C clause was added into the Privatization Law in 2004. This clause states that the downsized workers would be transferred to the personnel pool where they would be distributed to other state institutions. In the post-settlement period, those workers experienced significantly worse-off positions in terms of labour rights and wages.

employed as such would be given temporary contracts lasting minimum of two months and a maximum of 10 months and 28 days. As the extension of these contracts would require the decision of the government, it effectively deprived them not only of their job security, but also of redundancy payments (Yalman and Topal 2017, 6). As part of the 4-C clause, around 6,000 SOE workers were transferred to the Ministry of Education, while over 1,700 SOE workers were moved in the State Hospitals Institution.

A review of five major privatization transactions found that close to 30 per cent of workers in the five enterprises lost their jobs in few years after the privatization. The reductions ranged from 6 per cent in Erdemir iron and steel to 63 per cent in Tekel Alcohol (see Table 7). The cuts were made through layoffs, early retirements, and transfers of workers to other parts of the government. More importantly, while the number of workers was significantly reduced from pre-privatization levels, the new capitalist owners increased the amount of work that the remaining workers had to handle to ensure productivity gains. For example, the total steel production in İşdemir and Erdemir was 340 and 844 tons, respectively, just before privatization. In 2012, seven years after privatization, production per employee in İşdemir and Erdemir rose to 818 and 1,311 tons, respectively.[4] Likewise, the total sales per employee in Tüpraş increased from 4,538 tons to 5,404 tons between 2004 and 2012.[5] The promotion of privatization thus helped the power bloc to subordinate SOE workers to competitive and productivity imperatives.

Second, the power bloc supported privatization to reduce the power of organized labour, as the SOEs had historically provided the most powerful base for labour in Turkey. As a result of privatizations, privatized SOEs underwent massive de-unionization and flexibilization – the newly employed workers had been hired under flexible conditions and without union membership (Yücesan-Özdemir and Özdemir 2007, 467). Mustafa Türkel, the president of TEKGİDA-İŞ (Tobacco, Distillery, and Food Workers' Union of Turkey) affirmed that TÜRK-İŞ (Confederation of Turkish Trade Unions) drew its strength mainly from public sector unionism, which was severely hampered by privatization policies accelerated in the 2000s (Gürcan and Mete 2017, 97). In a similar direction, Nazmi Irgat, the president of the TEKSİF (Textile, Knitting, Clothing Industry Workers' Union), stated in a personal interview, "Before privatization, we had thirty-four thousand members in state-owned textile factories. At this

---

4   See İşdemir's and Erdemir's annual reports for 2004 and 2012, https://www.erdemir.com.tr/
    investor-relations/annual-reports/ (accessed on 16 September 2021).
5   See Tüpraş's annual reports for 2004 and 2012, https://www.tupras.com.tr/en/overview
    (accessed on 16 September 2021).

TABLE 7    Privatization and labor force reductions in Turkey

| Enterprise | Workers before privatization (2004) | Workers after privatization (2012) | % Change |
|---|---|---|---|
| İşdemir | 8,149 | 5,543 | −32 |
| Tekel Alcohol | 2,270 | 834 | −63 |
| Tüpraş | 5,398 | 4,700 | −13 |
| Erdemir | 7,022 | 6,630 | −6 |
| Türk Telekom | 53,472 | 37,524 | −30 |
| Total | 76,311 | 55,231 | −28 |

SOURCE: ANNUAL REPORTS OF COMPANIES

moment [2013], this number is marginal".[6] Furthermore, the liquidation of older workers with unionization experience through enforced retirement or dismissal enabled power bloc to impose flexible and other precarious forms of labour on younger generations who are characteristically devoid of a resistance culture and history (Gürcan and Mete 2017, 99). This helped to paralyze the Turkish labour class so that it failed to collectively oppose privatization and subordination of workers to competitive imperatives.

Third, the power bloc also pushed for privatization with the objective of achieving productivity gains by introducing new technologies and management techniques into the input-producing privatized enterprises (see Table 8).[7] The privatization of Tüpraş – Turkey's largest industrial enterprise – is an important example in this respect. While Tüpraş had difficulties in meeting even half of the $2.1 billion targets in the 1998–2004 Master Modernization Investment Plan under state ownership and management, the Koç-Shell consortium has invested more than $6 billion within ten years after privatization in 2005. The new fuel oil conversion facility, for instance, has enabled Tüpraş to increase productivity by converting low-value-added products such as fuel oil (for which demand in Turkey has been falling) to high-value-added white products including diesel, gasoline, and jet fuel.[8]

---

6  Interview with Nazmi Irgat, President of TEKSİF Union, 11 February 2013.
7  See the speech delivered by the Chairman of the Board of TÜSİAD, Tuncay Özilhan, on 12 December 2003 (https://tusiad.org/tr/konusma-metinleri/item/515-tusiad-yonetim-kurulu-baskani-tuncay-ozilhanin-yuksek-istisare-konseyi-toplantisi-acilis-konusmasi).
8  "Turkish Energy Giant Tüpraş Opens $3bln Refinery Facility", *Daily Sabah*, 14 December 2014.

TABLE 8        Privatization of key input providing SOEs

| Enterprise | Sector | Year of privatization | Price ($ million) |
|---|---|---|---|
| Çayeli Bakır | Copper Mining | 2004 | 49 |
| Tüpraş | Petroleum Refinery | 2005 | 4,140 |
| Erdemir | Iron and Steel | 2005 | 2,770 |
| Samsun Gübre | Fertilizer | 2005 | 41 |
| Petkim | Petrochemical | 2008 | 2,040 |

SOURCE: PRIVATIZATION AUTHORITY WEBSITE, HTTPS://WWW.OIB.GOV.TR

Privatization of Erdemir, which supplies 70 per cent of all iron and steel to the domestic private household appliances sector, is another significant example (Bilim, Sanayi ve Teknoloji Bakanlığı 2011, 5–7). Domestic private household appliance manufacturers such as Vestel, owned by Zorlu Holding, had been experiencing difficulty in responding to international client demand in a timely manner and were losing their competitive advantage because Erdemir's sale strategy under state ownership and management was based on long-term supply agreements. In a 2013 interview, the Director of Zorlu Holding's Strategy Department, Ali Yalçın, stated that, "After Erdemir's privatization in 2005, the new private owners introduced a more flexible management philosophy into privatized enterprise, which ensured the timely supply of iron and steel inputs to domestic household appliance manufacturers. This often fostered the export competitiveness of Turkish TVs, refrigerators and washing machines".[9]

The next important example is the petrochemical giant Petkim. The President of the Turkish Chemical Manufacturers Association, Timur Erk told the media that the government could count on their full support regarding Petkim privatization. However, he also warned that such a vital plant should not sold to Uzan Group, which was embroiled in financial difficulties and engaged in legal battle with multinational companies like Motorola and Nokia.[10] This means that Turkish power bloc preferred Petkim to be sold to a company (most likely foreign company) that would be able to complete an

---

9        Interview with Ali Yalçın, the Director of Strategy Department, Zorlu Holding, 2 February 2013.

10        "Turkish Petkim sale cancellataion delays vital investment", *www.icis.com,* 7 August 2003.

essential $2 billion modernization investment and improve productivity of the plant. It is important to note this preference was not unique to the Petkim case. Tuncay Özilhan and Ömer Sabancı, two successive Chairmen of TÜSİAD between 2001 and 2006, encouraged participation of foreign capital in the Turkish privatization process with the expectation that it would contribute to the introduction of new technologies and additional capacity investments (TÜSİAD 2003; TÜSİAD 2005). This demonstrates that the Turkish business community, which was very much against the sale of SOEs to foreign capital during the 1980s and 1990s, has now started to accept foreign capital to ensure the sustainable provision of high value added, quality and cheap inputs (discussed in more detail below).[11]

Fourth, the power bloc had backed privatization to create new investment opportunities with PPPs, which would be instrumental to meet the increasing infrastructure needs, especially in transportation and energy, of Turkish economy that was fully integrating with the global economy since 2001. Specifically, the passenger airport terminals and the hydro-wind electricity production plants opened further to the private sector with different forms of PPP including the BOT (Built-Operate-Transfer), BROT (Build-Rehabilitate-Operate-Transfer), and BOO (Build-Operate-Own) (see Table 9). From the perspective

TABLE 9      Major PPP projects in Turkey (2002–2009)

| Projects | Sector | Year | Project value ($ million) |
|---|---|---|---|
| Atatürk Airport Terminal | Airport | 2005 | 2,543 |
| Ankara Esenboğa Airport Terminal | Airport | 2005 | 305 |
| Antalya Airport Expansion | Airport | 2007 | 1,702 |
| Enerjisa Phases I and II Hydro and Natural Gas Plants | Electricity | 2008 | 1,539 |
| Zonguldak Coal Fired Power Plants | Electricity | 2008 | 1,500 |
| Sabiha Gökçen Airport Expansion | Airport | 2008 | 1,343 |
| Alkumru Hydroelectric Project | Electricity | 2009 | 466 |
| AkfenHes -11 hydro power plants | Electricity | 2009 | 309 |
| Osmaniye Wind Power Plant | Electricity | 2009 | 306 |

SOURCE: WORLD BANK PPI DATABASE, HTTPS://PPI.WORLDBANK.ORG/EN/SNAPSHOTS/COUNTRY/TURKEY

---

11      "Yabancı sermaye'ye bakışımız değişti", *Zaman,* 28 November 2005.

of the power bloc as a whole, these PPP projects were vital not only to enhance Turkish competitiveness and efficiency but also to provide new investment opportunities with various forms of state guarantees (e.g., revenue or usage guarantees, purchase agreements). In critical terms, PPPs embodies privatization of rewards and the socialization of the investment risks.

## 2      Privatization and Different Fractions of the Power Bloc

In the post-2001 era, the TÜSİAD-based holding groups and Islamic-influenced Anatolian capital fractions of the power bloc shifted their positions from resisting privatization to being supportive of privatization under the representation capacity of the AKP. Both the holding groups and the Anatolian capital fractions saw specific material benefits – in addition to the previously mentioned objective of completing internal restructuring of the domestic accumulation regime around competitive imperatives that was indispensable to the power bloc as a whole – and therefore supported privatization.[12] Moreover, a general consensus emerged that foreign capital, especially large multinational corporations with technical expertise, was warmly welcomed to participate the privatization process (Şahin 2010, 485). All these changed attitudes had significantly reduced the intra-capital conflicts (e.g., TÜSİAD vs. Anatolian; domestic vs. foreign) of the previous decades and created an unprecedented political drive for privatization.

### 2.1     *Privatization and TÜSİAD Holdings*
As a hegemonic fraction of the power bloc, the TÜSİAD-based holding groups saw privatization as a steppingstone to achieving their corporate restructuring strategy, which prioritized the competitive and high-value-added sectors at the expense of the secondary and low-value-added sectors. For holding groups, the corporate restructuring strategy was important to direct resources to those sectors where they can be used most effectively and integrate the world market as competitive and profit-making international players (Şenalp 2012, 355–357). The cases of Koç Holding and Sabancı Holding, Turkey's two largest conglomerates, help to provide concrete examples.

In the post-2001 era, Koç Holding prioritized the high-value-added and/ or export-oriented sectors (such as automotive, consumer durables, energy and finance) and withdrew from the low-value-added and secondary sectors

---

12      See TÜSİAD press release for the November 3, 2002 elections (https://tusiad.org/tr/com ponent/k2/item/2510-3-kasim-2002-genel-secimleri-sonrasinda-kurulacak-hukumetin -oncelikli-gundemini-olusturmasi-gereken-konular-hakkinda-tusiad-gorusleri).

(such as supermarket retailing and animal food).[13] As part of this strategy, Koç Holding turned its attention to the large-scale privatizations in the energy sector and secured the tender for the Tüpraş privatization in 2005 for a price of $4.1 billion. The takeover of Tüpraş, which was the biggest industrial enterprise and the top exporter of Turkey, had an epoch-making impact on Koç Holding's profitability and efficiency on a global scale, and helped the holding to soar in its rating in the list of the world's top five hundred companies.[14]

Koç Holding, on the other hand, withdrawn from sectors and companies where it saw a relatively smaller contribution to its portfolio in the long term and reduced the number of sectors in which it operates. This was vital to concentrate on core businesses like energy and automotive. First, Koç Holding agreed to sell its retailer Migros, Turkey's largest supermarket chain, to private equity firm BC Partners in 2008 for $1.7 billion.[15] Second, Koç sold Oltaş Spa, which distributes passenger car and commercial vehicle tyres in Turkey and has built up a franchise dealer network of 200 outlets, to Continental AG for an undisclosed amount in 2008.[16] Third, Koç and Allianz signed a share purchase agreement regarding the stakes in Koç Allianz Sigorta and Koç Allianz Hayat ve Emeklilik, held by Koç Holding. Thereby, Allianz acquired all the shares of Koç Holding in both companies for €373 million.[17]

Likewise, Sabancı Holding attempted to focus on the high-value-added information technology and energy sectors, instead of growing further in its traditional areas of labour-intensive textile and food production (Şenalp 2012, 356). In this regard, Sabancı Holding's vision was that the telecommunication and energy privatizations would be the centerpiece of its restructuring strategy. For example, the holding's president, Sakıp Sabancı, publicly asked the government in 2002, "What is the privatization of Türk Telekom waiting for? Isn't it on our agenda?"[18] In 2004, Sabancı Holding took it a step further and formed a consortium with its historical rival, Koç Holding, to participate Türk Telekom privatization.[19] Although Sabancı and Koç holdings agreed to appoint

---

13    See Koç Holding Annual Report, pp. 4–5, https://www.koc.com.tr/investor-relations/repo rts (accessed on 16 September 2021).

14    "Koç Tüpraş'la Dünyanın 200 Devi Arasına Girecek" [Koç will enter the list of the world's largest 200 companies with Tüpraş], *Hürriyet*, 14 September 2005.

15    "Turkey's Koc sells Migros in private equity deal", *Reuters*, 14 February 2008.

16    "Conti to Acquire 89.66% Stake in its Turkish Tyre Distributor", *Tyre Press*, 22 July 2008.

17    "Brief-Koc Holding sells insurance stakes to Allianz", *Reuters*, 21 April 2008.

18    "Sabancı: Türk Telekom'un Özelleştirmesi Neyi Bekliyor" [What is the Türk Telekom privatization waiting for?], *Zaman*, 8 February 2002.

19    See official website of Sabancı Holding, https://www.sabanci.com/tr/haber-detay/saba nci-ve-koc-telekom-ozellestirmesinde-goldman-sachs-i-yatirim-danismani-olarak-secti.

Goldman Sachs as their consultant for the Türk Telekom privatization, they announced the end to their consortium just days before the bidding for the tender begins.[20] In 2005, Sabancı Holding separately bid for, but failed to win, the Türk Telekom privatization tender.

Sabancı Holding then turned much of its attention to the upcoming energy privatizations. The holding growth strategy report in 2006 stated that it would evaluate electricity generation, distribution and trade as well as natural gas distribution and trade opportunities. To that purpose, the holding established its 'Energy Group Unit', signed a partnership agreement with Austrian electricity giant Verbund, and announced that it would invest at least $7 billion into energy sector.[21] Within four years, Sabancı Holding realized two important privatization projects in the energy sector (see Table 10). The first project, Enerjisa Phase I and II, constructed a portfolio of ten hydroelectric power plants in Seyhan, Ceyhan and Çambaşı basins and one natural gas-fired thermal plant in Bandırma with a total capacity of 1,920 megawatts.[22] This was one of the largest investments ever made in Turkish energy sector and had government support in the form of power purchase agreement. For example, Bandırma plant is expected to fulfill 3.5 per cent of Turkey's energy demand on its own. The second project involved the Başkent Electricity Distribution Company, of which Sabancı Holding won from the privatization portfolio offering the highest bid of $1,225 million in July 2008. The transfer of shares to Enerjisa (a joint venture of Sabancı-Verbund) was concluded in January 2009. Başkent Electricity Distribution Company maintains and operates the electricity distribution grid and provides electricity retail services as well as additional services to 3.2 million customers in Ankara, Bartın, Çankırı, Karabük, Kastamonu, Kırıkkale and Zonguldak.[23]

While the Sabancı Holding's strategic plans focused on the energy sector as a key growth area with privatizations, non-core businesses were sold off one after another. First, Sabancı completely withdrew from food sector and sold its

20    "Koç and Sabancı Telecom's consulting firm: Goldman Sachs", *Hurriyet,* 16 March 2004; "Koç and Sabancı Groups split on quest for Turk Telekom", *Hurriyet,* 6 May 2005.

21    "Sabancı Enerji'de Büyüyecek" [Sabanci will grow in the energy sector], *Zaman,* 14 February 2006; "Enerji'ye 7 Milyar Dolar Yatıracağız" [We will invest 7 Billion Dollar into Energy], *Zaman,* 21 December 2006.

22    See official website of Verbund, https://www.verbund.com/en-de/about-verbund/news -press/press-releases/2008/07/15/enerjisa-finanzierung.

23    See Sabancı Holding Annual Report for 2010, https://yatirimciiliskileri.sabanci.com/ en/financial-reports-publications/liste-report/Annual-Report/158/0/0 (accessed on 16 September 2021).

TABLE 10    Successful privatization projects of Sabancı Holding (2002–2009)

| Projects | Year | Type of privatization | Investment ($ million) |
|---|---|---|---|
| Enerjisa Phase I and II | 2008 | PPP | 1,539 |
| Başkent Electricity Distribution | 2009 | Divestiture | 1,225 |

SOURCE: WORLD BANK, TURKISH PRIVATIZATION AUTHORITY

food subsidiaries for cash – Danonesa to French Group Danone, and Gıdasa to MGS Marmara Gıda.[24] Second, Sabancı sold its 51.23% stake in Pilsa to Wavin, the world leader for plastic pipes, for $41 million in 2008. Third, Sabancı announced the sale of its 50% stake in Beksa, its joint venture in the steel cord business, to its partner Belgian Bekaert for €40 million in 2008. Fourth, Sabancı sold its majority stake in textile firm Bossa to a Turkish manufacturing company, Akkardan, for $76 million in 2008.[25] Fifth, Sabancı agreed to sell its 65% equity stake in Toyotasa, its passenger car distribution subsidiary, to Saudi Arabia-based ALJ Group for $85 million.[26]

Other TÜSİAD-based holdings were also actively involved in securing privatization projects (see Table 11). These holdings included Tekfen, Akfen, Akkök, Zorlu, and so on. From the mid-2000s, electricity production and distribution privatizations became particularly important to these holdings, as they embraced energy as one of their primary business areas. For example, Akkök Holding built Akocak Hydropower Plant with BOT subtype of PPP in 2006 and won the bidding opened by the Privatization Administration in 2008 for the privatization of the electricity distribution company Sakarya Electricity Distribution. Another example of this is Zorlu Holding, which won 2008 tender for privatization of nine power plants belonging to Ankara Doğal Elektrik

---

24    "Sabancı, Danonesa'yı 72 milyon dolara bıraktı", *Hürriyet,* 17 December 2003; "Sabancı, Gıdasa'yı Topbaş'a satıp gıdada üretim defterini kapatıyor", *Hürriyet,* 15 August 2008.
25    See Sabancı Holding Annual Report for 2008, https://yatirimciiliskileri.sabanci.com/en/financial-reports-publications/liste-report/Annual-Report/158/0/0 (accessed on 16 September 2021).
26    See Sabancı Holding Annual Report for 2009, https://yatirimciiliskileri.sabanci.com/en/financial-reports-publications/liste-report/Annual-Report/158/0/0 (accessed on 16 September 2021).

TABLE 11     Selected privatization projects of other TÜSİAD Holdings (2002–2009)

| Projects | Year | Type of privatization | Winner | Project value ($ million) |
|---|---|---|---|---|
| Samsun Gübre Sanayi | 2005 | Divestiture | Tekfen Holding | 41 |
| Atatürk Airport Terminal | 2005 | PPP | Tepe-Akfen Holding | 2,543 |
| Akocak Hydropower Plant | 2006 | PPP | Akkök Holding | 125 |
| Land in İstanbul Zincirlikuyu | 2007 | Divestiture | Zorlu Holding | 800 |
| Ankara Doğal Elektrik Üretim | 2008 | Divestiture | Zorlu Holding | 510 |
| Sakarya Electricity Distribution | 2008 | Divestiture | Akkök Holding | 600 |
| AkfenHes -11 hydro power plants | 2009 | PPP | Akfen Holding | 309 |
| Osmaniye Wind Power Plant | 2009 | PPP | Zorlu Holding | 306 |

SOURCE: WORLD BANK;= TURKISH PRIVATIZATION AUTHORITY

(including seven hydroelectric projects totaling 111MW) and constructed a 135MW onshore wind power project with BOT model in 2009.

### 2.2    *Privatization and Islamic-Influenced Anatolian Capital Groups*
Previously a rival fraction in the power bloc, Islamic-influenced Anatolian capital, also championed privatization in the post-2001 era. It should be said that two material forces made privatization the preferred option for Islamic-influenced Anatolian capital.

The first factor was the existence of the AKP government, ensuring the Islamic-influenced Anatolian capital's equal participation in the privatization process (Angın and Bedirhanoğlu 2013, 83). The AKP had always had an organic relationship with Islamic-influenced Anatolian capital. For example, ten MÜSİAD members were among the founders of the AKP, while twenty MÜSİAD members were elected to parliament as AKP deputies in the 2002 general elections (Atasoy 2007, 83). Though less in number, TUSKON and

ASKON-affiliated (i.e., two other representative bodies of Islamic-influenced Anatolian capital) individuals also served as AKP deputies (Atiyas, Bakış and Gürakar 2019, 95). In one of his first public speeches, the new Prime Minister, Recep Tayyip Erdoğan, emphasized that he wanted to ensure the equal participation of the different capital groups in state tenders (Ercan and Oğuz 2006, 652). This kind of statement by the AKP leadership and the organic ties with key AKP officials eliminated the concerns of Islamic-influenced Anatolian capital about the continuation of exclusionary state attitudes, which had effectively limited their participation in privatization tenders during the 1990s.

MÜSİAD was formed in 1990 and ASKON was founded in 1998. Both business associations are known to be close to the "*Milli Görüş*" (National Vision) movement and both used to have close relations with the Welfare Party of the Erbakan in the 1990s and the AKP later. TUSKON was established in 2005 and has been generally connected to the Gülen Community Movement, or *Fethullahçılar*. TUSKON has comprised of about 500 affiliated firms (e.g., Boydak Holding), many of them very profitable and fully integrated into the market economy.[27] Despite ideological differences among them, what unifies all three associations vis-à-vis TÜSİAD are their late participation in the capital accumulation process and their establishment, operation and expansion around Muslim business principles and political Islam.

The second and related factor that made privatization the preferred option for Islamic-influenced Anatolian capital was the expectation that the privatizations would present new opportunities for their long-waited transformation from generally medium-sized enterprises to large multisector conglomerates (Buğra and Savaşkan 2014, 80–90). Between 2002 and 2009, Islamic-influenced Anatolian capital groups mostly targeted the small and mid-scale privatizations – indicative of the size of those capital groups – in the privatization portfolio. First, Çalık Holding, a founding member of MÜSİAD, purchased Bursa Gas Distribution for a price of $120 million. Second, Cengiz Holding, originated from the hometown of Prime Minister Erdoğan, acquired mining plants Eti Bakır and Eti Aluminum, at a total cost of $327 million. Cengiz Holding also built the 600-MW Samsun Natural Gas Combined Cycle power plant with a PPP contract. Third, Albayrak Group, whose CEO (Ömer Bolat) acted as the

---

27    The relationship between the Gülen movement based TUSKON and the AKP government
      soured and eventually turned into open hostility after 2013 corruption scandal. The Gülen
      movement was declared a terrorist organization and, after the failed coup attempt in
      2016 for which the group was implicated, TUSKON was closed (Atiyas, Bakış and Gürakar
      2019, 92).

president of MÜSİAD between 2004 and 2008, took its first step into the manu-facturing and logistic sectors by winning three privatizations tenders – namely, Balıkesir Seka Paper, Trabzon Port, and Tümosan. Fourth, Sanko Holding, the most important enterprise of the southeastern Anatolian city of Gaziantep that had close relations with the TUSKON and the ruling AKP, commissioned 60MW Çatalca Wind Farm project with the BOT subtype of PPP. Fifth, Kiler Group, belonged to the family of AKP Deputy Vahit Kiler (2003–2015), pur-chased Kütahya Sugar Factory for a price of $23.8 million to complement its food retailing activities. Sixth, İC Holding, whose owner İbrahim Çeçen is con-sidered as one of the richest members of Islamic capital in Turkey and has close relations with Erdoğan, purchased Tekel Bomonti Land from the privatization portfolio and constructed one of the Europe's biggest hotels on it.[28] Moreover, İC Holding is one of the companies that has been very dominant with the share of the PPP projects (Transparency International Turkey 2017, 5–6). Some PPP projects of İC Holding include the Antalya Airport Renewal (Management) project with 17 years of operation rights, and Niksar Hydroelectric Power Plant that was built with BOO model (see Table 12).

Indeed, these privatizations helped the Islamic-influenced Anatolian capi-tal groups join in the ranks of big capital. While MÜSİAD had only three mem-bers in the list of Turkey's top five hundred industrial enterprises in 2004, by 2010, there were thirty-one MÜSİAD members on the list. TUSKON has also made significant headway, having forty-five TUSKON-affiliated companies among Turkey's top 500 industrial enterprises list in 2010 (Buğra and Savaşkan 2014, 105, 117–119; Çavdar 2014, 11; Tanyılmaz 2015, 107).[29] According to the monthly economy magazine *Capital*, there is also a significant increase in the number of holdings that were established in the Anatolian cities. The number of holdings in Anatolia thus increased from 144 in 2002 to 204 by 2009. Most of these new holdings were established in cities like Gaziantep, Denizli, Ankara, Kayseri, Konya, and Bursa.[30]

What underlies this increased participation by Islamic-influenced Anatolian capital in the privatization tenders is the diminishing of intra-capital con-flicts. While TÜSİAD-based holding groups and Islamic-influenced Anatolian capital had focused on blocking each other's participation as we see in the Petlas and TEDAŞ cases during the 1990s, they joined forces to participate in

28    "Bomonti ihalesini aldı, Arap yatırımcılar peşinde" [İC Holding won the Bomonti tender and the Arab investors is chasing], *Milliyet*, 23 October 2006.
29    The 500 lists have been provided by the İstanbul Chamber of Industry.
30    Ayşe Tarcan Aksakal, "Anadolu'nun Yükselen Holdingleri" [The Rising Holdings of Anatolia], *Capital*, February 2010.

TABLE 12    Selected privatizations (divestitures and PPPs) of Islamic-influenced Anatolian
            capital groups (2002–2009)

| Privatizations | Company | Year | Value ($ million) |
|---|---|---|---|
| Balıkesir Seka | Albayrak Group | 2003 | 1.1 |
| Trabzon Port | Albayrak Group | 2003 | 22.4 |
| Tümosan | Albayrak Group | 2004 | 27.2 |
| Bursa Gas Distribution | Çalık Holding | 2004 | 120 |
| Eti Bakır | Cengiz Holding | 2004 | 22 |
| Kütahya Sugar Factory | Kiler Group | 2004 | 23.8 |
| Eti Aluminum | Cengiz Holding | 2005 | 305 |
| Tekel Bomonti Land | İc Holding | 2006 | 42 |
| Antalya Airport Renewal (Management) Project | İc Holding | 2007 | 1,700 |
| Çatalca Wind Farm | Sanko Holding | 2008 | 100 |
| Meram Electricity Distribution | Cengiz-Alarko Holding | 2009 | 440 |
| Niksar Hydropower Plant | İc Holding | 2009 | 170 |
| Samsun Gas Fired Power Plant | Cengiz Holding | 2009 | 105 |

SOURCE: WORLD BANK; PRIVATIZATION AUTHORITY; COMPANY ANNUAL REPORTS

privatizations in the post-2001 era. For example, Alarko Holding (a TÜSİAD member) and Cengiz Holding (Anatolian capital) cooperated to secure the Meram Region Electricity Distribution (involving central Anatolian cities such as Konya, Aksaray, Niğde, Kırşehir, Nevşehir, and Karaman) privatization tender for a price of $440 million in 2008.[31]

A more interesting example is the partnership between leading TÜSİAD member Koç Holding and founding MÜSİAD member Yıldız Holding (Ülker) in their $5.7 billion bid for a highway privatization.[32] This partnership acquired a deeper meaning when we remember that the same Yıldız Holding had been among the companies that had been excluded not only from privatization process but also from public procurements during the 1990s as a result of the

---

31    See official website of Cengiz Holding (http://www.cengiz.com.tr/en-us/Sectors/Energy/
      Pages/Meram-Elektrik-Dagitim-Anonim-Sirketi.aspx).
32    "Koç Group wins Turkish Highway Concession", *Financial Times*, 17 December 2012.

interventions of TÜSİAD members. Even the former United States ambassador to Turkey from 1997 to 2000, Mark Parris, who also served as a deputy chief of mission at the U.S. embassy in Israel and political counselor at the U.S. embassy in Moscow, stated in a late 2005 speech: "Turkey is now joined together politically as never before".[33]

## 2.3    Privatization and Foreign Capital

Turkey had been unsuccessful in attracting foreign direct investment (FDI) during the 1980s and 1990s. However, this situation clearly changed in the post-2001 era. The Turkish power bloc that was aiming to integrate with world capitalism and increase commodity exports after the crisis became more receptive to foreign capital, as an important vector for getting access to new technologies, developing manufacturing capabilities and financing new investments. It was also in this period when foreign capital that was seeking new areas to invest with the accelerated global liquidity cycle showed genuine interest in Turkey and its privatization opportunities. The successful implementation of structural reforms (TSE program) in 2001 and 2002, the election of a single-party AKP government in the November 2002 general elections, the enactment of the FDI Law in 2003 and the EU's decision to begin membership negotiations with Turkey in December 2004 convinced foreign investors and helped FDI inflows to bounce. While the FDI inflows amounted to less than $1 billion before 2001, it reached a record level of $10 billion in 2005. FDI inflows continued to increase to $20 and $22 billion in 2006 and 2007, respectively. Despite the global financial crisis, the FDI inflows stayed around $20 billion in 2008.[34]

Founded in 1980 as an independent and non-profit business association, YASED (International Investors Association of Turkey – *Uluslararası Yatırımcılar Derneği*) represented more than 200 international companies operating in the country. One of the most important missions of the association is the improvement of the investment environment to encourage free investment and movement of capital. Through official visits, conferences and meetings, the association creates opportunities for its members to come together with government officials. We did see that YASED were becoming more effective in influencing policy makers and policy in the 2000s. For example, YASED hired university scholars in 2004 and 2005 to prepare reports on

---

33    "Türkiye'yi hiç bu kadar iyi görmemiştim" [I never seen Turkey as well as it is now], *Zaman,* 13 October 2005.

34    The FDI data is taken from UNCTAD.

FDI strategy of Turkey, which then submitted to government officials.[35] YASED officials also recommended that Turkey should take a leap forward in the privatization to promote foreign investment.[36]

The rise in FDI has gone hand in hand with the privatization boom. Major privatization deals of the 2002–2009 period demonstrate a significant foreign presence – over 25 per cent of total sales and/or investment.[37] Foreign companies participating alone or acting in joint ventures with powerful domestic partners succeeded to acquire the ownership of some-large scale SOEs and/or to realize some of the significant PPP projects (see Table 13).

Turkey's biggest ever privatization materialized in 2005 as the 55 per cent stake in the country's fixed-line telecommunications operator, Türk Telekom, was sold to a Saudi Oger Telecom for a fee of $6.55 billion dollars. The government then had real success with a 15 per cent initial public offering (IPO) for Türk Telekom in 2008. Despite a downturn in the market, foreign investors showed a strong interest in the deal, and it netted the government $1.9 billion. Next, French Groupama has acquired Başak Sigorta, a general insurance company and Başak Emeklilik, a life insurance company, following a privatization process in 2006 that involved national and international bidders. Those acquisitions cost Groupama $267 million and allowed it to significantly strengthen its presence in Turkey, thereby making it the sixth largest insurer on the Turkish market.[38]

Petkim Petrokimya Holding A.S. (Petkim) was established in 1965 by the Turkish state under the auspices of Turkish Petroleum Corporation. In May 2008 the privatization of Petkim was finalized. The State Oil Company of Azerbaijan (SOCAR) and Turkey's TURCAS consortium bid $2.04 billion and acquired 51 per cent of Petkim's shares. The effort to privatize Turkey's cigarette maker TEKEL also ended when British American Tobacco (BAT) offered the highest bid for the company at $1.72 billion. The Privatization Administration first tried to sell TEKEL in 2003 and the latest tender was its third attempt. The sale included factories in Adana, Ballıca, Bitlis, Malatya and Tokat, while facilities in Istanbul were leased.

---

35   See TUSİAD and YASED, "FDI Attractiveness of Turkey: A Comparative Analysis", February
      2004; Kamil Yılmaz, "Towards a Foreign Direct Investment Strategy for Turkey", Koç
      University, Paper prepared for YASED, İstanbul, 27 October 2005.
36   "Özelleştirme pahalıya satmak değil" [Privatization does not mean selling at a high price],
      Zaman, 21 July 2004.
37   The participation of foreign investors into the privatization process between 1984 and
      2000 was around 10 per cent of total sales (Doğan 2012, 51–57).
38   See https://www.groupama.com/en/analyst/groupama-acquires-basak-sigorta-and
      -basak-emeklilik-turkish-insurance-companies/ (accessed on 16 July 2020).

TABLE 13     Selected privatizations involved by foreign capital (2002–2009)

| Privatizations | Involved by | Foreign share (%) | Year | Value ($ million) |
|---|---|---|---|---|
| Türk Telekom | Oger Telecom (Saudi) | 100 | 2005 | 6,550 |
| Başak Sigorta and Emeklilik | Groupama International (France) | 100 | 2006 | 267 |
| Motor Vehicle Inspection | TUV SUD (Germany) | 33 | 2007 | 552 |
| Halkbank | Various investors | 100 | 2007 | 1,289 |
| Petkim Petrokimya | SOCAR (Azerbaijan) | 75 | 2008 | 2,040 |
| Tekel Tobacco | British American Tobacco | 100 | 2008 | 1,720 |
| Sakarya Electricity Distribution | CEZ (Czech Republic) | 50 | 2008 | 600 |
| Enerjisa Phase I and II | Verbund (Austria) | 50 | 2008 | 1,539 |
| Baskent Electricity Distribution | Verbund (Austria) | 50 | 2009 | 1,225 |
| Izmit Gas Distribution | GDF Suez (France) | 90 | 2009 | 232 |
| Niksar Hydropower Plant | AES Corporation (USA) | 51 | 2009 | 170 |
| Essentium Hydropower Plant | Essentium Group (Spain) | 100 | 2009 | 78 |

SOURCE: WORLD BANK; PRIVATIZATION AUTHORITY OF TURKEY; ANNUAL REPORTS OF COMPANIES

The process of privatization of energy sectors opened up new investment opportunities for foreign investors (see Table 13). As I mentioned above, Verbund, one of the leading electricity companies in Europe, signed a joint venture agreement (based on equal share and management principle) with

Sabancı of Turkey. Verbund Sabancı Joint Venture won the privatization tender for the block sale of 100 per cent of the shares of Başkent Electricity Distribution Company as well as completing the Enerjisa Phase I and II electricity production investments with PPP model. Moreover, GDF Suez won the bid for the privatization of Izmet Gaz Dağıtım (Izgaz), a Turkish natural gas distribution and retail network owned by the city council of İzmit, which lies in the Kocaeli region 80km east of Istanbul. Izgaz is Turkey's third largest gas distributor after Istanbul and Ankara distributors.[39] Furthermore, AES Corporation in partnership with Turkey's IC Holding built Niksar Hydroelectric Power Plant Project (40 MW) with build, own, and operate (BOO) model in 2009. The project cost was $170 million. Through Akcez Energy, a joint venture with a Turkish partner (i.e., Akkök Holding), CEZ, one of the leading energy companies in Central and Eastern Europe, won the bidding opened by the Privatization Administration in July 2008 for the privatization of the electricity distribution company Sakarya Elektrik Dagitim AS (SEDAS) at a cost of $600 million.

### 2.4   Privatization and the AKP Government

The AKP has been an enthusiastic supporter of privatization in Turkey since its establishment in 2001. According to the AKP's founding party programme, 'privatization is important for the development of a more rational economic order'.[40] In January 2003, the newly elected AKP government published its 'Emergency Action Plan' and declared that a series of state assets including major industrial and banking enterprises would be privatized as soon as possible with a well-designed strategy and calendar.[41] At the same time, the Deputy Prime Minister has conveyed his government's strong intentions by announcing, 'these are privatizations which have been planned for years and should have been taken care of a long time ago'.[42] In May 2003, the AKP government introduced the 'Turkish Privatization Strategy Plan' with the direct participation of representatives from the state bureaucracy, business associations, and academics. Domestic and foreign consulting firms such as ARGE, Investa, and JP Morgan were also among the participants. The plan set out government's privatization vision and identified potential obstacles and strategies to

---

39   "GDF Suez wins bid for Turkish gas distributor Izgaz", *Oil & Gas Journal,* 19 August 2008.

40   See AKP (2002), "Kalkınma ve Demokratikleşme Programı", https://acikerisim.tbmm .gov.tr/xmlui/bitstream/handle/11543/926/200205071.pdf?sequence=1&isAllowed=y (accessed on 17 July 2020).

41   See "T.C. 58. Hükümet Acil Eylem Planı" [T.R. 58th Government Emergency Action Plan], 2003, p. 49.

42   "Turkey reveals privatisation plans", *BBC News,* 13 January 2003.

follow.[43] A few days later, Prime Minister Erdoğan stated that they have been actively working on the issue of privatization while asking labour unions not to stand against the privatization program.[44]

The AKP eventually kept its promises and generated more receipts from privatization than all previous administrations combined. Privatization was among the most important conditionalities of the IMF, WB, and the EU, and was welcomed by these international organizations. However, it would be delusive to argue that the AKP was externally forced to accelerate the privatization process in the post-2001 era (Erol 2018, 5).

It is important not to underestimate the AKP's domestic preferences. First, the AKP internalized the common interests of TÜSİAD and MÜSİAD to drive the acceleration of privatization and strove to balance the conflicting involvement of the two groups as well as the participation of foreign capital in the privatization tenders. Joint partnerships between TÜSİAD and MÜSİAD members (and between Turkish companies and large foreign capital groups), as shown above, were crafted under the representation capacity of the AKP government. Thanks to its pro-market and pro-privatization stance, the AKP could successfully establish itself as the representative of both wings of the Turkish bourgeoisie.

The AKP's commitment to privatization can also be rethought in relation to its politically vulnerable position within the power relations, particularly during its first two terms in the office (2002–2009). This was a period in which the AKP government was in office but lacked confidence considering the fate of a previous Islamic-based party – the RP. At the domestic and international level, there was a welcoming but cautious attitude toward the AKP's rise to power. Within such an atmosphere, the AKP had a special imperative to remain loyal to the neoliberal agenda and to accelerate the privatization process to demonstrate to domestic and international actors that it was the right party to govern Turkey (Angın and Bedirhanoğlu 2012, 150). In other words, the AKP government pushed forward the privatization program in its quest for gaining legitimacy in the eyes of liberal circles both at home and abroad. The commitment of the AKP to privatization is, therefore, inscribed with the interests of the power bloc, but it is also rooted in its own strategies and struggles.

After 2009–2010, the AKP government increased its relative autonomy vis-à-vis the hegemonic fraction of the power bloc (i.e., the TÜSİAD-based holding

---

43    "Turkish Privatization Strategy Plan", 18 May 2003, https://slideplayer.biz.tr/slide/2809
      169/ (accessed on 17 July 2020).

44    "Erdoğan'dan sendikalara: Lütfen özelleştirmenin karşısına dikilmeyin" [From Erdoğan to
      labour unions: Please do not stand against privatization], *Zaman*, 25 May 2003.

groups), thanks to its strong relationship with petro-dollar Gulf capital originating from Saudi Arabia and Qatar, and mobilization of mass support for government policies in a plebiscitary fashion (Oğuz 2016). This represented a turning point in the AKP's attitude toward privatization. Although the AKP continued to support privatization as a policy, the AKP started to use privatization tenders as reward-punishment mechanism for individual capital groups to consolidate its own strategies and power base. Some Islamic-influenced Anatolian capital groups such as Cengiz İnşaat, Bereket Enerji, Limak Holding, and IC Holding, which had proven their closeness to the AKP government, received preferential treatment and won several privatization tenders after 2009.

Yet this does not mean that other, more neutral, capital groups of TÜSİAD and/or foreign investors were totally excluded from privatization tenders or PPP investments, as happened to the Islamic-influenced Anatolian capital groups during the 1990s (Aykut 2015). For example, prominent TÜSİAD member Sabancı Holding won several privatization tenders after 2009. Similarly, many TÜSİAD members were heavily involved in the PPP projects in the post-2009 period as financial lenders, input suppliers and engineering contractors (as is discussed in Chapter 5 in more detail).

3      Privatization and Resistance

The general weakening of the organized labor in the neoliberal era should not be allowed to obscure the fact that class struggle continues, albeit in a peculiarly asymmetric form (Callinicos 2016, 58). As Benjamin Selwyn's fascinating article clearly demonstrates with concrete case studies, 'collective action by laboring classes can generate tangible development gains for themselves and their communities' (2016, 1). So, the narrative above should not lead one to see Turkey's privatization process between 2002 and 2009 as a simple series of exchanges in buying and selling SOEs with no resistance. Despite the shared interests of the power bloc fractions in privatization and a committed AKP government, the privatizations were contested by organized labor.

Yet it is fair to say that, by and large, the resistance of Turkish labor to privatization turned out to be local in nature and relatively mild. In addition to the systemic damage of neoliberalism and finance on the capacity of organized labor across the world, I see a few specific reasons for the limited resistance of Turkish labor. To begin with, the 1980 military coup and its aftermath have seen a heavy suppression of the labor movement, which has ended up paralyzing union organizing for decades (Gürcan and Mete 2017, 6). The military coup environment of the 1980–1983 period dealt a heavy blow to

organized labour particularly via the temporary prohibition of unions, introduction of an authoritarian labor regime, and persecution of leading union
cadres, because of which unions could never regain their membership base
and organized consciousness in the 1980s and 1990s (Gürcan and Mete 2017,
95). According to a prominent Turkish labour researcher, Demet Dinler, the
unionization rate for waged workers was around 6 per cent in the mid-2000s
(2012, 2). As such, the rule of the AKP in the 2000s coincides with the weakest
period of collective labour rights and the unions in the last 50 years of Turkey
(Çelik 2015, 618).

The ideological diversionism further weakened the power of organized
labour and resulted in its inability to open a collective labor front against privatization. It is undeniable that the AKP government encouraged such ideological diversionism. Workers are forced to resign from their unions and become
members of a confederation close to the government.

In Turkey, there are three labor confederations with different ideological
positions over privatization in particular and socio-economic issues in general (see Table 14). HAK-İŞ (Confederation of True Trade Unions of Turkey)
was close to the Islamist ideology and emphasized a non-confrontational
approach based on symbiotic harmony between employers and employees.
Unsurprisingly, HAK-İŞ adopted a clearly pro-privatization stance during the
AKP rule. In contrast, the left-wing DİSK (Confederation of Revolutionary
Workers' Unions) was more critical in its standing vis-à-vis the AKP government. It has also taken clearly and ideologically anti-privatization stand.
TÜRK-İŞ (Confederation of Trade Unions in Turkey), as the largest confederation, is composed primarily of right-wing unions and occupies a center-right
position. TÜRK-İŞ was the confederation that traditionally monopolized the
representation of the public sector blue-collar employees and perhaps best
equipped to play a central role in establishing coordination between different public sector unions, but it has avoided such a role. Although TÜRK-İŞ
leadership had certain criticisms and objects particularly to the erosion of job
security and potential job losses (i.e., bread-and-butter issues) resulting from
privatization, it took milder attitude vis-à-vis privatizations and cautiously
collaborated with the AKP government. Hence, TÜRK-İŞ leadership with such
an attitude could even be considered as an implicit proponent of privatization. However, this should not be taken to mean that the strategies of TÜRK-İŞ
affiliated unions have been uniform. For example, a cluster of unions (e.g.,
Petrol-İş, Liman-İş, Gıda-İş, and Selüloz İş) within TÜRK-İŞ has overtly against
privatization. As I will show later, the leading union among those, Petrol-İş,
showed a great capacity to organize activities against the privatization of
Tüpraş petroleum refineries.

TABLE 14    Official membership figures of labor confederations in 2009

| Confederation | Number of members | Number of unions |
|---|---|---|
| TÜRK-İŞ | 2,239,341 | 33 |
| HAK-İŞ | 431,550 | 7 |
| DİSK | 426,232 | 17 |

SOURCE: DINLER (2012), P. 2

Organized labor in Turkey also had difficulties in reaching out to the non-unionized new working class – which comprises urban workers engaged in precarious work, dispossed people, migrant workers, and the rural poor (Chang 2015, 190). These divergent elements of the new working class are important because they have been active participant in struggles against privatization in different parts of the world (Spronk 2007, 8). It has become increasingly clear that the unions, which are based on the concept of a solid/fixed/coherent working class, can no longer act on their own within the context of the fragmented labor relations and employment conditions prevalent in these neoliberal times (Chang 2015, 190). The advocates of privatization in Turkey more easily defeated the organized labour because the unions acted in opposition to privatization in the cause of defending the rights of their members in full and secure employment, without finding ways to work in parallel with the new working class. The TEKEL resistance that began in December 2009 might be seen, in this sense, as an exception that succeeded in articulating different labor practices to a common struggle. The place of TEKEL resistance, which defined as 'tent city' by Metin Özuğurlu (2011), became in a short time a hub of laborer solidarity for organized, unorganized, collective, and individual initiatives generated from every part of Turkey. But TEKEL resistance cannot be generalized, as organized labor in Turkey is far from establishing alliances with non-unionized new working class.

Despite its assault on labor and the deteriorating conditions of the workers because of the neoliberal policies including privatization, the AKP government's charity distributions and populist social aid networks recruited support from the new working class (Gürcan and Peker 2015, 334–336). The social policy measures and social assistance measures such social assistance based on local municipalities, faith-based charitable organizations and public poverty reduction programs have played key roles to contain class struggle to a certain extent in the 2000s and co-opting the rampant discontent of the laboring classes (especially informal workers and the urban poor) with deteriorating working conditions (Erol 2018, 9). The AKP's colonization of the new working class led to contestation/fractures within the laboring classes, which in turn significantly weakened organized labor's resistance to privatization. As Demet Dinler recommends, labor unions in Turkey need to reach out to workers in precarious employment by using many kinds of venues such as homes, coffee houses, city centers, and public transport as well as the workplaces (2012, 20).

### 3.1    Sporadic Labor Resistances: Seka, Tüpraş ...

For all these reasons, Turkish labor did not form a collective front against privatization. There were, however, important sporadic examples of organized labor's resistance to privatization, some of which achieved considerable success in the cancellation or delay of specific privatization implementations. Some major flashpoint instances include the 2003–2004 Petkim demonstrations, the 2003–2005 Seydisehir struggle, the 2004–2005 Seka workplace occupations, the 2003–2006 Tüpraş resistances, and the 2009–2010 Tekel resistance. These experiences have become the greatest symbol of the labor struggle against the AKP's privatization agenda.

The SEKA experience was a landmark in the history of Turkey's labour struggle against the AKP's rush to privatization. SEKA's paper factory in İzmit, northwest Turkey, used to be one of the country's important industrial enterprises, until the AKP government decided to privatize this facility in November 2004 (Gürcan and Mete 2017, 19). After sustained protests in December 2004 with iconic slogans like "everywhere is SEKA, everywhere is resistance", more than 700 SEKA workers together with family members occupied the factory on 20 January 2005 to prevent its privatization.[45] The workplace occupation of the SEKA paper workers also received a lot of public support. While tens of thousands of workers from several sectors remained at their workplaces on 4 March 2005 to demonstrate their solidarity and support for the SEKA paper workers, university professors like Erinç Yeldan announced that an investment of $5.8 million would allow all the SEKA factories to produce various grades of paper and make the company globally competitive.[46] The 51-day workers' occupation came to an end on 11 March, after workers accepted an offer by the Turkish government. Under the terms of the agreement, the SEKA factory would be transferred to the Greater Kocaeli municipality, which would ensure that production at the plant is to continue and workers who transferred along is to keep their social security and rights (Özveri 2005). Although the factory eventually

45    See "Turkey: paper workers occupy factory", *World Socialist Web Site,* 25 February 2005 (https://www.wsws.org/en/articles/2005/02/turk-f25.html).

46    "Turkey: union bureaucracy works to sabotage paper workers' occupation", *World Socialist Web Site,* 10 March 2005 (https://www.wsws.org/en/articles/2005/02/turk-f25.html).

closed, the SEKA workers maintained their social security and rights (Yalman and Topal 2017, 6).

Another landmark in the history of the Turkish labor is the worker's resistance against the privatization of Tüpraş between 2003 and 2006. Most of the Tüpraş workers were members of the Petrol-İş (the Turkish Petroleum, Chemical and Rubber Workers Union) union.[47] At the time, Petrol-İş opposed privatization of Tüpraş on two grounds: (1) strategic importance, and (2) public interest. According to union, foreign ownership of such a critical enterprise would jeopardize Turkey's long-term strategic position and render the country even more dependent on external forces in the energy sector (Petrol-İş 2005, 48). The head of Petrol-İş Ankara Branch, Mustafa Özgen, for example, stated:

> Under a private monopoly in the refinery sector, it is highly likely that Turkey's domestic production will fall beyond the rising demand; the country's import dependence will rise, and this will put other sectors at risk making Turkey vulnerable to world markets. This is a threat to our national interest.
>
> ŞAHİN 2010, 491–492

Petrol-İş also argued that Tüpraş is very important for the future and social welfare of the general populace in Turkey, and therefore should be removed from the privatization program and meticulously protected (Petrol-İş 2005, 7, 50). As the Petrol-İş Central Committee Member, İbrahim Doğangül, stated in a 2012 interview, 'we fought for preventing privatization of Tüpraş because it would lead to a resource transfer to a rich minority and cause the large public masses including Petrol-İş workers to suffer in every sense, such as employment losses, high commodity prices, declining quality of workplace and so on'.[48] Thus, in the eyes of the some union leaders, privatization of Tüpraş was likely to impose a heavy burden on the general populace of Turkey in different ways.

Having identified arguments against privatization, Petrol-İş hotly contested the privatization of Tüpraş via a series of actions including legal action, demonstrations, media campaign, and creative forms of industrial action and work stoppages. Contrary to the elite development theories – including neoliberal, statist, and some Marxist theories – that remains rather exclusively focused

---

47    As of 2002, Petrol-İş has counted on the 85 per cent of 4,700 Tüpraş workers as members (Petrol-İş 2007).

48    Personal Interview with İbrahim Doğangül, Petrol-İş Central Committee Member, 12 October 2012.

on the agency of elites, the actions of the Petrol-İş confirmed empirically that under particular circumstances laboring classes can also assume primary agency in pursuing and achieving their own material interests (Selwyn 2016).

It is indeed remarkable that the media campaign that Petrol-İş launched quickly increased the level of public awareness and discussion around Tüpraş privatization. The campaign involved pamphlets, brochures, billboards, and booklets as well as print and television announcements, which were all designed by a private advertisement agency. As a Political Science Professor, Peride K. Blind, so accurately captures, 'one of these advertisements displayed a gas pump held as a revolver by a hand, against the neck of a lady wearing a golden necklace, the latter representing the economic well being of a family in the Turkish culture' (2008, 99). The slogan read, "Tüpraş is our future. It cannot be sold". Another advertisement even tried to relate Tüpraş privatization with the 2003 US-led invasion of Iraq. From the point of view of Petrol-İş union, such a connection between two issues would provide opportunities for fuelling a public backlash against privatization, especially considering the fact that the Turkish public strongly opposed the war and the Turkish government decided not to allow coalition forces to enter Iraq from the north.

The most effective action of the Petrol-İş, however, was the legal battle. Petrol-İş knew the existing Turkish institutional and legal framework, to some extent, still reflected a different logic of accumulation based on public interest and national interest that could potentially be used against the market logic of privatization. Therefore, the strategic purpose of the union was to use the state legal apparatus as a contested space through which it could engage in efforts countering privatization. This reminds us of one of the to core arguments of the distinguished Marxist, Nicos Poulantzas: that the state is the heart of the exercise of political power, structured in a particular way, where different social and political forces struggle (1978, 258).

The legal battle mounted by Petrol-İş was long and contested. It lasted from June 2003 to November 2004 and involved three different lawsuits. In June 2003, Petrol-İş filed a lawsuit against the tender announcement of the PA at the Ankara 10th Administrative Court in June 2003. Petrol-İş contended that the tender announcement was unlawful because it failed to define the golden share in a privatized enterprise that would allow the state to maintain its veto on strategic decisions such as military fuel supply (Petrol-İş 2005, 24–34). The establishment of the golden share is based usually on public and national interest considerations and many countries that privatized state enterprises maintained golden shares (Papadopoulos 2015).

In January 2004, Petrol-İş filed a second lawsuit at the Ankara 10th Administrative Court, this time against the Privatization Tender Commission

(PTC). Petrol-İş argued that the PTC had acted against the public interest by failing to make clear that the tender would be concluded with a closed offer. This led to fatal flaws in the tender strategy of most participants as they refrained from making high offers initially with the expectation that the auction procedure might follow. In the same lawsuit, Petrol-İş identified two technical errors that the PTC had made during the tender process. On the one hand, the PTC had allowed Turkey's Zorlu Holding to join German-based Efremov-Kautschuk GmBH (which represented the interests of Russia's Tatneft) as a partner after the tender process had already started (Şahin 2010, 491). On the other hand, the PTC had permitted participants to put forward clauses in the tender proposal (for example, the enactment of the Petroleum Market Law) (Petrol-İş 2005, 40).

In February 2004, the union filed a third lawsuit, this time against the Privatization High Council (PHC) on the grounds that it had approved the contested decisions of the PTC mentioned above.

The PTC (second) lawsuit received most attention and was heard at different times by a variety of courts. The Ankara Regional Administrative Court favored the completion of the tender, while the Ankara 10th Administrative Court opposed and rejected the tender. The Supreme Administrative Court, the Council of the State (*Danıştay*), then stepped in to give the final decision and restore the crisis. The Council of the State ruled in November 2004 that the sale of Tüpraş to the Efremov-Kautschuk-Zorlu consortium was illegal. It thus declared the decisions of the PTC to be null and void and cancelled the sale of Tüpraş (Petrol-İş 2005, 74–95). Tüpraş was ultimately privatized in early 2006, and soon after, the AKP government implemented a series of legal-institutional reforms to avoid similar cancellations, which we will detail below.

### 3.2    Türk-Metal Union and Domestic Private Iron-Steel Companies: Erdemir

Unlike Petrol-İş union, the right leaning and nationalist Türk-Metal (Union of Metallurgy Workers; Türk Metal İşçileri Sendikası) union did not develop independent capacity to pursue the interest of its own workers and stop Erdemir privatization. Rather than organizing more than six thousand Erdemir workers against privatization, Türk-Metal institutionally subordinated itself to the nationalist strategy of the domestic private iron-steel companies (mostly small and medium size).

Türk-Metal union promoted a national sentiment, particularly over the prospect of ownership of Erdemir being sold to foreign capital, which naturally supported the cause of domestic private iron-steel companies. As Angın and Bedirhanoğlu narrated in their article, the President of Türk-Metal, Mustafa

Özbek, pointed out that 'none of the advanced industrialized countries, neither Japan nor Germany, had allowed foreign companies to take control of their integrated iron and steel industries. He added that Erdemir was supplying 40% of Turkey's flat steel demand, and that, by 2025, Turkey would need nine more enterprises of Erdemir's capacity. Therefore, if Erdemir were sold to foreign companies, Turkey's future and growth would be left to the mercy of foreigners' (2012, 158). As such, Türk-Metal fuelled debate over the nationality of the potential buyers of Erdemir.

It was the domestic private iron-steel companies dependent upon Erdemir's iron and steel products to make business that originally created and pursued such a nationalist strategy against the sale of Erdemir to foreign steel giants such as Arcelor and Mittal. The most important companies include Diler Iron & Steel Industry and Trade, İCDAS A.S., Kibar Foreign Trade, Toscelik A.S., and Assan Iron & Steel. Some of these companies had institutionalized special connections to purchase inputs from Erdemir below market prices; and some of these enjoyed privileges to distribute (or export) Erdemir's final products to the world market and thereby making large profits. Even the Eight Five-Year Development Plan of Turkey (2001–2005) clearly demonstrated that the operations of Erdemir directly influence the profitability and sustainability of those domestic private iron-steel companies (DPT 2000a).

To illustrate, two examples are instructive for understanding the indispensable relationship between Erdemir and domestic private iron-steel companies. The first example concerns the Kibar Holding that operates within the iron-steel sector with two subsidiaries – Assan Iron & Steel, and Kibar Foreign Trade. The former subsidiary has long been acquiring flat steel from Erdemir to manufacture various iron and steel products demanded by industrial companies and final customers (DPT 2000b, 41). The latter subsidiary has been exporting considerable amount of Erdemir's production to different parts of the world since the mid-1980. The second case concerns Borusan Holding, which has continued to grow in the iron and steel sector with Borusan Mannesmann (a steel pipe manufacturer) and Borçelik (a cold rolled and galvanized flat steel producer). Most importantly, Borusan Mannesmann and Borçelik were purchasing raw steel from Erdemir to produce steel pipes and galvanized steel. For example, the cost of steel roll, the only domestic supplier of which was Erdemir, constituted 65 per cent of the total production cost of Borusan Mannesmann (DPT 2000b, 40, 105). I highlighted these two examples because both demonstrate the importance of Erdemir to domestic private iron-steel companies.

Those domestic private iron-steel companies dependent upon Erdemir were seriously concerned that the new owner of Erdemir might harden their access to inputs and put an end to special privileges. In a personal interview, the advisor of steel giant Arcelor (2003–2005), Kemal Özden, told me that 'domestic private iron and steel companies aimed at shaping privatization process of Erdemir in order to protect their well-established privileges'.[49] The domestic private iron-steel companies thus pursued a strategy of tying Erdemir privatization to nationalist sentiment as a means of shaping the outcome in such a way that their privileges and strategic relationships with Erdemir would not be harmed. To that purpose, they intervened on two fronts.

To begin with, the domestic private iron-steel companies influenced high-ranking employees of Erdemir such as Kerim Dervişoğlu and Atamer Giyici to protest the sale of Erdemir to a foreign company. Precisely because Dervişoğlu[50] and Giyici[51] previously worked in the private iron-steel sector and established personal links with the sector leaders, it was possible for domestic private iron-steel companies to be influential in shaping the political trajectory of these officials on Erdemir privatization. Dervişoğlu and Giyici attempted to create a discourse around the perceived threat of foreign control over Erdemir by delivering interviews and speeches to media and the general public. They suggested that, instead of a block sale to foreign companies, the shares of Erdemir could be privatized via public offering method, citing the South Korean POSCO model as an example. Subsequently, they quit their jobs to protest the government's decision to allow foreign companies to enter Erdemir privatization tender (Angın and Bedirhanoğlu 2012, 158).[52]

Having understood that the privatization of Erdemir and the participation of foreign companies to the tender could not be halted, domestic private iron-steel companies joined together and formed a national consortium under the coordination of TOBB to bid for Erdemir (Oxford Business Group 2007, 50). This consortium is known as the 'Erdemir Consortium'. The participant of the consortium included some of the major private iron-steel companies in Turkey including Kibar Holding, İçdaş Çelik, Tosçelik, Borusan Holding and Diler

---

49    Personal interview with Kemal Özden, Advisor of Arcelor (2003–2005), 29 January 2013.
50    Before being appointed to Erdemir, Kerim Dervişoğlu worked as an advisor of the Borçelik of Borusan Holding between 1993 and 2003. After he resigned from Erdemir, he became board member of Kibar Holding.
51    Before being appointed to Erdemir, Atamer Giyici acted as a general director of Assan Aluminum of Kibar Holding between 1999 and 2003. After resigning from Erdemir, he went back to Assan Aluminum.
52    For more information about Dervişoğlu and Giyici and their attempt to shape Erdemir privatization, see: (http://www.makinastore.com/-1-85-atamer-giyici-yillik-uretim-kapas itemizi--250000-tona-cikaracagiz.html), and (http://www.demircelikstore.com/-1-2129 -turk-demir-celik-sektorunun-duayeni-a-kerim-derv3043500286lu.html) (accessed on 12 August 2020).

Holding. In a personal interview, the spokesperson of Erdemir Consortium, Serdar Koçtürk, clarified to me that 'the consortium was specifically interested in preventing foreign steel giants, such as Arcelor and Mittal, from acquiring Erdemir'. The consortium participants reasoned that 'Erdemir was providing vital inputs for the Turkish iron and steel sector and the access to inputs would be difficult if a foreign owner bought the plant'.[53]

It is important to note that, although consortium geared against the foreign acquisition of Erdemir, it was not advocating categorical opposition to foreign investment. For example, the President of TOBB, Rıfat Hisarcıklıoğlu, made it clear that the consortium was neither against privatization nor foreign investment. For him, Turkish companies had to unite and struggle to win the tender of Erdemir to become global players rather than mere subcontractors (Angın and Bedirhanoğlu 2012, 159). Moreover, a quick review of the consortium participants reveals a picture that is striking – almost all of them had foreign partners from different sectors. While Borusan Holding had partnerships with German Mannesmann in its iron and steel investments as well as with the German BMW in the automotive sector, Kibar Holding formed partnerships with South Korean companies POSCO and Hyundai in its iron and steel and automotive investments.

Both domestic and foreign companies showed strong interest in the Erdemir privatization tender in October 2005. The domestic company OYAK made the highest bid ($2.77 billion) in the tender and managed to acquire 49.29 per cent of Erdemir's shares ahead of Erdemir Consortium, Arcelor, and Mittal. The resulting price tag was 86 per cent higher than the stock-exchange value of the Erdemir. Although the participants of Erdemir Consortium were so happy about the sale of Erdemir to a component of national capital that is also connected to the Turkish military, it is difficult to reliably measure the role and extent of their interventions over the result. What we can be sure of is that the labour unions especially Türk-Metal gave positive responses to the sale of Erdemir to OYAK and turned out to be enthusiastic supporters of this privatization on the grounds that Erdemir stayed in the hands of national capital. The President of Türk-Metal union, Mustafa Özbek, announced right after the tender that 'he applauded the sale of Erdemir to OYAK'.[54]

53  Personal interview with Serdar Koçtürk, Board Member of Kibar Holding and Spokesperson of the Erdemir Consortium, 6 February 2013.
54  "Özbek Erdemir'in satışını alkışlamış" [Özbek applauded the sale of Erdemir], *Evrensel,* 21 Ekim 2005.

## 4      Institutional Reforms and Overcoming Barriers

Although Türk-Metal was not opposed the privatization of Erdemir, it was concerned with the sale of Erdemir to foreign capital and therefore allied with
domestic private iron-steel companies to prevent Erdemir's foreign acquisition. Such a struggle runs contrary to what is expected by conventional labour
union, but it put great pressure on the Turkish government to privatize with
care, and to some extent slowed privatization process. Moreover, as discussed
above in the Tüpraş case, some unions like Petrol-İş have become more serious
opponents of privatization, and directly engaged in anti-privatization struggles through legal actions. They also supported legal actions with media campaign that caused a public sentiment against privatization.

Despite causing slight and temporary setbacks in privatization plans, these
struggles were not successful in pressuring the power bloc and government to
abandon privatization strategy. Rather, the power bloc and the AKP acted in
concert to reshape the legal and institutional state apparatus so as to weaken
the resistance of labour and to facilitate the participation of potential investors in the privatization tenders. Immediately after the legal challenges of
Petrol-İş began in January 2004, the Prime Minister, Recep Tayyip Erdoğan, and
Koç Holding's president, Mustafa Koç, emphasized the urgent need to resolve
the legal shadows looming over the privatization process.[55] At the same time,
Sabancı Holding's president, Güler Sabancı, stated in a newspaper interview: "I am worried about the latest legal decisions on Tüpraş privatization.
Unfortunately, Turkey still did not learn how to handle privatizations. It started
with Özal, but it is still on our agenda. Markets are expecting to see swift conclusion of privatizations".[56] This brings us back to one of the book's core theoretical premises: that the institutional-legal framework is often a consequence
of a series of conflicts between different classes, and nature of the strategies
that these classes undertake in furthering their interests (Poulantzas 1978, 115;
Saad-Filho 2008, 344). I will explore the institutional-legal reforms below.

First, the Foreign Investment Law (4875) was enacted by the AKP government
in 2003 with the aim of eliminating the barriers to the participation of foreign
capital in the privatization process since foreign investors was indispensable in

---

55   "Özelleştirmenin önündeki iki engel: Bürokratlar ve yargıya güvensizlik" [Two obstacles
     to privatization: The bureaucracy and distrust of the judiciary], *Zaman*, 20 January 2004;
     "Özelleştirme Kanunu mutlaka değiştirilmeli" [The Privatization Law must change],
     *Zaman*, 18 July 2004.
56   "Sabancı: Özelleştirmeyi bir türlü halledemedik" [We did not still complete privatiza-
     tion], *Zaman*, 4 June 2004.

securing international competitiveness for the economy. The Finance Minister, Kemal Unakıtan, summarized the intent of the new law: "The government welcomes FDI to Turkey because it could contribute to national development, investment in fixed assets, and job creation".[57] Such statements from high-ranking government officials and the uniformly supportive positions of the key state institutions including the State Planning Organization, the Privatization Administration and the Undersecretary of Treasury were decisive in marginal-izing the above-discussed nationalist discourses against foreign capital.

The state authorities then established the Investment Advisory Council (IAC) of Turkey in 2004 to better implement the provisions of the recently enacted Foreign Investment Law. The IAC acted as an institutional platform for the senior executives from multinational companies to meet with the leading Turkish busi-ness associations (TÜSİAD, TOBB, YASED) along with upper-level state officials for the purpose of overcoming the administrative barriers to FDI. An inaugu-ral IAC meeting was held in March 2004. This high-level meeting included the participation of CEOs of 19 leading multinational companies, the president of World Bank James Wolfensohn, the director of the IMF's European Department Michael Deppler, presidents of TÜSİAD, TOBB, YASED as well as the Prime Minister Erdoğan, State Minister for Economic Affairs Ali Babacan, and Treasury Minister Kemal Unakıtan (IMF 2004). State officials, who gained experience with each meeting with institutional learning, did what was necessary to pave the way for the involvement of foreign capital in the Turkish privatization process.

As an extension of IAC activities, the Privatization Administration (PA) of Turkey started to organize investor roadshows abroad. In the 2013 interview, a senior PA official, Arzu Atik, stated that investor roadshows aimed to enhance dialogue and information exchange with foreign investors and contribute their stable participation in the privatization tenders.[58] Between 2004 and 2009, Turkey has become a key participant in many international roadshows in Dubai, London, Vienna, New York, Boston, and Frankfurt. In those roadshows, Turkey often represented by the Head of Privatization Administration, Metin Kılcı, and the Finance Minister, Kemal Unakıtan. One example of this was the meeting of Metin Kılcı with potential buyers in London and New York in 2005 to discuss the privatization of Petkim.[59] It is interesting to note that Unakıtan

---

57    "Unakıtan: Yabancıya tek sözümüz Welcome" [We only say welcome to foreigners], *Milliyet,* 28 September 2005.

58    Interview with Arzu Atik, Project Group Head at Privatization Administration (1992–2012), 8 February 2013. Currently, she is working as Director of Strategy and Planning at Kolin Group, which has won several important privatization tenders.

59    "Petkim'de roadshow zamanı" [Roadshow time for Petkim], *Hürriyet,* 5 April 2005.

was named 2008 Finance Minister of the Year by the Financial Times and the Citigroup, while he was doing one of his privatization roadshows in London.[60]

Second, the Independent Regulatory Authorities (IRAs) were reorganized to transform their institutional materiality such that they were favourable to privatization, which also enabled them to better communicate with potential investors in privatization tenders. Although most of the IRAs such as the Energy Market Regulatory Authority (EMRA), the Banking Regulation and Supervision Agency (BRSA), and the Telecommunications Agency (TA) were established prior to the onset of the 2001 crisis, they were largely ineffective and highly politicized. Under the banner of "structural reforms" that was influenced by the IMF agreements and EU conditionality, IRAs began to significantly transform during the first years of the AKP government. It is true that this transformation achieved a degree of success in reining in arbitrary political intervention into the economy for a period.[61] For example, the Petroleum Market Law (5015) of December 2003 shifted some regulatory powers (e.g., carrying out investigations, examining licenses) in the energy sector from the Council of Ministers to the autonomous EMRA. This resulted in the insulation of the regulation of the energy sector from other layers of government as well as from popular forces and democratic pressures (Oğuz 2008, 182).

Yet the autonomy of EMRA was not applied to those social actors such as capital groups and wealthy investors, which could establish connections with EMRA independent of the democratic political process, and the classical bureaucratic structures, potentially through lobbying the EMRA's board of governance and the extensive use of management consultants and business appointees. Ben Fine and David Hall explains that: "These consultancies are themselves made up of a small group of multinational firms such as PriceWaterhouseCoopers, Deloitte, Ernst and Young, which act as a policy replication mechanism" (2012, 61). In addition, the IRAs like EMRA could also be subject to a well-recognized process of "capture" by the large Turkish corporations in the sector, which are prominent supporters of privatization.

Another form of the institutionalization of the policy and ideology of privatization within the EMRA capacity is the appointment of increasing numbers of pro-privatization bureaucrats from other state departments (e.g., Privatization Administration) to EMRA policy positions, which would normally be held by

---

60    "Yılın Maliye Bakanı Unakıtan" [Finance Minister of the Year is Unakıtan], BBC Turkish, 7 March 2008.
61    However, few years later the AKP proceeded to limit these agencies' autonomy and jurisdiction through new laws and regulations. The AKP also attempted to politicize certain IRAs, increasingly in its third term in power since 2011 (see next chapter).

career civil servants within the EMRA. For example, Hasan Köktaş, who had been vice president of the Privatization Administration between 2003 and 2007, was appointed president of EMRA in 2008. Moreover, Gülefsan Demirbaş, who had started her career as an expert in the Privatization Administration, appointed as the head of strategy development department of EMRA in 2009. It is crucial to underscore that these top-level appointments to the EMRA coincided with the start of the government's efforts to privatize Turkey's electricity distribution and production assets discussed above.

Third, the state judicial apparatus and institutions were restructured to weaken the organized labor's resistance to privatization by legal means. As noted, the state apparatus is itself a specific political field of power and struggle in which dominated forces and actors (e.g., unions, local communities) could operate, up to certain extent, to counter privatization efforts of the dominant classes (e.g., power bloc fractions) (Poulantzas 1978). For example, as discussed above, Petrol-İş union opposed privatization of Tüpraş by recourse to laws and judicial institutions, and considerably heightened the internal divisions and contradictions within the state. The restructuring of the state judicial apparatus and institutions aimed at mitigating dominated classes' resistance and minimizing those contradictions.

The AKP government initially changed the composition of the Constitutional Court, which took a very active stance against privatization policies in the 1990s and the early 2000s. Judges who had embraced the hegemonic principles of the market slowly replaced those judges who had been opposed to neoliberal policies in general and to privatization in particular on the grounds that they would be detrimental to the public interest and national interest (Şahin 2010, 494). In other words, these changes restructured the Constitutional Court in such a way that judges could no longer base their rulings on public interest and national interest, but on the basis of the new market imperatives characterized by increased economic efficiency and competitiveness and centrality of private ownership to development. Lawyer Gökhan Candoğan, who had been using the Constitutional Court to thwart the government's efforts to privatize SOEs since the mid-1990s, described the consequences of this succinctly: "Because more pro-market and pro-privatization judges appointed to the Constitutional Court, the role of the Constitutional Court in guarding against privatization significantly weakened or undermined. As their decisions are increasingly in favour of privatization, the doors of the Constitutional Court now closed to the opponents of privatization".

The judicial restructuring process clearly did not stop with the changed composition of the Constitutional Court. On the contrary, the government also made changes to the Privatization Law (4046) in 2005 and centralized the administrative legal decision making for privatization matters within the Council of the State – *Danıştay*. The Council of the State, the supreme administrative court that used to deal only with appeals from other administrative courts, thus is authorized to act as the court of first instance for all privatization-related cases.[62] The process of judicial centralization has been given further impetus as the government changed the Council of State Law (2575), thereby selecting the 13th Chamber of the Council of State to be the expert chamber responsible for all privatization-related cases. In the meanwhile, the fourteen other chambers of the Council of the State have increasingly forced to move away from privatization-related cases.[63] This means that the administrative judicial review of privatization-related cases has been centralized into one institution – 13th Chamber of the Council of the State.

One of the consequences of this was that the opponents of privatization have lost their opportunity to file claims against privatization in the local and regional administrative courts and the fourteen other chambers of the Council of State. This undermined their capacity to generate conflicting decisions in different courts, as we had seen in the Tüpraş example. It also made it much easier for the government to institutionalize the logic of privatization in just one chamber – 13th Chamber of the Council of the State – than to do the same task for the whole administrative judicial apparatus. In a personal interview, a Privatization Administration employee said to me: "As the same judges reviewed all the privatization cases, they have, over time, effectively internalized the logic of privatization and stopped causing problem".[64]

Last, but not least, the AKP government incorporated a new clause 4-C into the Privatization Law in 2004 for the workers to be made redundant as part of the privatization of the SOEs. This clause states that the SOE workers who become unemployed because of privatization must be employed in other state institutions and ministries. This means that laid off workers are provided a guaranteed opportunity to move elsewhere in the state apparatus – albeit with temporary status, wage cuts, and fewer labor rights (Doğan 2012, 59–60). As such, workers with 4-C would be given temporary contracts lasting minimum of two months and a maximum of 10 months and 28 days. The extension of these contracts would also require the decision of the government, which effectively deprived workers of their job security (Yalman and Topal 2017, 6).

62    See "Özelleştirme Uygulamaları Hakkında Kanun" [Privatization Law], 4046, Article 27 (https://www.mevzuat.gov.tr/MevzuatMetin/1.5.4046.pdf) accessed on 21 August 2020.
63    At the time, the Council of State had fifteen chambers in its institutional structure.
64    Interview with Yeşim Kurna, Head of Project Group, Privatization Administration, 13 February 2013.

The introduction of 4-C, however, has weakened the organization capacity of the unions and their ability to mobilize workers against privatization because 4-C has driven a wedge between those soon-to-be-unemployed workers who wish to benefit from it, those who rejected 4-C, and those who will maintain their positions after privatization. Put differently, it not only boosted a form of precarity in the public sector, but also denied these workers the capacity to struggle for their rights (Yalman and Topal 2017, 7).

In brief, each of these four institutional-legal reforms thus helped to enable a rapid privatization of the leading Turkish SOEs during the following years.

## 5      Conclusion

After a long period of limited action on major privatizations, Turkey succeeded to move forward with its largest privatization items – including Turkey's telecom monopoly, Türk Telekom; petroleum refining company, Tüpraş; Tekel's tobacco arm; Atatürk and İstanbul Sabiha Gökçen Airport Expansions; petrochemical complex, Petkim; and steel conglomerate, Erdemir. As a result, the accumulated privatization value of Turkey, which had reached only about $19 billion from 1984 to 2001, rose dramatically to $70 billion at the end of 2009.

It was only when the competing interests of the power bloc fractions aligned after the initial hostility to provide strong support, in the more favourable and constitutive context of the post-2001 domestic capital accumulation regime, that the legal and institutional state apparatus was restructured, labor resistance was weakened, and privatization was finally accelerated. Because the dominant literature on the acceleration of privatization in Turkey confined its scope of analysis to coalitions and/or networks between the government and favourable business groups that have participated in the privatization tenders, its analysis failed to capture the bigger and a more nuanced picture of the acceleration of privatization in Turkey, one that should be involving the above mentioned complex interplay of interrelated factors – power bloc, domestic capital accumulation, and state. The following chapter explores in detail how these interrelated factors (albeit in ways modified by changing context) shaped the latest phase of Turkish privatization process (2010–2018), which will further enable us to continue demonstrating too narrow focus of the dominant literature.

CHAPTER 5

# The Expansion of Privatization

*Public-Private Partnerships: 2010–2018*

The 1st Istanbul PPP Summit took place in Turkey between 2 November and 5 November 2015 with 25 delegates from 19 countries. The event was organized with significant contributions of international organizations such as the World Bank and the Islamic Development Bank along with the participation of several PPP experts and private sector representatives from around the world. The Turkish President Recep Tayyip Erdoğan and key AKP officials also attended the event. David Baxter, a former PPP advisor of USAİD and World Bank, remarked in his blog post: "The presence of President Recep Tayyip Erdoğan at the 1st Istanbul Summit is an indication that PPPs are long being discussed at by the top decision makers in Turkey, [which] is in itself a promising development".[1]

I think this was an accurate reflection of the growing importance of PPPs to political and economic policymaking in Turkey. The size of the overall PPP investment portfolio in Turkey has been increasingly rapidly since 2009. Between 2010 and 2018, Turkey has implemented over $100 billion worth of PPP projects along with nearly $30 billion worth of divestiture.[2] This chapter explores this latest phase of Turkish privatization process characterized by the rise of PPPs. I argue that the rise of PPPs in the 2010s is due to the complex and sometimes contradictory background with three dynamics. First, as Turkey failed to increase relative surplus production and international competitiveness during the 2010s, PPP projects became increasingly important to create new financial resources to postpone crisis dynamics. Second, although the Turkish power bloc was not unified anymore as the internal contradictions between fractions of capital sharpened in the 2010s, the capitalist class' support for privatization and PPP projects remained strong. This is because PPP projects elevated the general interest of capital above the interests of the popular and laboring classes. Third, the exceptional state formed under the AKP government during 2010s has increasingly managed to bypass legal and institutional checks and balances that enabled the implementation PPP projects without delays.

---

1   "New Horizons for PPPs in Turkey", *Linkedin*, 11 October 2015 (https://www.linkedin.com/pulse/new-horizons-ppps-turkey-david-baxter/), accessed on 16 October 2020.
2   For the list of divestitures realized during 2010s see Appendix 3.

The chapter is divided into four sections. The first section conceptualizes the PPP phenomenon. In the second section, I provide broad contours of PPP implementations in Turkey during 2010s. In the third section, I discuss in detail the above-mentioned three dynamics that lie behind the acceleration of PPPs in Turkey. In the last section, I outline six showcase PPP projects to provide concrete and specific details.

## 1    Conceptualization of the PPP Phenomenon

Public-private partnerships (PPPs) have enjoyed a global resurgence and have become icons of modern public administration over the past few decades (Hodge and Greve 2009, 34). PPPs have been used by both the developed world and developing countries like Turkey. There is certainly a huge amount of money at stake in today's PPPs. As Hodge, Greve and Boardman (2012) put it, "despite its popularity and its iconic status as a visible pillar of contemporary public management practices, the PPP phenomenon remains an enigma". The section below conceptualizes the PPP phenomenon.

There were wide ranging debates during the 1990s and 2000s about how to understand PPPs. Several researchers have tried to provide clear-cut definitions of PPP, but few people agree on what PPP actually is. Many still debate its definition and its historical origins. So, there is a need to establish a modest definition.

I think we can define a public-private partnership (PPP) as a long-term contract (sometimes up to 30 years) between a public entity and a private party under which a private party finances, designs, builds, and operates some element of a infrastructure asset or public service; and the private party gets paid over a number of years, either through charges paid by users, or by payments from the state authority, or a combination of both (Hall 2015, 5). A key factor in PPP is the government's acceptance of a private sector role in infrastructure asset or public service provision. Many PPPs involve private companies in financing, building, and managing new public assets – often called *greenfield* investments – from highways and airports to hospitals. PPPs are also used to transfer responsibility for upgrading and managing existing assets to a private company – *brownfield* investments (World Bank 2017, 6).

PPPs cover a wide range of arrangements include, for example, the build-own-operate (BOO), build-own-operate-transfer (BOOT), build-operate-transfer (BOT), rehabilitate-operate-transfer (ROT), and build-lease-transfer (BLT), along with a host of other acronyms (Hodge, Greve and Boardman 2012, 6).

The range of PPP arrangement types is described by the functions transferred to the private sector.

Under a BOT project, the private company owns the project assets until they are transferred at the end of the contract. BOOT is often used interchangeably with BOT. ROT is a variant of BOT and refers to a rehabilitation of an existing facility. In contrast, in a BOO contract, the private company owns the project and does not have to transfer it to the government entity at the end of the term (World Bank 2017, 7). Under the BLT model, the private company builds a facility and then leases it to the relevant public authority, with the state providing the public service and private company has limited number of operational activities consisting of support services. The BLT model is customized for certain sectors such as health and education where the involvement of the state during the operation phase is crucial.[3]

Although PPPs have been used in a wide range of sectors to provide different kind of services, there are four sectors where it is most common to see examples of PPP arrangements worldwide: (i) transport sector to build roads, tunnels, bridges, ports and airports, (ii) water and waste sector to improve water distribution, sewerage systems and solid waste management services, (iii) energy sector to support generation and distribution systems, (iv) social and government infrastructure sectors to build hospitals, health care and school facilities.

Geographically, East Asia and the Pacific region (led by China) that dominates global investments in PPP accounts for around 25 per cent of total PPP investments during the last decade (World Bank 2019). Almost equally important, Europe and Central Asia region has seen more than 700 PPP projects of an investment value of $270 billion over the last two decades. This would be much higher without the global financial crisis that began in late 2008 and set back ambitious development plans among many countries in the region (Hall 2015, 9). As we will see below, one exception to this was Turkey, where PPP investments significantly increased during the same period.

Advocates of PPPs include the international financial institutions, regional development banks, consulting firms, banks, and construction companies. The World Bank and its private sector funding arm, the International Finance Corporation (IFC), play a leading role in promoting and funding PPPs. In the last 20 years, the IFC has worked on over 350 PPPs in 99 different countries (Hall 2015, 13–14). Recently, most consulting firms such as McKinsey, Citi, PWC,

---

3  "The Build-Lease-Transfer Model: First Health Campuses, What's Next?", *Lexology*, 5 May 2016. See https://www.lexology.com/library/detail.aspx?g=b320c119-e425-4b8e-9ff9-70f03 1e52119 (accessed on 30 December 2020).

and Deloitte began aspiring to a larger role in promoting the principles of PPPs. In fact, they claim to provide balanced evaluations of PPP policy options through their professional reports, while simultaneously and openly lobbying for PPP because of its importance to their core revenues (Hodge, Greve and Boardman 2012, 8).

Unsurprisingly, this PPP-promoting network is facing popular opposition from many workers organizations, consumers groups, and major NGOs that emphasize the negative effects of PPPs including rising long-term debt, loss of transparency, exclusion from or reduced access to basic services, increased environmental problems, and a host of corruption related scandals. Significant protest movements occurred in countries like France, Germany, Canada, Argentina, El Salvador, Brazil, Indonesia, and India (Kishimoto and Petitjean 2017). In El Salvador, on May Day 2012 more than 80,000 workers, students, indigenous, feminist, and social movement activists marched under the banner 'No More Privatisations, No to Public Private Partnerships'. This forced state authorities to exclude healthcare, education, water, public security, and prisons from the scope of a new PPP law, and to require all contracts over $10 million to be presented to parliament before signing (Hall 2015, 28).

Before moving on to the discussion of actual PPP implementations in Turkey during 2010s, one more conceptual proposal should be made. This means that a primacy needs to be placed on the wider processes and social relations set in motion by a PPP project. Most of the studies have so far employed a narrow and technocratic perspective that defined PPP as an agreement between the two signatories – public party (contracting authority) and private party (project company) – and therefore have devoted much of their attention to the identity of the private project company and its special relations with the public contracting authority.

Once again, it is important to emphasize that a PPP project involves and influences not just the public contracting authority and private project company, but also lenders, engineering-design contractors, input suppliers, and community in the form of users and workers. Such a broader conceptual model allows for an interpretation of PPP as a highly complex arrangement that can bring together multiple stakeholders. This is illustrated in Figure 1.

One of the critical roles played by the public contracting authority, which often subordinated to the broader economic policy objectives of the government, is to offer legislation enabling PPPs. On most PPP projects, the public contracting authority also sets up schemes that support PPPs through mechanisms of providing government guarantees and identifies the site on which the asset will be built and operated (Hall 2015, 19). But the most obvious role of the public contracting authority is to select the private project company that will

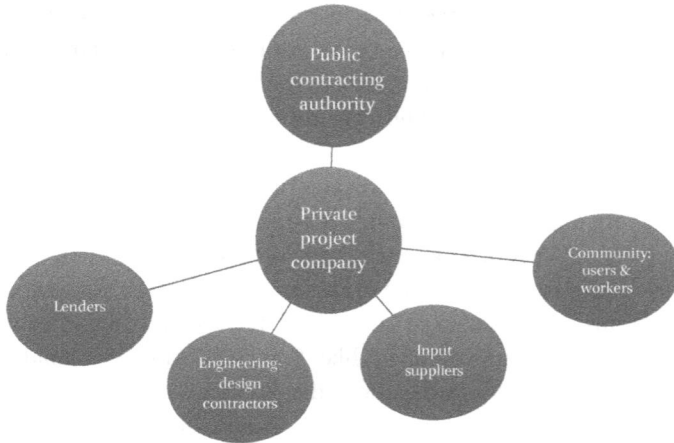

FIGURE 1     Typical PPP project stakeholders

implement the PPP and sign a PPP contract that regulates rights and obligations of the private project company to whom the development of the project
will be contracted out (ADB, EBRD, IDB, IsDB and WBG 2016, 84).

By the contract signature, the private project company, usually in the form of
a Special Purpose Vehicle (SPV), assumes the obligations described in the contract from designing and financing to construction and eventually operating
and maintaining the actual asset. For the private company or a consortium of
companies that constitute the SPV, PPP represent an extremely attractive business opportunity – a single contract may give a flow of income for 25 years or
more (often guaranteed by the government itself) (Hall 2015, 8). This explains
why critiques of PPPs (e.g., media, unions, academics) have constantly ques-
tioned the intimate (and sometimes corrupt) relationship between companies
that constitute the SPV and the government officials. Yet a PPP project is a far
more complicated and complex than outward appearance suggested. We need
to penetrate beneath a surface level analysis and look at other actors that are
heavily involved in the project.

Lenders, which may include commercial domestic and foreign banks,
regional development banks, IFIs, export credit agencies, and institutional
investors such as pension funds constitute a significant component of any
PPP project (World Bank 2017, 40). The World Bank (2015) research that ana-
lysed the sources of financing for 163 PPP projects in low-to-middle income
countries in 2015 found that the total investment commitment of $52.3 bil-
lion comprised of about 67 per cent in debt ($35.2 billion). Exactly half of
this debt ($17.6 billion) was financed by commercial banks; about a quarter

($9 billion) by public lenders; and the remainder by regional development banks and IFIs ($7.9 billion) and, to a lesser extent, institutional investors ($0.7 billion). Lenders sometimes acquire step-in rights – a power to take control of the project in certain situations – that come into effect if the SPV fails to meet its debt service obligations (World Bank 2017, 48).

Engineering-Design Contractors (EDCs), which are reputable engineering, design, and manufacturing firms, also work on PPP projects. EDCs are generally managed complex technical and design work (such as bridge design and construction of tower foundations, anchorage structures and piers in motorway projects) that are technologically demanding and require superior known-how and expertise at a fixed price and schedule through subcontracting from SPV (Yescombe 2007, 8). The largest EDC contracts in the world (and Turkey) tend to go to giant companies from the United States, Europe, and East Asia. Increasingly, however, Asian firms – from South Korea, Taiwan, and China – are winning these lucrative contracts.

Input, equipment, and raw material suppliers are important participants of PPP projects. Large-scale infrastructure PPPs became particularly large driver of the demand for key input providing sectors such as cement, iron and steel, and petroleum. For example, the road and airport PPPs placed heavy demand on petroleum product – bitumen – that is used as the binder in asphalt roads and other paved areas. Similarly, those PPP projects have fuelled demand for heavy equipment such as excavators, bulldozers, and graders. In many cases, the SPV signs numerous contracts with suppliers to acquire machinery, materials, and other inputs vital to implement PPP project.

In a typical PPP, stakeholders include the community in the form of workers and users, which are likely to be affected by the project. While the interest of a single user is to maintain her/his access to certain service after the implementation of PPP project, the users as a consumer group could have relatively high level of interest such as avoiding higher price charges (Wojewnik-Filipkowska and Wegrzyn 2019, 9). The PSIRU (Public Services International Research Unit) report, commissioned by the EPSU (European Federation of Public Service Unions), demonstrates that PPPs worsen the employment conditions of workers and their collective organizations in unions. According to the report, "these effects are caused by firstly, the employees being transferred to a separate private employer, and secondly, by the dominant role of the PPP contract itself, which forces public authorities to prioritize payments to the PPP company over all other expenditure" (Hall 2008, 2). Yet, users and workers should not be seen as the passive victims of changes draconically imposed by those who dominate the PPP implementations. User and worker groups have material resources, organizational capability, and ability to struggle against PPPs.

2      Broad Contours of PPP Implementations in Turkey during the 2010s

Turkey has launched an ambitious PPP program in the 2010s. According to
the Turkish Presidency of Strategy and Budget, 134 PPP contracts with a total
contract value of just over $110 billion were delivered from the 2010 towards
the end of 2020. As could have been expected, this makes Turkey one of the
top countries using PPPs both among the European countries and the developing countries. The World Bank's PPI Database demonstrates that Turkey
ranked fourth after Brazil ($242 billion), India ($173 billion), and China ($135
billion) among 139 countries in terms of total PPP investment between 2010
and 2020.[4]

During this period Turkey has implemented many large-scale PPP projects,
with a concentration in the transportation, energy, and health sectors (See
Table 15). The transportation sector (mostly mega motorways and airports)
remained by far the largest in value terms. These transportation projects are
mainly tendered within BOT (Build-Operate-Transfer) scheme. The Third
International Airport for İstanbul ($35.58 billion), for example, is the largest
PPP project closed in Europe since 2002 (discussed in more detail below in the
case study section) (EPEC 2015, 5).

In the energy sector, Turkey's PPPs aimed to focus more on the localization and diversification of the electricity generation mix by realizing local coal
and renewable projects. For example, the Turkish Coal Operations Authority
granted a private entity the rights to operate the Tufanbeyli lignite mine on
the condition that it will construct a minimum 600 MW power plant to use lignite resources (Türkiye Kömür İşletmeleri Kurumu 2019, 31). The construction
activities of the Tufanbeyli lignite power plant have been completed in 2016 by
Enerjisa – the Turkish private electricity producer owned by Turkish Sabancı
Holding and German E.ON. As part of its next target of increasing the use of
renewable sources of energy, Turkey introduced Renewable Energy Resources
Areas (YEKA – *Yenilenebilir Enerji Kaynak Alanı*) model in 2016. The REZ model
is in essence an auction mechanism where the winner of the tender is granted
the right to set up large scale renewable energy generation facility on publicly
owned lands and sell the electricity with guaranteed feed-in-tariffs for 15 years.
The tender involves the condition of the establishment of local manufacturing
and R&D facilities or using locally manufactured equipment with an aim to
ensure localization. The first round of YEKA auctions for solar and wind was

---

4   "The World Bank PPI Database". See https://ppi.worldbank.org/en/customquery (accessed
    on 7 August 2021).

TABLE 15    Large-scale PPP projects of Turkey between 2010 and 2020

| Project | Sector | Capacity | Contract value[a] ($ bn) |
|---|---|---|---|
| Bosphorus (Eurasia) Tunnel | Transportation/ Roads | 15 km | 1.23 |
| Gebze-Orhangazi-İzmir Motorway (incl. Osmangazi Bridge) | Transportation/ Roads | 433 km | 9.75 |
| Third International Airport for İstanbul | Transportation/ Airports | 150 m passengers | 35.58 |
| Northern Marmara Motorway-Third Bosphorus Bridge | Transportation/ Roads | 114 km | 3.89 |
| Northern Marmara Motorway – European Sections | Transportation/ Roads | 95 km | 1.04 |
| Northern Marmara Motorway – Asian Sections | Transportation/ Roads | 178 km | 1.63 |
| Dardanelles Bridge & Kınalı-Balıkesir Motorway | Transportation/ Roads | 385 km | 2.84 |
| YEKA SOLAR-1 | Energy | 1,000 MW | 1.30 |
| YEKA WIND-1 | Energy | 1,000 MW | 1.00 |
| YEKA WIND-2 | Energy | 1,000 MW | 1.00 |
| Enerjisa Tufanbeyli Power Plant | Energy | 600 MW | 1.35 |
| Healthcare Campus Projects[b] | Healthcare | 44,309 beds | 16.1 |
| Total | | | 76.71 |

a   Contract value is the sum of investment in physical assets and fees to government.
b   In total, 32 integrated healthcare campuses will be built.
SOURCE: KALKINMA BAKANLIĞI (2016); WORLD BANK PPI DATABASE (WEBSITE); PRESI-
DENCY OF THE REPUBLIC OF TURKEY INVESTMENT OFFICE (2019)

held in 2017. Two of 1,000 MW size capacities were awarded to two distinct consortiums consisting of national and international partners.[5]

In terms of PPPs, the healthcare sector observed the upward trend over the last few years. This was due to the Turkish government's healthcare campus projects to raise the quality of the healthcare services across the nation. The government announced that 32 integrated healthcare campuses with an estimated total capacity of 44,309 beds and aggregate value of $16.1 billion would be built within BLT (Build-Lease-Transfer) scheme (PWC 2017). As of today, 13 healthcare campus projects are completed and operating. 7 healthcare campus projects are at various stages of construction (discussed in more detail below in the case study section).

Although Turkey has implemented tens of billions worth of PPP projects in different sectors, the national legislation does not have one single framework law. In the current situation, the legislative mechanism is composed of a list of specific laws for different kinds of models (See Table 16). The most used BOT model is regulated by a BOT Law No. 3996, which empowers private actors to undertake investment and service delivery in different infrastructure areas like transportation, energy, and water supply.[6] The BO Law No. 4283 regulates the provision of electricity generated by existing thermal power plants. The implementation of this law, however, was suspended for new projects after the electricity market liberalization in 2001 with the enactment of Electricity Market Law (No. 4628). The BLT Law No. 6428 that came into force in 2013 provided a unified legal instrument to be applied for the PPP projects in health sector. This law enabled the private sector to construct and make hospitals available for the use of the Ministry of Health in exchange for availability payments made by the government (Emek 2015).

While there is no central PPP Unit in Turkey, the PPP Department in the Strategy and Budget Office under the Presidency performs essential functions that include: assessment of PPP projects from sectoral, financial, fiscal, and legal aspects and their compliance with the national macroeconomic priorities, and formulating PPP policies for the government via the National Development Plans and Medium Term and Annual Programs.[7] Of

---

5   "Opportunities to strengthen the YEKA auction model for enhancing the regulatory framework of Turkey's power system transformation", *Shura Energy Transition Center*, 2018. See www.shura.org.tr (accessed on 7 August 2021).

6   There are other separate BOT laws regulating investment in the electricity sector (Law No. 3096) and in the road transport sector (Law No. 3465).

7   Prior to the transition to the presidential system of government in 2018, there was a PPP department under the Ministry of Development. Most of the personnel and functions of the new department under the Presidency transferred from there.

TABLE 16     Some PPP laws and models in Turkey

| Year of enactment | Legislation | Model |
|---|---|---|
| 1994 | Law No. 3996 on the Procurement of Certain Investments and Services under the BOT Model | BOT |
| 1997 | Law No. 4283 on the Regulation of the Establishment and Operation of Electrical Energy Generation Facilities and the Sale of Energy under the BO Model | BO |
| 2013 | Law No. 6428 on the Construction, Renovation and Purchase of Services by the Ministry of Health by way of the Public-Private Cooperation Model and Amendments to Certain Laws and Decrees with the Force of Law | BLT |

SOURCE: PRESIDENCY OF THE REPUBLIC OF TURKEY, INVESTMENT OFFICE (2019)

course, this PPP Department can hardly be viewed as a centralized institution effectively coordinating the process from inception towards delivery of contracts. Instead, there is a trend towards a more sector-specialization in a dedicated PPP teams in line ministries, which are implementing and managing PPPs falling in their sector. In the current situation, three-line ministries including the Ministry of Transport, the Ministry of Health, and the Ministry of Energy are directly involved in PPP projects. For example, in the event of a highway project, the General Directorate of Highways, which is subordinated to the Ministry of Transportation, becomes the PPP procuring authority.

Another important entity facilitating the PPP program in coordination with the PPP Department and the line ministries is the Ministry of Treasury and Finance. As noted earlier, participation into PPPs has not been a purely market-driven process – it has driven by different forms of state intervention. In that sense, the Ministry of Treasury and Finance provides incentives in the form of debt assumption, demand guarantee, and tax incentives to support the bankability of the PPP projects and persuade the investors to enter the PPP market.

The planned PPP projects in Turkey must comply with policy priorities set out by government in five-year development plans, medium term program, and yearly program. Both the 10th (2014–2018) and 11th (2019–2023) five-year development plans of Turkey included a national strategic PPP infrastructure plan, which was prepared by the contributions of the PPP Ad Hoc Committee that had more than 100 participants both from public and private sectors including contractors, financial institutions, NGOs, consultants, and university professors. It has been suggested in the plan that the use of PPP model in Turkey should not only be expanded in the existing sectors but also extended to new sectors like education, healthcare, drinking water and wastewater, science and technology, transportation, irrigation, and defense industry, which would increase the share of PPP investment to 30 per cent of total investment.[8]

Up until the transition to the presidential system in 2018, the ultimate decision-making body for PPPs in Turkey had been the HPC (High Planning Council – *Yüksek Planlama Kurulu*), which was comprised of Ministers in charge of different parts of economy who were supervised by the Prime Minister. The key function of the HPC in that period was to approve PPP projects before launching tender. A formal approval process used to begin when the implementing (or procuring) ministry (e.g., Ministry of Transport) submitted its preliminary project together with feasibility reports, technical analysis, and other documents to the HPC. Acting as the secretariat of HPC, the PPP Department in the Ministry of Development evaluated the project with a view to ensuring that the project is economically, financially, and socially value-adding, and in line with sectoral and national policy priorities. Based on the analysis carried out by the PPP Department in the Ministry of Development, the HPC then evaluated the project and approved it to be included in the pipeline (World Bank Group 2017). It has, however, to be noted that following the recent changes to Turkey's constitution and with the transition to the presidential system in 2018, the duties of the HPC have been transferred to the President. Accordingly, the newly formed PPP Department in the Strategy and Budget Office under the Presidency has replaced the PPP Department in the Ministry of Development as the new secretariat.

Another interesting facet of the PPPs in Turkey is the source of finance. The World Bank (2015) report demonstrates that domestic private financiers are the most active in Turkey.[9] Most of the PPP projects implemented in Turkey, where domestic Turkish banks lifted the burden mostly and financed a large portion of investments (with the important exception of healthcare PPPs). To create further funding options, the Turkish Wealth Fund (*Türkiye*

---

8  "11th Development Plan (2019–2023): Effective Management in PPP Implementations in Turkey", *Ministry of Development*, Ankara.

9  After Turkey comes India, where domestic private financiers are also very active.

*Varlık Fonu*) was created in 2016 by an emergency rule with an initial capital of $50 billion. The Turkish Wealth Fund can be seen as a development fund to utilize state-owned assets to raise capital to finance infrastructure projects. The fund, owned and managed by the Turkish state, contains three of Turkey's state-owned banks (Ziraat Bank, Halkbank, Vakıfbank), two largest power generation and distribution companies (Botaş and Turkish Petroleum), Turkish Airlines and other 17 companies from 8 different sectors.[10] The President Erdoğan was made the chairman with his son-in-law appointed as the deputy chair of the fund, whose governance mechanism is criticized for being non-transparent, unaccountable, centralized and personalized (Bedirhanoğlu 2020, 34).

The international financial institutions, such as the IFC, the EBRD, the EIB, and the IDB, also become more active in the Turkish PPP market in recent years. This has been particularly evident in the hospital PPPs in the healthcare sector. For example, the EIB has provided significant finance to PPP projects like Bursa Health Campus and Gaziantep Health Campus.

## 3 Dynamics behind Acceleration of PPPs in Turkey during the 2010s

As previously mentioned, I argue that this rise of PPPs in Turkey in the 2010s is due to the complex background with three dynamics. First, as Turkey failed to increase relative surplus production and international competitiveness, PPP projects became increasingly important for domestic capital accumulation regime to create new financial resources to postpone crisis dynamics. Second, although the Turkish power bloc was not unified anymore as the internal contradictions between fractions of capital sharpened in the 2010s, the capitalist class' support for PPP projects remained strong because these projects elevated the general interest of capital above the interests of the popular and laboring classes. Third, the exceptional state formed under the AKP government has increasingly managed to bypass legal and institutional checks and balances and enabled the implementation of PPP projects without any delays. The section below discusses these three dynamics – domestic capital accumulation, power bloc, state – that lie behind the acceleration of PPPs in Turkey during 2010s.

---

10    See the official website of the Turkish Wealth Fund, https://www.tvf.com.tr/en/our-portfo lio (accessed on 8 August 2021).

3.1    *Domestic Capital Accumulation*

Shortly before the 2008–2009 global financial crisis, the domestic capital accumulation regime in Turkey became increasingly unstable. There was growing difficulty in ensuring the rise of relative surplus production (or 'high-valued added' industries) and international competitiveness required to maintain adequate export performance. While Turkey has dramatically increased its medium-technology exports, it stagnated in high-tech export. The share of high technology exports in Turkey's total manufactured exports remained less than 2 percent between 2002 and 2008, which was well below the world average (Kutlay 2015). Trade figures also suggested that Turkey exported mainly consumption goods, while importing investment and intermediary goods, which gradually increased current account deficit from 2.5 per cent of GDP in 2003 to 5.1 per cent in 2008.

Coupled with the slowdown in foreign markets that have been affected by the 2008–2009 crisis, the ability of the AKP government to sustain capital accumulation by means of exports and foreign direct investment (FDI) greatly reduced. The Turkish economy shrank by 4.8 percent in 2009. FDI inflows declined significantly to $7 billion in 2009, edging down from $18 billion average during the three-year period 2006 to 2008. Export earnings declined by more than 20 per cent in 2009 because of the decreasing demand from Europe, which is the most significant trade partner of Turkey (Cömert and Yeldan 2018). The 2008–2009 global financial crisis thus exposed the limitations of export-based accumulation strategies. The severity of the situation acknowledged even by the AKP officials as they made the following grim observation in an industrial strategy document: "Despite its rapid growth after the crisis in 2001, the Turkish economy falls short of expectations with respect to global competitiveness" (cited in Yalman 2016, p. 259). The chairperson of TÜSİAD, Arzuhan Doğan Yalçındağ, expressed the same opinion in a short letter to Private View (publication of TÜSİAD), noting that "in the current period of economic downturn, rising unemployment and declining exports, Turkey is in need of looking for alternatives to finance its growth in the post-crisis period" (TÜSİAD 2009, 5).

In response, the AKP government stepped in to revive domestic demand. As part of this strategy, the AKP began to prioritise the construction sector as a locomotive to boost the economy as it involves many other sub-sectors. Every city in Turkey witnessed a building boom. Table 17 demonstrates that the share of construction sector in Turkey increased from 5.6 per cent of total GDP to 7.2 per cent from 2009 to 2018. It is important to note, however, that if we take

TABLE 17    The share of the construction sector in GDP

| Year | Total debt stock ($ billion) | GDP ($ billion) | Share of construction sector in total GDP (%) |
|------|------------------------------|-----------------|-----------------------------------------------|
| 2009 | 268.9 | 646.9 | 5.6 |
| 2010 | 291.8 | 772.4 | 6.1 |
| 2011 | 305.4 | 831.7 | 6.8 |
| 2012 | 342.2 | 871.1 | 7.0 |
| 2013 | 392.7 | 950.4 | 7.4 |
| 2014 | 405.7 | 934.9 | 7.4 |
| 2015 | 400.3 | 861.9 | 7.3 |
| 2016 | 409.3 | 862.7 | 7.5 |
| 2017 | 455.0 | 851.7 | 7.6 |
| 2018 | 444.6 | 787.1 | 7.2 |

SOURCE: GÜNGEN (2020)

its supporting industries into account, the share of construction sector rose to about a 30 per cent share of GDP.[11]

This construction-oriented model of accumulation was made possible through huge capital inflows and cheap credit from the core capitalist countries. Especially up until 2013 the international dynamics of the valorization of money capital had been favourable for emerging economies like Turkey, mainly due to FED's policy of low interest rates (Ercan and Oğuz 2020, 110). Turkish companies borrowed heavily in foreign hard currency loans like US Dollar and Euro to finance the construction boom. The Central Bank of Turkey data shows that foreign exchange liabilities of non-financial companies increased rapidly from $146.8 billion in 2009 to $336 billion in 2018.[12] Loans received abroad by the domestic banks also increased significantly from $33.8 billion in 2009 to $94.3 billion in 2018.[13] As Ali Rıza Güngen (2020) partly noted, the above data

---

11    Tekfen Holding, Annual Report 2017, pg 29. See http://www.tekfen.com.tr/en/Uploads/pdfs/2882020225812217fr2017.pdf (accessed on 11 February 2021).

12    The Central Bank of Turkey, Foreign Exchange Assets and Liabilities of Non-Financial Companies. https://www.tcmb.gov.tr/wps/wcm/connect/EN/TCMB+EN/Main+Menu/Statistics/Monetary+and+Financial+Statistics (accessed on 11 February 2021).

13    The Central Bank of Turkey, Outstanding Long-Term/Short-Term Loans Received from Abroad by Private Sector. See https://www.tcmb.gov.tr/wps/wcm/connect/EN/TCMB+EN/Main+Menu/Statistics/Balance+of+Payments+and+Related+Statistics/Outstanding+Loans+Received+from+Abroad+by+Private+Sector-/Data/ (accessed on 11 February 2021).

reveals that the domestic banking sector borrowed from international markets and lend to non-financial companies (e.g., contractors, manufacturers of construction materials such as steel, cement and so on), which supported construction boom in the wake of the 2008–2009 global financial crisis.

There were three components to the construction boom. First, the state-owned Housing Development Administration of Turkey (TOKİ – *Toplu Konut İdaresi Başkanlığı*) became a massive capitalist land/property developer and commodified housing and land across the country with urban transformation projects. Between 2003 and 2016, the TOKİ initiated the construction of more than 700,000 housing units (Tansel 2019, 322). The second component of the construction boom was unprecedented private investments in the energy sector, especially through hydro, solar and wind power generation plants built in the valleys and rivers of Anatolia. From 2008 to 2017, the total investment volume in the energy sector surpassed $75 billion.[14] Finally, the most important of these components was PPP-based infrastructure investments on a massive scale like a third airport in İstanbul's northern forests, and a third bridge to span the Bosporus (Ercan and Oğuz 2020, 109).

These PPP-based infrastructure investments could not only energize the Turkish construction sector but also could serve as a short-term boost to economic growth. This is not a novel observation specific to Turkey, as global consultancy firms and multinational banks argued in different reports that infrastructure spending, which has significant forward and backward linkages, can boost economic activity everywhere. For example, a 2016 report by Citibank's Global Perspectives and Solutions team concluded that 1% increase in infrastructure investment is associated with a 1.2% increase in GDP growth.[15] Similarly, the McKinsey Global Institute suggested that in the shorter term, increasing infrastructure investment by one percentage point of GDP could generate millions of direct and indirect jobs (e.g., 3.4 million in India, 1.5 million in the USA, and so on).[16] Confirming the importance of

---

14    Invest in Turkey: Why Invest in Turkish Energy Sector. See https://www.invest.gov.tr/
      en/library/publications/lists/investpublications/energy-industry.pdf (accessed on 15
      February 2021).

15    "Infrastructure for Growth: The dawn of a new multi-trillion dollar asset class", *CITI GPS*,
      October 2016. See https://www.citivelocity.com/citigps/infrastructure-growth/ (accessed
      on 15 February 2021).

16    "Bridging Global Infrastructure Gaps", *McKinsey&Company*, June 2016. See https://www
      .mckinsey.com/business-functions/operations/our-insights/bridging-global-infrastruct
      ure-gaps# (accessed on 15 February 2021).

PPP-based infrastructure investment for economic growth and capital accumulation, the G20 and the World Bank established the PPP-oriented Global
Infrastructure Facility (GIF) in 2014, with the goal of addressing funding shortages and doubling developing country investment in infrastructure through
to 2020 (Cammack 2020, 421). The GIF platform coordinates and integrates
the efforts of multilateral development banks, private sector investors, financiers, and governments to ensure that well-structured and bankable PPP-based
infrastructure projects are brought to market.

The AKP government was aware of the situation, and it was seeking to accelerate PPP-based infrastructure investments to boost economic growth in the
post-crisis period of export hardship – as mentioned above, this was partly
because of 2008–2009 crisis, and partly due to Turkey's failure to increase
export competitiveness that is heavily reliant on productivity gains and the
use of technology. When looking at official documents, the report of the PPP
Ad Hoc Committee for the 11th Development Plan of Turkey suggested that
infrastructure investments with PPP model set up a potentially significant avenue for economic development and is expected to become central engine for
economic growth.

As a result, PPP contract value in Turkey rose sharply as a percentage of
GDP, from 0.42 per cent between 1984 and 2009 to 1.34 per cent between 2010
and 2018.[17] The increase takes on a new meaning when we consider that the
same figure remained relatively low – 0.44 per cent on average – in other
emerging markets and developing economies from 2010 to 2015.[18] As such,
the PPP-oriented and construction-based growth strategy created an incredible source of opportunities for domestic capital accumulation regime in
Turkey: (1) the super exploitation of labour without an upgrading of workers'
skills and technology; (2) the commodification of nature, land, urban space,
and public services such as transportation and health; (3) the acceleration of
external borrowing from international money markets with state guarantees;
and (4) increased demand for sectors which provide input to infrastructure
projects and sectors which use infrastructure projects as input.

A major concrete example to see how these capital accumulation opportunities created by the PPP-infrastructure projects is the Third International

---

17    Based on my own calculations from the Turkish Ministry of Development and Republic of
      Turkey's Presidency Strategy and Budget Office data.
18    "The State of PPPs: Infrastructure Public-Private Partnerships in Emerging Markets &
      Developing Economies 1991–2015", *The World Bank Group*, June 2016. See https://ppiaf
      .org/documents/3551/download (accessed on 16 February 2021).

Airport for Istanbul, which was built between 2014 and 2019.[19] First, most of a total of 32,000 workers employed on the construction site, who are sub-contracted workers working for over 500 different subcontracting firms, fall outside collective bargaining, have issues over wages, and experience super exploitation under poor working conditions and incessant pressure to meet project timelines.[20] According to official figures, about 57 workers had died as a result of various health and safety violations happened in the site.[21] Second, according to data compiled by the Independent Architects' Association of Turkey, the airport (located along the coast of Black Sea) covers a gigantic area of 7,650 hectares of land in the Northern Forests of İstanbul that involves woods, forestlands, farmlands and lakes. As such, the construction of airport paved the way for commodification of these natural areas and created value that was not supplied through the capital accumulation process. Third, a group of six Turkish banks raised more than \$5 billion financing package from international investors for the construction of the first stage of the airport, which enabled capital inflows into Turkey. Fourth, the construction of airport increased the demand for inputs such as cement, concrete, machinery, asphalt, aluminium, steel, and other building materials. During the construction, 3,159 construction machines operated non-stop, 6.5 million cubic meters of asphalt and 10 million cubic meters of concrete was poured.[22] Table 18 clearly demonstrates how large-scale infrastructure investments with PPP model became the main drivers for cement consumption in Turkey.

### 3.2    *Power Bloc*

Although the Turkish power bloc was not as unified as before due to the sharpened contradictions between different fractions of capital over issues like Turkey's accession to the European Union, direction of country's foreign

---

19    This is only for the construction of the first stage. The airport will be fully completed by 2025.

20    "New Istanbul airport: Turkey's refusal to respect labour standards is costing lives", *International Trade Union Confederation,* 28 March 2019. See https://www.ituc-csi.org/ new-istanbul-airport-turkey-s (accessed on 16 February 2021).

21    "Individual Case (CAS) – Discussion: 2019, Publication: 108th ILO Session", *International Labour Organization,* 2019. See https://www.ilo.org/dyn/normlex/en/f?p=NORMLEX PUB:13101:0::NO::P13101_COMMENT_ID:4000367 (accessed on 16 February 2021).

22    "Limitlerin Zorlandığı Proje: İstanbul Havalimanı", *Şantiye Dergisi,* Sayi 383, pp. 36–49. See https://www.santiye.com.tr/edergi/383/52/ (accessed on 18 February 2021). "İstanbul 3. Havalimanı Projesinde Tek Tercih: MEKA Beton Santralleri", *MEKA.* See https://www .mekaglobal.com/tr/galeri/istanbul-3-havalimani-projesinde-tek-tercih-meka-beton -santralleri (accessed on 18 February 2021).

TABLE 18    Domestic cement consumption in Turkey and infrastructure projects

| Year | Cement consumption (mn tons) | Share of infrastructure projects in cement consumption (%) |
|------|------------------------------|------------------------------------------------------------|
| 2010 | 48 | 30 |
| 2011 | 53 | 33 |
| 2012 | 55 | 31 |
| 2013 | 62 | 33 |
| 2014 | 63 | 34 |
| 2015 | 64 | 39 |
| 2016 | 67 | 41 |
| 2017 | 72 | 43 |
| 2018 | 76 | 46 |

a    "Sabancı Holding Cement Day" 14 March 2018. See https://yatirimciiliskileri.sabanci.com/en/images/pdf/sbu_cement_day_v6.pdf (accessed on 18 February 2021).
SOURCE: TURKISH CEMENT MANUFACTURERS ASSOCIATION AND SABANCI CEMENT GROUPA

policy and the rule of law, it has remained strongly committed to PPPs during 2010s. This position could possibly stem from the fact that PPPs represented potentially lucrative opportunities – including profit, reputation, increased demand for credit, access to state guarantees – for all fractions of Turkish power bloc.

While Turkish construction companies expected to build and operate several roads, bridges, and hospitals with PPP model, domestic construction material producers believed that the rise of PPPs would increase demand for their manufactured goods.[23] Banks and holdings that assumed greater presence in the control of banking capital in Turkey were also uniquely suited (and happy) to seize PPP's promises such as higher interest rates and higher degree of confidence that loans will be repaid or recovered. A report by the Sabancı Holding owned Akbank clearly demonstrates that PPP investments led to significant growth in the Turkish banking sector. To a considerable extent, the unprecedented increase in Akbank's loans from a total of $29 billion to $56 billion between 2009 and 2018 would not have been possible without the financing

23    Türkiye İMSAD Yapı Sektörü Raporu 2018, p. 57. See http://www.imsad.org/Uploads/Files/Turkiye_IMSAD%20_Yapi_Sektoru_Raporu_2018_web.pdf (accessed on 1 March 2021).

of PPP projects.[24] Commercial capitalists that are active in moments of the commodity circuit as agents and distributors of imports (such as foreign made heavy machinery and sophisticated technological goods) promoted PPPs to benefit from lucrative contracts provided by their construction.

It can hardly come as a surprise that the major business associations in Turkey have also strongly supported PPPs. For example, TÜSİAD, as the main representative body of the first-generation İstanbul-based big holdings that are known to be more internationalized, secular, and pro-European, asserted that policy measures to bring about liberalization and private participation in infrastructure investments should be sought.[25] The 2011 report, where TÜSİAD collated the recommendations of its members to be discussed with the leaders of political parties prior to the General Elections on June 2011, recommended that "Projects to improve private businesses should be prioritised ... Public private partnership based models should be promoted in provision and financing of the health services".[26] Moreover, MÜSİAD, as the representative association of the second-generation Anatolian-based capital groups that organize around Muslim business principles and have close connections with the AKP government, also reiterated its support for PPPs during one of its board meetings in 2012.[27]

The PPP Ad Hoc Committee, which had convened two times in 2014 and 2018 with hundreds of participants from public and private sectors under the umbrella of the Ministry of Development and contributed to the preparation of national development plans, could be seen as a platform that brings together different fractions of power bloc (despite their differences) to produce a common discourse on the progress of PPP projects in Turkey. Some of the participants were: TÜSİAD members such as Enerjisa (Sabancı), Akfen Holding, Gama Holding, and TAV; Islamic-influenced Anatolian companies with close links to AKP such as İçtaş Holding, Otoyol A.ş., and Dia Holding; representatives of foreign capital including the World Bank, Denizbank, ICBC

---

24      Akbank Annual Report 2016. See https://www.akbankinvestorrelations.com/en/images/ pdf/2016_akbank_annual_report.pdf (accessed on 28 February 2021).

25      TÜSİAD Yönetim Kurulu Başkanı Ümit Boyner'in "Türkiye Sanayi Stratejisi Belgesi" Tanıtım Toplantısı Açılış Konuşması, 5 January 2011. See https://tusiad.org/tr/konusma -metinleri/item/2108-tusiad-yonetim-kurulu-baskani-umit-boynerin-turkiye-sanayi-str atejisi-belgesi-acilis-konusmasi (accessed on 2 March 2021).

26      "İş Dünyasının Yeni Yasama Dönemine İlişkin Beklentileri 2011–2015", March 2011, Publication No: TÜSİAD-T/2011/03/514. See https://tusiad.org/en/reports/item/5213 -expectations-of-the-business-world-in-the-new-legislative-term-2011-2015 (accessed on 2 March 2021).

27      "MÜSİAD Toplantısı Sonuç Bildirisi", *SonDakika.com*, 25 November 2012.

(China), PWC, EBRD and QNB Finansbank (Kalkınma Bakanlığı 2014; Kalkınma Bakanlığı 2018).

Although different fractions of power bloc produced a collective political will to push for PPPs, they nevertheless warned the government about the problems that they experienced during the concrete application process. First, the government authorities should not rush and allow enough time between different tenders because the simultaneous promotion of billions of dollars projects could cause excess demand in the loan market and put investors under pressure (Kalkınma Bakanlığı 2014, 54–55). Second, the authorities should use more instruments such as investment conferences and roadshows to encourage foreign capital involvement in PPP projects (Kalkınma Bakanlığı 2018, 53). Third, the authorities should consider clarifying the application framework of the lenders' step-in rights and address various challenges associated with it (Kalkınma Bakanlığı 2018, 49–51). Fourth, the authorities should devote more attention to the transparency and fair competition in tenders. This was particularly expressed by TÜSİAD members, which felt uncomfortable with the close relations between the government and some capital groups. President of the High Advisory Council of TÜSİAD, Tuncay Özilhan, told in a speech that: "A loose regulatory framework that gives too much discretionary power to the administration is neither conducive to fair competition ... Proper use of the citizen's money requires that public tenders should be awarded in accordance with the principles of transparency and accountability".[28]

Such statement coming from a high-ranking TÜSİAD member was an indicator of the increasing polarization within the power bloc especially after the Gezi Uprisings in 2013 (Akça 2014, 24–25). There were three components to this polarization, reflected in the different ways that the power bloc was organized within the state. First, TÜSİAD lost its hegemonic leadership of the power bloc, meaning that its specific interests on issues like EU relations and rule of law were not anymore prioritized by the policies of the state. Much of this stemmed from the increased relative autonomy of the state (under the AKP rule) vis-à-vis the TÜSİAD, thanks to AKP's strong relationship with petrodollar Gulf capital and mobilization of mass support for government policies in a plebiscitary fashion (Oğuz 2016). Second, as Turkey's relations with the west have worsened since 2015 because of the significant differences on the issues of the future of Syria, the refugee crisis, and S-400 procurement, foreign investors that are invested in the country (such as German, French, and

---

28    48th General Assembly Meeting of TÜSİAD, 18 January 2018. See https://tusiad.org/en/press-releases/item/9931-48th-general-assembly-meeting-of-tusiad (accessed on 4 March 2021).

Dutch multinationals) began commenting critically on the AKP government and pulling their money out of Turkey.[29]

Third, the rising struggle for controlling state resources and the new direction of Turkish foreign policy opened profound fissures within the Islamic-influenced Anatolian capital fraction. Particularly important battle waged by the Gülen Movement, a well-organized community of people named after the US-based Turkish cleric Fethullah Gülen who is known to be one of the allies of the AKP as it took power in 2002. The Gülen Movement runs schools and dorms all over Turkey, and its members hold influential positions in critical state institutions including judiciary and secret services (Öztürk 2015). The busines association that linked to the movement – TUSKON – founded in 2005 and reached more than 50,000 members at its peak.[30] The confrontation between the Gülen Movement and the AKP government began with the 17–25 December 2013 corruption inquiry organized by the Gülenist prosecutors and police forces, in which three AKP ministers were detained on allegations of bribery and money laundering. And the confrontation ended with the coup attempt of the Gülenist faction within the military and police on 15 July 2016. After the failed coup, the AKP closed hundreds of Gülenist schools and dormitories, prosecuted thousands of TUSKON members, and seized their companies (e.g., Boydak Holding, Naksan Holding, Bank Asya, Koza-İpek Holding).[31]

Yet these polarizations within the power bloc have not reached to a level that would give rise to intra-class conflicts over PPPs (as happened in the 1990s). TÜSİAD-based capital groups succeeded to establish some cooperation with the Islamic-influenced capital groups, which were almost completely represented by MÜSİAD after the closure of TUSKON, to maintain the conditions for the good of PPPs. The DEİK (Foreign Economic Relations Board of Turkey – *Dış Ekonomik İlişkiler Kurulu*), in particular, played critical roles in providing the key nodes of cooperation. Prominent TÜSİAD (e.g., Tuncay Özilhan, M. Ali Yalçındağ) and MÜSİAD (e.g., Abdurrahman Kaan, Ümit Kiler) members have assumed responsible positions in the business councils of DEİK.[32] The

---

29    "Comment: Turkey's myriad uncertainties worry investors", *International Investment*, 9 May 2019. See https://www.internationalinvestment.net/opinion/4002131/comment-tur key-myriad-uncertainties-worry-investors (accessed on 10 March 2021).

30    "Jale Özgentürk: TUSKON eksiliyor, MÜSİAD büyüyor", *Hürriyet*, 10 January 2016. See https://www.hurriyet.com.tr/yazarlar/jale-ozgenturk/tuskon-eksiliyor-musiad-buyuyor -40038361 (accessed on 9 March 2021).

31    TUSKON reports claim that the value of confiscated companies and assets is more than $50 billion.

32    See DEİK's Board of Directors https://www.deik.org.tr/deik-organizational-structure -board-of-directors (accessed on 18 March 2021).

President of DEİK, Nail Olpak, who also served as the Chairman of MÜSİAD before, expressed in his speech that "DEİK supports PPP projects".[33] As part of this commitment, DEİK PPP Committee was founded in 2015 to provide a platform for different fractions of capital and like-minded state elites to cooperate on PPPs. Participants of PPP Summits organized by the DEİK PPP Committee included: Ernst and Young, Philips, PWC, STFA Construction, Akfen Holding, İçtaş Holding, Makyol and Yapı Merkezi.[34]

A review of the coverage of newspapers and business annual reports demonstrated how all three fractions of capital – Islamic influenced Anatolian companies that have close relations with AKP and MÜSİAD, TÜSİAD based capital groups, and foreign capital – benefited from the PPP projects. I begin with the Islamic-influenced Anatolian capital groups that increased their annual turnover between two and five-fold during 2010s through involvement in PPP projects (See Appendix 2 for more information).

The first group is the Kalyon Group (founded in Gaziantep in 1974) which had close relations with the National Vision Movement of the Welfare Party in the 1990s and the AKP later. In 2019, President Erdoğan personally attended the wedding ceremony of Haluk Kalyoncu, who is the vice Chairman of the group.[35] Those political connections helped the group to participate in several large-scale PPP projects such as Third Airport for İstanbul and North Marmara Motorway as one of the project companies, and thereby increased its annual turnover from $105 million in 2010 to about $500 million in 2018.[36] Another group is the İçtaş Holding, which was founded by İbrahim Çeçen, a close friend of Erdoğan, that involved in Third Bridge and Menemen-Aliağa-Çandarlı motorway PPPs as a project company. As a result, holding's annual turnover more than quadrupled during the last decade.[37] Third, Limak Holding, which

33 Virtual PPP Week 2020, 2 November 2020. See https://www.deik.org.tr/uploads/deik-bask ani-nail-olpak_virtual-ppp-week-2020-2.pdf (accessed on 18 March 2021).

34 See "2015 İstanbul PPP Week Sonuç Raporu", https://issuu.com/phdconsulting/docs/ istanbul_ppp_week-_sonu___raporu-. See also "2016 İstanbul PPP Week Final Report", https://issuu.com/phdconsulting/docs/pppweek_2016_final_report (accessed on 18 March 2021).

35 "Turkey's Kalyon, Demirören heirs tie the know in Istanbul wedding", *Daily Sabah,* 14 April 2019.

36 Kalyon İnşaat, Sanayi ve Ticaret holded 419th position in the Fortune 500 Turkey list in 2010 (https://www.fortuneturkey.com/fortune500?yil=2010&tip=1). For 2018 turnover see https://nbn.business/kalyon-holding/ (accessed on 22 March 2021).

37 For holding's annual turnover at the end of 2009 see "Yeni zengin değilim 96'da da ilk 120'deydim", *Hürriyet Kelebek,* 1 November 2009. For holding's annual turnover later on see Fortune 500 Turkey list in 2017. (https://www.fortuneturkey.com/fortune500?yil =2017&tip=1) (accessed on 25 March 2021).

was awarded several PPP projects with its partners, more than doubled its annual turnover from $2 billion in 2010 to 4.2 billion in 2017.[38] The fourth group is the Çarmıklı family's Nurol Holding that has won numerous state contracts including Gebze-Orhangazi-İzmir PPP and achieved a net sales revenue increase of 100 per cent between 2008 ($0.6 billion) and 2017 ($1.2 billion).[39] Fifth, the Ankara-based Kolin Group that was founded in 1977 has done significant work in the contracting sector with the Third Airport and Northern Marmara Motorway PPPs. As a result, the Group achieved $1.5 billion sales revenue in 2019, which represented nearly 100 per cent rise from the 2010 level.[40] The last group is the Cengiz Holding that originated from the hometown of Erdoğan in 1987. During 2010s holding involved in building airports, highways, and electricity infrastructure with PPP model and increased its annual revenue from $3 billion in 2012 to $5 billion in 2018.[41]

Contrary to liberal-cum-institutionalist accounts noted earlier, TÜSİAD-based capital groups were not excluded from PPP projects. To the contrary, these PPP projects helped these capital groups to grow in size and influence (See Appendix 1 for more information). A major example is the Koç Holding – the largest Turkish conglomerate and the founding member of TÜSİAD. Although Koç Holding did not directly win any PPP tender as a project company, it nevertheless benefited from the acceleration of PPP projects through significant control over energy, automobile, and finance sectors. One of Koç Holding's flagship companies, Tüpraş Refinery, increased its asphalt/bitumen and jet fuel sales because of the growing demand resulting from highways, bridge, and airport investments with PPP model (See Table 19). Another company of Koç Holding, Yapı Kredi Bank, recorded strong loan growth from $26 billion in 2009 to $65 billion in 2017, thanks to demand created by the PPP-based investments (as is discussed in below case studies in detail). Not

38    For Limak's annual revenue in 2010 see "Asistanlıktan patron koltuğuna", *Radikal*, 20 June 2011. For revenue in 2017 see https://www.statista.com/statistics/970408/limak-group-revenue/ (accessed on 25 March 2021).

39    "M. Rauf Ateş: 20 yılda kaç büyük holding yaratabildik?", *Hürriyet*, 8 July 2009. Nurol Holding 2017 Annual Report (https://www.nurol.com.tr/dergi/faaliyet-raporu-en-2017/mobile/index.html) (accessed on 25 March 2021).

40    "Kolin İnşaat kimin, İstanbul Havalimanı ortaklığından niye çekiliyor?", *InternatHaber*, 9 January 2019 (https://www.internethaber.com/kolin-insaat-kimin-istanbul-havalimani-ortakligindan-niye-cekiliyor-1933126h.htm). Kolin Group 2010 Annual Report (http://www.kolin.com.tr/english/files/kolin-in-numbers/annual-reports/1_57243936_kolin-ing.pdf) (accessed on 29 March 2021).

41    "Vehap Munyar: Seydişehir'e 565 milyon dolar yatırdı, yeni teşviklerle 200 milyon dolarlık plan hazırladı", *Hürriyet*, 8 July 2012. Cengiz Holding official website (https://www.cengiz holding.com.tr/hakkimizda/?lang=en) (accessed on 29 March 2021).

TABLE 19    Sales of Tüpraş, 2010–2017 (mn tons)

| Year | Asphalt/Bitumen | Jet fuel |
|------|-----------------|----------|
| 2010 | 2.74 | 2.64 |
| 2017 | 3.52 | 4.53 |

SOURCE: KOÇ HOLDING ANNUAL REPORTS

surprisingly, Koç Holding maintained its dominance of the Turkish economy with its annual revenue of $30 billion in 2018.

Another example is Sabancı Holding – the second largest Turkish conglomerate and the founding member of TÜSİAD. Unlike Koç Holding, Sabancı Holding directly participated in PPP projects, as a project company, including Enerjisa Tufanbeyli Power Plant (600-MW) and YEKA wind energy tenders for Çanakkale (250-MW) and Aydın (250-MW) regions.[42] Sabancı Holding also provided inputs and finance to other PPP projects through its subsidiaries (Akbank, and cement producers Akçansa and Çimsa). As holding's annual reports demonstrate, Akbank's loans in support of the Turkish economy that includes several PPP projects grew from $29 billion in 2009 to $56 billion in 2018.[43] In short, all these activities helped the holding to increase its annual revenue from $12 billion in 2009 to $18 billion in 2017.

Next example is Borusan Holding, whose founder Asım Kocabıyık served 15 years in the board of TÜSİAD. The holding operates a large network of subsidiaries in manufacturing and energy sectors that benefited from the rise of PPPs in Turkey. Borusan EnBW Energy grew 11-fold in ten years and reached 505MW installed capacity in 2019, thanks to the licences won in the state PPP tenders for wind capacity.[44] Borusan Steel Group – Mannesmann and Borçelik – played key roles in the supply chains of many PPP projects. Borusan Machinery increased its market share with sales of hundreds of units of heavy equipment to PPP projects. Borusan Power Systems became an important

42    https://www.conexioconsulting.com/results-of-the-yeka-2-wind-tenders/ (accessed on 29 March 2021).

43    Sabancı's annual reports are available at (https://yatirimciiliskileri.sabanci.com/en/ financial-reports-publications/liste-report/Annual-Report/158/o/o) (accessed on 29 March 2021).

44    See https://www.borusan.com/_Media/tr/AnnualReports/2019/borusan-energy.html (accessed on 29 March 2021).

supplier of healthcare PPPs. Consequently, holding's annual sales revenue rose from $3 billion in 2009 to about $5 billion in 2017.

Furthermore, Tekfen Holding, whose co-founder Feyyaz Berker served as the first chairman of TÜSİAD, were heavily involved in PPP projects. Tekfen won the tender for the construction of the 509km section of the Trans-Anatolia Natural Gas Pipeline and Afyonkarahisar-Uşak section of the Ankara-İzmir Rapid Train Project in 2014 and 2016 respectively. It then won the EDC contract for the 1915 Çanakkale Bridge and Malkara-Çanakkale Motorway PPP project in 2017.[45] One year later, holding booked a historically high level of total turnover worth $2.3 billion, which demonstrated 40 per cent increase from the turnover posted a decade earlier.[46]

The last example is the Akfen Holding, whose top executives such as Hamdi Akın and Pelin Akın Özalp, are all active TÜSİAD members. In the space of just two decades beginning in 2001, Akfen became a leading infrastructural investment holding through numerous privatization tenders and PPP projects. In terms of PPP, Akfen constructed Doğançay (31-MW) and Çamlıca 3 (26-MW) hydroelectric plants with BOT model in 2010 and 2011 respectively. It then won the BLT tenders for three healthcare campus projects (Isparta, Tekirdağ, Eskişehir) with a commitment to make a total investment of $1.1 billion.[47]

Foreign capital also benefited considerably from the acceleration of the PPP projects. Italian Astaldi and South Korean SK Engineering & Construction participated as project companies in some technologically demanding PPP projects like Eurasia Tunnel and Gebze-Orhangazi-İzmir Motorway. Foreign-owned Turkish banks such as Denizbank (owned by Dubai based Emirates NBD), ING Bank, QNB Finansbank, and TEB (half owned by BNP Paribas) as well as multinational banking giants Deutsche Bank, UniCredit, and Bank of China profited from the loans provided to Turkey's PPP projects. In energy sector, German firms Enercon and Siemens, Danish manufacturer Vestas, and South Korean Hanwha Q Cells won several YEKA tenders for installing solar and wind power plants. In healthcare sector, as the production of medical devices and technologies is limited in Turkey, increasing demand due to PPP-based hospital investments is chiefly met by foreign companies like Abbott, Siemens, Bayer, GE Healthcare, and Baxter. It is thus not surprising that the GE Healthcare

45    Tekfen Holding, Annual Report 2017. See https://www.tekfen.com.tr/en/annual-reports -4-26 (accessed on 3 April 2021).
46    Tekfen Holding, Annual Report 2019. See https://www.tekfen.com.tr/en/Uploads/pdfs/ 2882020221112557fr2019-en.pdf (accessed on 3 April 2021).
47    Akfen Annual Report 2019 https://www.akfen.com.tr/activity-reports (accessed on 5 April 2021).

has decided to move its headquarters for the eastern and African growth markets region to İstanbul,[48] while Siemens opened a new production plant in İstanbul,[49] and Baxalta of the USA has entered into a joint venture agreement with the leading Turkish pharmaceutical company Eczacıbaşı Holding.[50]

## 3.3    *State*

The then Turkish prime minister Erdoğan launched his campaign for June 2011's parliamentary election with the announcement of, in his own words, "crazy projects" – the ambitious programme of PPP-based new construction if elected.[51] Those projects included a 50 km long canal from the Black Sea to the Aegean, and new bridges, airports and hospitals.[52] As Özcan cited, "it is a very common global behaviour for politicians to use mega urban projects as a powerful tool to claim votes" (2018, 530). The persuasive element can be seen in the building of these PPP-based mega projects, in the 'rock star' or 'pharaonic' appeal of politicians who can produce historical results, open a bridge, and solve a problem. Those who deliver them are our leaders (chief or *'reis'* as Erdoğan known to his followers), their mark left on the landscape in enduring legacy (Sturup 2013, 142).

Yet the implementation of these projects is no easy task. They are highly contested inside and outside of the state. Various groups such as local communities, environmental groups, professionals, civil society groups, politicians, and unions would oppose PPPs at different stages of implementation: during legislative approval, land expropriation, displacement of people, planning permission, and environmental clearances. For example, obtaining planning permission includes having the relevant zoning plan amended, which can be a challenge. As Magnus and Ekin (2013) explains: "Even if changes to the zoning plan approved by the relevant ministry and municipality, the approval is open

---

48   "GE Healthcare to manage its operations from Turkey", *Hürriyet*, 13 June 2008.

49   "German business giant Siemens opens new low voltage switchgear plant in Gebze", *BusinessTurkey*, 2 January 2018. See https://businessturkeytoday.com/german-business -giant-siemens-opens-new-low-voltage-switchgear-plant-in-gebze.html (accessed on 6 April 2021).

50   "Global Biopharmaceutical Leader Baxalta Selects Eczacıbaşı", *Eczacıbaşı*. See https:// www.eczacibasi.com.tr/en/press-room/news/global-biopharmaceutical-leader-baxalta -selects-eczacibasi (accessed on 6 April 2021).

51   İlhan Tekeli, "Siyasetçiler ve Mega Projeler Üzerine", Mega Projeler ve İstanbul Paneli, MSGSÜ Şehir ve Bölge Planlama Bölümü, 12.02.2014. See https://www.academia.edu/27999 587/SİYASETÇİLER_VE_MEGA_PROJELER_ÜZERİNE (accessed on 19 April 2021).

52   "Turkey ruling party wins election with reduced majority", *BBC News*, 12 June 2011. See https://www.bbc.com/news/world-europe-13740147 (accessed on 19 April 2021).

to challenges in courts". Not surprisingly, there were reportedly 1,514 objections raised to changing the İstanbul Metropolitan Municipality zoning plan for the Northern Marmara Motorway PPP.

All these struggles linked together in a specific conjuncture of the Gezi Park protests that began as a movement to defend a tiny urban park that AKP government wanted to replace with a late-Ottoman revivalist shopping mall (Adaman et al. 2014). On 27 May 2013 Gezi Park protests turned to a wide-scale uprising where different societal groups collectively articulated and organized against PPP-based mega projects (Ercan and Oğuz 2015; Akçay 2021). As Adaman et al. (2014) narrated, it was not a coincidence that the construction of the third bridge in İstanbul with connections to the planned third airport began with a fanfare just two days before the uprising.

Although Gezi protesters that were mainly comprised of members of Taksim Solidarity, Taksim Gezi Park Protection and Beautification Association as well as some unaffiliated but concerned individuals committed to pursue resistance,[53] it was the Northern Forests Defence (NFD – Kuzey Ormanları Savunması) that launched an organized campaign to stop all kinds of PPP projects (including 3rd bridge, Canal Istanbul, and the 3rd airport) falling within the Northern forests, watersheds, and farmlands of İstanbul. The NFD also established connections with TEPAV (Economic and Policy Research Foundation of Turkey), TEMA (Turkish Foundation for Combatting Soil Erosion), and BETAM (Bahçeşehir University Economic and Social Research Center) to prepare reports on PPP projects and demonstrate mistakes made in site selections and the problems identified in the Environmental Impact Assessment reports.[54]

The NFD, in alliance with the TMMOB (Union of Chambers of Turkish Engineers and Architects) and local community, started a long and contested legal battle to block the construction of PPP projects. It was argued by these organizations that PPP projects had dramatic effects on farmlands, natural habitat, and climate change, and violated the Turkish Constitution, the applicable laws (e.g., Istanbul Environmental Plan, 10th Article of the Environmental Law) and international conventions. After several

---

53    "How the Gezi Park struggle sparked an uprising, and why it could happen in Vancouver", *The Mainlander,* 6 June 2013. See https://themainlander.com/2013/06/06/how-the-gezi -park-struggle-sparked-an-uprising-and-why-it-could-happen-in-vancouver/ (accessed on 26 May 2021).

54    "The Third Airport Project Vis-à-vis Life, Nature, Environment, People and Law" *Kuzey Ormanları Savunması [Northern Forests Defense],* March 2015. See http://hlrn.org/img/ documents/3rdAirportProject_24052015.pdf (accessed on 16 February).

challenges, in 2014, İstanbul 4th Administrative Court gave a stay of execu-
tion order. However, this decision did not prevent the continuation of the
PPP projects.[55]

The importance of PPP projects for domestic capital accumulation, power
bloc and AKP leadership meant that any popular challenge to those projects
must be avoided at all costs. Therefore, the AKP government started to significantly transform the state's administrative and legal apparatuses to prevent
any opposition group from slowing down the PPP programme. In the aftermath of the Gezi protests of 2013, higher level of executive centralization was
encouraged to consolidate and expand the arms of the executive in shaping key
decision-making processes around PPPs (Tansel 2019, 324–325). Particularly
since the failed coup attempt of July 2016, a state of emergency has been
declared, under which an AKP and the far-right Nationalist Action Party alliance won the 2017 constitutional referendum and changed the regime from a
parliamentary to presidential system (Akçay 2021). Under this strong Turkish-
style presidential system, where most essential institutions and values of even
a nominal democracy are downgraded that sometimes resembles Poulantzas's
concept of 'exceptional state' (Erol 2018, 2), the government increasingly relied
upon governmental decree laws such as 'Urgent Expropriation' to speed up
and/or by-pass the normal parliamentary and judicial processes of the PPP
projects.[56]

Yet, these exceptional practices can hardly be viewed as interventions
that go against capital. As a matter of fact, the President Erdoğan himself
clearly announced on several occasions that the state remained market-
friendly, and the state of emergency was enforced to benefit markets (Kutun
2020, 145). For example, Erdoğan said at a commemoration ceremony of the
first anniversary of the failed coup attempt: "We are enforcing emergency
laws in order for our businesses to function more easily. So, let me ask. Have
you got any problems in the business world? Any delays?" (Ercan and Oğuz
2020, 114).

---

55   "The Third Airport Project Vis-à-vis Life, Nature, Environment, People and Law" *Kuzey
      Ormanları Savunması* [*Northern Forests Defense*], March 2015. See http://hlrn.org/img/
      documents/3rdAirportProject_24052015.pdf (accessed on 16 February).
56   "Fuat Ercan: Bir Yasanın İşaret Ettiği Türkiye'nin Bileşenleri-II: Zeytin mi Tesis mi?", *Yeşil
      Sol,* Eylül-Ekim 2017. See https://www.academia.edu/42853977/Bir_Yasan%C4%B1n
      _%C4%B0%C5%9Faret_Etti%C4%9Fi_T%C3%BCrkiyenin_Bile%C5%9Fenleri_II_Zey
      tin_mi_Tesis_mi (accessed on 11 May 2021).

## 4       Case Studies

So far, we have looked at the broad contours of PPPs in Turkey and discussed the dynamics that lied behind their acceleration during 2010s. In this section, I will outline six showcase PPP projects as small case studies to provide concrete and specific details.

### 4.1     *Bosporus (Eurasia) Tunnel*
The project is a PPP for the design, financing, construction, operation, and maintenance of the İstanbul Strait Road Tunnel Crossing with a total length of 14.6km, which was designed to provide continuous flow of traffic between Asian and European sides of Istanbul. It has been tendered by the Turkish State at the end of 2008 and has been awarded with a contract period of 30.5 years to a Turkish-Korean joint venture.[57]

Yapı Merkezi of Turkey and SK E&C of South Korea founded ATAŞ (Eurasia Tunnel Operation Construction and Investment Inc.) in 2009 to be responsible for the project. Construction that began in 2011 was completed in less than six years with $1.23 billion investment cost. By December 2016 the Eurasia Tunnel began operating.

The project represented a truly international effort with participants from all around the world. It was constructed by an equal partnership of Turkish Yapı Merkezi and South Korean SK E&C. It was financed by $960 million loans from three main sources: (1) IFIs such as European Investment Bank, EBRD, and Korea Exim Bank ($550 million); (2) Foreign banks like Sumitomo Mitsui Banking Corporation, Standard Chartered Bank, and the Mizuho Bank ($210 million); and (3) Domestic banks including Yapı Kredi Bank, Türkiye İş Bank, and Garanti Bank ($200 million).

There were other domestic and foreign participants of this significant project too. Arup from the UK retained by the lenders as their technical advisor. WSP USA (formerly Parsons Brinckerhoff) was the lead design and structural engineer for the project. HNTB of the USA was the project's independent design verification engineer. Herrenknecht from Germany supplied a specially designed tunnel Boring Machine to dig the tunnel around 100 meters below sea level. Bosch Security Systems installed 5,500 innovative fire detectors and 500 video cameras as well as more than 100 emergency phones on each level to

57      "Eurosia Tunnel (PPP)", *European Investment Bank,* 10 December 2010. See https://www .eib.org/en/projects/pipelines/all/20090678# (accessed on 8 June 2021).

ensure the safety of the underwater traffic connection. OYAK Concrete Industry and Trade Inc. of Turkey provided 450.000 m3 heavy concrete for the project.

### 4.2    Gebze-Orhangazi-İzmir Motorway (incl. Osmangazi Bridge)

The road PPP project connects İstanbul and the İzmir in the Aegean region of Turkey with a 426-km-long motorway. The most complex part of the project is the 3.3km İzmit Bay suspension bridge – Osmangazi Bridge – requiring over 77,000 tons of steel and numerous tunnels and viaducts.

The consortium consisting of five Turkish companies (Nurol Holding, Makyol Holding, Özaltın Construction, Göçay Construction, and Yüksel Holding) and one Italian company (Astaldi) was selected as the preferred bidders in 2009 tender in which only two consortiums submitted offers. The Turkish-Italian consortium was awarded a 22-year and 4-month BOT contract and incorporated Otoyol Yatırım ve İşletme A.ş. as a special purpose joint stock company under the laws of Turkey (i.e., project company) in September 2010 to implement the project. The project broke ground in October 2010 and completed in August 2019.

According to World Bank's PPI database, total investment in the project was $9.75 billion including $6.95 billion from debt and $2.8 billion from equity.[58] The debt financing was made available by eight domestic banks (i.e., Akbank, Finansbank, Garanti Bankası, Halk Bankası, İş Bankası, Vakıflar Bankası, Yapı ve Kredi Bankası, and Ziraat Bankası) as well as Deutsche Bank AG London Branch. The $1.1 billion EPC contract for the suspension bridge was sub-contracted to a consortium of IHI Infrastructure Systems (i.e., a subsidiary of Japanese construction corporation IHI) and Itochu Corporation (i.e., one of the leading corporations in Japan). IHI Infrastructure Systems and Itochu consortium further subcontracted different segments of the project to other companies including: COWI of Denmark for the bridge design, STFA of Turkey for the construction of tower foundations in sea and land, German multinational conglomerate Siemens for the development, installation and commissioning of the bridge's structure, traffic and central components and systems, Çimtaş of Turkey for fabricating the steel tower blocks and tower and girder panels, and OYAK Concrete Industry and Trade Inc. of Turkey for providing 140.000 m3 heavy concrete for the bridge construction.[59]

---

58    "Gebze-Orhangazi-İzmir Motorway", World Bank PPI Database. See https://ppi.worldb ank.org/en/snapshots/project/gebze-orhangazi-izmir-motorway-8175 (accessed on 10 June 2021).

59    "Osmangazi Suspension Bridge, İstanbul, Turkey", Road Traffic Technology. See https:// www.roadtraffic-technology.com/projects/osman-gazi-suspension-bridge-istanbul/ (accessed on 10 June 2021).

### 4.3    Third International Airport for İstanbul

As one of the most significant projects in the history of Turkish Republic, the new İstanbul airport is planned to be amongst the world's largest and the busiest with 76.5 million square meters surface area and a yearly capacity of 150 million passengers. The airport is located 35-km outside of İstanbul and expected to be integrated to other PPP projects such as Northern Marmara Motorway and the Third Bridge that were completed in 2016.

The PPP tender for the airport took place in May 2013. The consortium of five Turkish companies (Cengiz Holding, Kolin Group, Limak Holding, Mapa Group, and Kalyon Group) bid $29 billion for the project, which included a 25-year lease, outbidding rivals including Turkey's TAV Holding and Germany's Fraport. In addition to $29 billion for 25-years of lease, the airport would cost $13 billion to construct ($6.5 billion of this would spend on the construction of the first stage).[60] The winning consortium formed İstanbul Grand Airport (IGA) in October 2013 as a project company to be responsible for constructing and operating the airport for 25 years. Construction commenced in June 2014 in the presence of the then prime minister Erdoğan. The first stage of construction that enabled the airport to initially serve 90 million passengers annually completed in October 2018.

Multiple domestic and foreign companies were involved with the project. State-owned banks (Ziraat Bank, Halkbank, and Vakıfbank) and foreign-owned domestic banks (Denizbank, Garanti Bank, and Finansbank) provided $4.89 billion worth of loan to cover the first stage of investment.[61] British Arup Group developed the master plan for the project. Arcadis Nederland provided earthwork design services (i.e., designed the stable platform for the runways, taxiways, aprons, and terminal areas). UK-based Grimshaw Architects, Nordic Office of Architecture, Scott Browning, in partnership with Turkish companies Fonksiyon and Kiklop/TAM, provided the conceptual design of the airport. American AECOM and Italian Pininfarina designed the regional Air Traffic Control tower and technical buildings. Swiss equipment manufacturer Liebherr supplied 58 tower cranes to help construction that represented the largest single order in the history of the company. Turkish Borusan Machinery and Power Systems delivered 400 Caterpillar heavy machines and 8 Genie

---

60      "Turkish firms win 22 billion euro Istanbul airport tender", *Reuters,* 3 May 2013. See https://www.reuters.com/article/us-turkey-airport-idUSBRE9420RL20130503 (accessed on 14 June 2021).

61      "IGA Airport", *World Bank PPI* Database. See https://ppi.worldbank.org/en/snapshots/project/iga-airport-7711 (accessed on 12 August 2021).

diesel-powered articulating boom lifts. Systemair Turkey supplied 650 air handling units and 7,200 fan-coil units to the new airport.[62]

**4.4      *Northern Marmara Motorway (incl. Third Bosporus Bridge)*
The 387-km long Northern Marmara Motorway is intended to boost transport
connectivity between the European and Asian sides of Turkey. The motorway consists of three main sections: (i) 178-km long section located between
İstanbul's eastern Kurtköy district and Sakarya's north-western Akyazı district
on the Asian part of the motorway (Asian Section), (ii) 95-km section located
between Kınalı in the west of İstanbul and Odayeri neighbourhood of Eyüp
district on the European part of the motorway (European Section), and (iii)
114-km long section between Odayeri and Paşaköy that includes the Third
Bosporus bridge connecting Asian and European parts of the motorway.

The 114-km long section with the Third Bridge, often considered to be the
major component of the motorway, was put out on to tender in 2012. A consortium of Italy's Astaldi and Turkey's iç içtaş placed the winning bid with a construction and operation period of 10 years and 2 months.[63] The construction
work that started in May 2013 completed in August 2016 with an investment
amounted to $3.89 billion. A mixture of state-owned and private Turkish banks
such as İşbank, Yapı Kredi Bankası, Vakıfbank, Garanti Bankası, Halkbank, and
Ziraat Bankası provided $2.3 billion loan for the construction.

The remaining two sections, the 95-km long Kınalı-Odayeri (European) and
178-km long Kurtköy-Akyazı (Asian), were tendered in May 2016 by the General
Directorate of Highways (KGM). A consortium of Limak Holding and Cengiz
Holding won the BOT contract (6 years and 9 months) for the Asian section,
while a consortium of Kolin Group, Kalyon Holding and Hasen Construction
consortium acquired the BOT contract (7 years and 9 months) for the
European part.[64] The construction work on both sections completed in May
2021 with a total investment cost of $1.63 billion and $1.04 billion respectively.

62    "Turkey's $12.7bn Istanbul New Airport to open this year", *Construction Week*. See https://
       www.constructionweekonline.com/article-48898-turkeys-127bn-istanbul-new-airport
       -to-open-this-year (accessed on 12 August 2021). "Istanbul New Airport: A hub for the 21st
       century", *Airport Review*. See https://www.internationalairportreview.com/article/23303/
       istanbul-new-airport-a-hub-for-the-21st-century/ (accessed on 12 August 2021).
63    "Astaldi-IC Ictas make best bid for Turkish road project", *Reuters,* 29 May 2012. See https://
       www.reuters.com/article/astaldi-turkey-marmara-idINL5E8GT5N120120529 (accessed on
       16 June 2021).
64    "Dev projenin ihalesi sonuçlandı", *Bloomberg HT,* 18 May 2016. See https://businessht.bloo
       mberght.com/piyasalar/haber/1241105-dev-projenin-ihalesi-sonuclandi (accessed on 16
       June 2021).

The financing for construction was arranged by offshore branches of leading Turkish banks: Garanti Bank, İş Bank, QNB Finansbank, Ziraat Bank, Halk Bankası and Vakıflar Bankası.

Apart from the above-mentioned project companies, the Northern Marmara Motorway project with its three sections is being involved by key market players in the international and domestic construction sector. For example, South Korean based Hyundai E&C and its South Korean partner (SK Engineering & Construction) has won $697 million engineering sub-contract to build the bridge.[65] Belgian Greisch, Turkish Temelsu International Engineering, Swiss Lombardi, French CSTB and Dutch Fugro contributed to the design of the bridge. OYAK Concrete Industry and Trade Inc. of Turkey provided 1.3 million m3 concrete for the bridge construction. Akçansa, a subsidiary of Sabancı Holding, provided 2.5 million tonnes of ready-mix concrete (RMC) and 750,000 tonnes of cement for the project.[66] Borusan Holding of Turkey sold nearly 200 heavy equipment in the project.

### 4.5    *Dardanelles Bridge and Kınalı-Balıkesir Motorway (Malkara-Çanakkale Section)*

The 101-km Malkara-Çanakkale section (including Dardanelles Bridge) of the 322-km long Kınalı-Balıkesir Motorway project on the North-western region of Turkey was tendered in October 2016. The KGM awarded the BOT contract to a Turkish-Korean consortium comprising SK Engineering & Construction and Daelim Industrial Corporation of South Korea, and Limak Holding and Yapı Merkezi Construction of Turkey.[67] According to contract, the consortium would first construct and then manage and operate the completed bridge for 16 years and 2 months.

Construction of motorway started in March 2017 and scheduled to be completed in 2023 at an estimated cost of $2.84 billion. The World Bank PPI sources demonstrate that the funding of $2.65 billion has been finalised with 24 lenders, including domestic and international banks. Approximately 70 per cent of the funding secured from international banks such as Bank of China,

65    "Hyundai consortium wins $697m Turkey bridge deal", *Construction Week,* 10 July 2013. See https://www.constructionweekonline.com/article-23321-hyundai-consortium-wins-697m-turkey-bridge-deal (accessed on 16 June 2021).

66    "Turkish Cement Sector: Grey constituent of growth", *Garanti Securities,* June 2014. See https://rapor.garantibbvayatirim.com.tr/arastirma/sector_reports/CementSector0614.pdf (accessed on 16 June 2021).

67    "Project Information" See https://www.1915canakkale.com/en-us/about/project-information (accessed on 16 June 2021).

Deutsche Bank, DZ Bank, ING, Siemens Bank, Export-Import Bank of Korea, Standard Chartered, and Shinhan Financial Group. The remaining 30 per cent of the funding was provided by Turkish banks including Akbank, Garanti Bank, Finansbank, İş Bank, Yapı Kredi, and Vakıfbank.[68]

Serving as the centrepiece of the motorway project, the Dardanelles Bridge will break the world record for the longest span of any bridge in the world when finished. In addition to SK Engineering-Daelim-Limak-Yapı Merkezi consortium selected as project companies, many leading engineering and consultancy firms are involved. For example, American Parsons and Turkish Tekfen Holding joint venture secured a TL165 million contract to provide engineering and construction support, along with supervision and inspection services for the motorway and bridge (Tekfen Annual Report 2017, 48). South Korean based Pyunghwa Engineering Consultants provided a feasibility study and basic design for the bridge. London based Pell Frischmann and Danish COWI helped to design the bridge, while Dutch Fugro undertook geotechnical works.[69]

Input suppliers were also participated the project. For instance, steel elements of the bridge were provided by the strategic partnership between Turkish and South Korean suppliers, with Çimtaş (ENKA Holding) and POSCO agreeing to supply 35,000 tonnes of heavy steel for the tower structures, cabling systems and road surface. That partnership also supplied 52,000 tonnes of steel plate for the bridge deck and 41,000 tonnes of steel wire roads for the suspension system that will support it (ENKA Annual Report 2018, 60). Turkey's cement giants Akçansa and Çimsa (both are subsidiaries of Sabancı Holding) provided the ready-mixed concrete for the project.

**4.6    Healthcare Campus Projects (City Hospitals)**
The Turkish government initiated the landmark Health Public-Private-Partnership (PPP) program in 2010, aiming to improve the quality of Turkey's health infrastructure. The PPP program involved the construction of 32 integrated healthcare campus projects (known as 'city hospitals' in Turkey) across the country, delivering between 40,000–50,000 hospital beds with an estimated investment cost of $20 billion (Investment Support and Promotion Agency of Turkey 2014, 89).

---

68   "Malkara-Canakkale Motorway PPP", *World Bank PPI* Database. See https://ppi.worldb ank.org/en/snapshots/project/malkara-canakkale-motorway-ppp-9458 (accessed on 21 June 2021).
69   "Canakkale 1915 Bridge", *Road Traffic Technology*. See https://www.roadtraffic-technology .com/projects/canakkale-1915-bridge/ (accessed on 15 August 2021).

Designed along the lines of the United Kingdom's private finance initiative, the healthcare projects follow a typical PPP-based BLT model with an average concession period of 28 years (Pala 2018, 8). Let me go into detail. First, the Project Company secures the financing required for the completion of the project. If the land on which the facility will be built is state-owned, the Ministry of Health (MoH) then arranges the land to be used by the Project Company free of charge. Once the health facility is built and all medical and nonmedical equipment are procured by the Project Company according to the contract standard (usually within three years), the MoH will lease the facility for a period of twenty-five years. The MoH will pay the Project Company a yearly lease adjusted annually for inflation and collected independently of hospital occupancy. During this period, the Project Company operates the facility and has the right to develop non-healthcare services, but it cannot not provide any core medical services and cannot be liable for services that are to be performed by the doctors, nurses, or administrative personnel. These remain the sole responsibility of the MoH. At the end of the contract term, the Project Company returns the healthcare facilities built to the MoH in good working condition and without any encumbrances (Investment Support and Promotion Agency of Turkey 2014, 91).

To date, 13 healthcare campuses have become operational with PPP-based BLT model (See Table 20). Each of these campuses has capacities of roughly 500 to 4,000 beds. Project companies that invested around a total of $7 billion included Turkey's Rönesans Holding, iç Holding, Akfen Holding, YDA Construction as well as foreign entities like Inso Sistemi (Italy), Meridiam (France) and Sojitz (Japan). Although the PPP legislation adopted in 2013 requires at least 20 per cent of the medical equipment used in healthcare campuses to be manufactured locally, the production of medical devices is limited in Turkey and the increasing demand is chiefly met by global healthcare giants like GE Healthcare and Siemens.

Most of these healthcare campus projects were conducted by the active TÜSiAD members such as Rönesans Holding and Akfen Holding. For example, Rönesans Holding, which was founded by Erman Ilıcaklı who acted as the TÜSiAD vice president before and has recently established close relations with Erdoğan, is the dominant actor among healthcare campus builders and operators.[70] The company and its partners (built) and operate five healthcare campuses with a combined capacity of nearly 7,000 beds. For example,

---

70   Before establishing his own company, Erman Ilıcaklı worked for ENKA Holding, a leading member of TÜSiAD.

TABLE 20   Healthcare campuses (PPP) in operation

| Healthcare campus | Capacity (beds) | Investment value ($ mil) | Project company | Operation year |
|---|---|---|---|---|
| Adana | 1,550 | 687 | Rönesans-Meridiam-Sıla-Şam | 2017 |
| Mersin | 1,294 | 385 | DIA Holding-CCN Sağlık (iç Holding) | 2017 |
| Isparta | 755 | 264 | Akfen | 2017 |
| Yozgat | 475 | 184 | Rönesans-Şentürkler-Sıla-Şam | 2017 |
| Kayseri | 1,607 | 498 | YDA-Inso Sistemi | 2018 |
| Manisa | 558 | 217 | YDA-Inso Sistemi | 2018 |
| Elâzığ | 1,038 | 390 | Rönesans-Meridiam-Sıla-Şam | 2018 |
| Ankara Bilkent | 3,711 | 1,288 | DIA Holding-CCN Sağlık (iç Holding) | 2018 |
| Eskişehir | 1,081 | 461 | Akfen | 2018 |
| Bursa | 1,355 | 399 | Rönesans-Meridiam-Sıla-Şam | 2019 |
| İstanbul Başakşehir | 2,682 | 1,559 | Rönesans-Sojitz | 2020 |
| Konya | 1,250 | 269 | YDA-Inso Sistemi | 2020 |
| Tekirdağ | 486 | 252 | Akfen | 2020 |
| TOTAL | 17,842 | 6,853 | | |

SOURCE: TC SAĞLIK YATIRIMLARI GENEL MÜDÜRLÜĞÜ (HTTPS://SYGM.SAGLIK.GOV.TR); TC SAĞLIK BAKANLIĞI 2020 FAALIYET RAPORU (HTTPS://SAGLIK.GOV.TR)

Rönesans-led (i.e., holds majority ownership) consortium that also includes, Şam, Sıla and international leading infrastructure firm Meridiam completed the construction of $687 million Adana Healthcare Campus in 2017. A further nine international financial institutions – EBRD, IFC, DEG, Proparco, Siemens, BBVA, HSBC, Mitsui Banking Corporation, Korea Development Bank – provided €433m long-term loan package for the project.[71]

[71]   "Transforming Turkey's health", *World Finance,* 2 December 2015. See https://www.world finance.com/infrastructure-investment/project-finance/transforming-turkeys-health (accessed on 04 July 2021).

Islamic-influenced Anatolian companies also participated in PPP-based healthcare campus projects. For example, DİA Holding-CCN Sağlık, which operates two significant healthcare campuses with a combined capacity of nearly 5,000 beds, is owned by Murat Çeçen, a family member of İbrahim Çeçen (the founding chairman of İç Holding) known to be a close friend of Erdoğan.[72] Murat Çeçen's DİA Holding-CCN Sağlık implemented the $1.28 billion Ankara Bilkent Healthcare Campus that holds the title of being the largest hospital in Europe, as well as the largest hospital constructed under a single contract in the world.[73] Siemens has entered into a €100 million worth contract with DİA Holding-CCN Sağlık to supply and operate the laboratory services within the campus for five years. Alarko-Carrier of Alarko Holding provided the health campus with a package of products including liquid chillers, air-cooled chillers, and cooling towers.[74] Unlike Adana Healthcare Campus, Ankara Bilkent Healthcare Campus Project was financed by mainly domestic creditor banks such as Garanti Bank, Deniz Bank, Finansbank, İş Bankası and Yapı Kredi Bankası.

There are 7 more healthcare campuses with a total bed capacity of 13,479 beds that are at various stages of financing and construction (See Table 21). The total investment cost of these campuses is expected to be about $4.4 billion. TÜSİAD-based Rönesans Holding, which had completed several healthcare campuses before, has been constructing Physical Therapy and Rehabilitation (PTR) & High Security Forensic Psychiatric (HFSP) hospitals. Another TÜSİAD member, GAMA Holding, has invested in two major healthcare PPPs (i.e., İzmir Bayraklı and Kocaeli) with its partners – Turkish corporation Türkerler Holding and global industrial giant General Electric. The development of these two projects that together valued at around $1 billion were financed by the EBRD, Export Development Canada, and the Overseas Private Investment Corporation of US.[75]

Foreign project companies such as Astaldi (Italy), Salini (Italy), General Electric (US), and Samsung (South Korea) also heavily involved in these healthcare PPPs under construction. For example, Astaldi, an Italian construction

---

72    Murat Çeçen is the oldest son of İbrahim Çeçen.

73    "Turkey prepares to welcome its largest health complex", *World Finance*, 20 July 2016. See https://www.worldfinance.com/infrastructure-investment/project-finance/turkey-prepa res-to-welcome-its-largest-health-complex (accessed on 04 July 2021).

74    "Bilkent City Hospital Chooses Alarko Carrier". See https://www.alarko-carrier.com.tr/ en/corporate/media/news/bilkent-city-hospital-chooses-alarko-carrier (accessed on 7 October 2021).

75    "EBRD, Canada's EDC and OPIC of US finance Izmir hospital in Turkey", *EBRD*, 20 October 2016. See https://www.hurriyetdailynews.com/ebrd-canadas-edc-and-opic-of-us-fina nce-izmir-hospital-in-turkey--105275 (accessed on 16 August 2021).

TABLE 21    Healthcare campuses (PPP) under construction

| Campus | Capacity (beds) | Investment ($ mil) | Project company |
|---|---|---|---|
| Ankara Etlik | 3,624 | 1,166 | Astaldi-Türkerler |
| PTR & HFSP | 2,400 | 696 | Rönesans-Sıla-Şam |
| İzmir Bayraklı | 2,060 | 614 | Gama-Türkerler-General Electric |
| Gaziantep | 1,875 | 932 | Samsung-Kayı-Salini-PEIF |
| Şanlıurfa | 1,700 | 405 | YDA |
| Kocaeli | 1,210 | 396 | Gama-Türkerler-General Electric |
| Kütahya | 610 | 186 | Güriş |
| TOTAL | 13,479 | 4,395 | |

SOURCE: T.C. CUMHURBAŞKANLIĞI STRATEJI VE BÜTÇE BAŞKANLIĞI (2019); PRESIDENCY OF THE REPUBLIC OF TURKEY INVESTMENT OFFICE (HTTPS://WWW.INVEST.GOV.TR)

company and experienced hospital operator, established a partnership with Turkish company Türkerler Holding, in which Astaldi is the majority stakeholder. Astaldi-Türkerler partnership won the tender for constructing, supplying, and maintaining 3,624-beds Ankara Etlik hospital. When complete the $1.16 billion hospital will be among the largest of mega hospitals funded under a PPP model.[76] Another example is the 1,875-beds Gaziantep Healthcare PPP project that is in southern Turkey, which has recently seen a sharp increase in population, mainly due to influx of refugees from neighbouring Syria. Samsung Corporation from South Korea and Salini Impregilo from Italy entered a partnership with Turkey's Kayı Construction to design, construct, supply and maintain the hospital.

Although President Erdoğan and the AKP officials have described these healthcare PPPs as a "dream" come true, they can hardly be viewed as perfect projects. Indeed, outspoken critics such as opposition MPs Kayıhan Pala and Mehmet Bekaroğlu as well as journalists Mustafa Sönmez, Can Teoman and Bahadır Özgür based their critique on the three dimensions (Pala 2018, 11). First, they argued that the average cost per bed of healthcare PPPs was higher than other private and/or public hospital investments. For example,

76  "Ankara Etlik Hospital PPP Project", EBRD, 6 November 2014. See https://www.ebrd.com/work-with-us/projects/psd/central-anatolia-(etlik)-hospital-ppp.html (accessed on 4 July 2021).

Can Teoman stated that Koç University Hospital and Medicana Bursa, which ranked among the Turkey's top ten hospitals in terms of quality and luxury, had an average per bed cost of $341,000 and 333,000 respectively (compared with the 389,000 in healthcare PPPs).[77] Unexpectedly, a study conducted by the North Anatolia Development Agency (2016), which is affiliated with the Turkish Ministry of Industry and Technology, calculated the average per bed cost for a mid-level hospital to be between $85–100,000.

Second, they argued that because healthcare PPPs are mostly located on the outskirts of big cities due to their big size, those old and poor patients, who do not have personal car possessions, are struggling to access the hospitals to meet their healthcare needs.[78] A research prepared by the Mersin Medical Chamber found that people who live in some areas of Mersin has to take nearly 2 hours public transport to reach Mersin City Hospital. The research also found that 49 per cent of the participants think that the distance of city hospital to the place they live at is "very bad" (Uğurhan 2018). As Emek (2017) stated in his publication on PPPs in Turkish healthcare sector, "this is contrary to the main objectives of the [Turkey's] Health Transformation Programme which intended to provide effective, equitable, accessible and high-quality services for all citizens (p. 11)".

Third, critics described the healthcare PPPs as the "biggest black hole" for the budget in the Turkey's modern history.[79] In 2020, the project companies operating the PPP hospitals were paid about 10 billion liras ($1.3 billion) by the Ministry of Health for rent (i.e., for the use of the health facilities) and services (e.g. furnishing, grounds maintenance, clinical equipment, imaging, laboratory, sterilization, rehabilitation, waste management, laundry, security, car parking and so on), with the two categories representing roughly equal sums. In 2021, the companies will receive around 17 billion liras ($1.9 billion), which will make nearly 20 per cent of the ministry's total budget expenditures of 77 billion liras (Trade Union of Public Employees in Health and Social Sciences

77    "Çılgın şehir hastanelerinin maliyetleri daha da çılgın", *Ahval,* 30 January 2018. See https://ahvalnews.com/tr/hastaneler/cilgin-sehir-hastanelerinin-maliyetleri-daha-da-cilgin (accessed on 7 July 2021).
78    "Demet Parlar: Sağlığımıza 2021 Sağlık Bütçesi merceğinden bakmak", *Gazete Karınca,* 25 November 2020. See https://gazetekarinca.com/2020/11/sagligimiza-2021-saglik-butcesi-merceginden-bakmak/ (accessed on 8 July 2021).
79    "Mustafa Sönmez: Turkey's city hospitals threaten a financial black hole", *Al-Monitor,* 31 August 2020. See https://www.al-monitor.com/originals/2020/08/turkey-city-hospitals-threaten-financial-black-hole-pandemic.html (accessed on 8 July 2021).

2021, pp. 6–8).[80] More importantly, those payments will continue for up to 25 years, and are adjusted for inflation and for the foreign exchange (FX) fluctuations, which mitigates the FX risk for project companies.

These criticisms and the strain of fiscal deficits after a 2018 currency crisis have forced the Turkish government to stop a costly PPP healthcare program for some time. Speaking in Ankara on 14 November 2019 during budget talks, Health Minister Fahrettin Koca said 10 new hospitals including İstanbul Sancaktepe, Denizli and Antalya, which were originally planned to be PPP projects, will be built through government tender.[81] According to the "2020 Investment Program" of the Presidency of the Republic of Turkey, Strategy and Budget Office, the government adopted a public procurement method and allocated about $1.7 billion to fund these ten hospitals with a total of 12,400 beds.[82]

## 5       Conclusion

The size of the overall PPP investment portfolio in Turkey has been increasingly rapidly since 2009. Between 2010 and 2018, Turkey has implemented over $100 billion worth of PPP projects mainly in transportation, energy, and healthcare sectors. Throughout the chapter I argued that the rise of PPPs is due to complex background with three dynamics. First, as Turkey failed to increase relative surplus production and international competitiveness, PPP projects became increasingly important for domestic capital accumulation regime to create new financial resources to postpone crisis dynamics. Second, although the Turkish power bloc was not unified anymore as the internal contradictions between fractions of capital sharpened in the 2010s, the capitalist class' support for PPP projects remained strong because these projects elevated the general interest of capital above the interests of the popular and laboring classes.

---

80    "Rant hastanelerine 16 milyar TL'lik bütçe", *Birgün*, 4 February 2021. See https://www.bir gun.net/haber/rant-hastanelerine-16-milyar-tl-lik-butce-332953 (accessed on 8 July 2021). For more information, check the Turkish Ministry of Health's Strategic Plan for 2019– 2023. See https://stratejikplan.saglik.gov.tr/files/TC-Saglik-Bakanligi-2019-2023-Stratejik -Plan.pdf (accessed on 8 July 2021).

81    "Turkey seals biggest budget 'black hole' in U-Turn on Hospitals", *Bloomberg*, 15 November 2019. See https://www.bloomberg.com/news/articles/2019-11-15/turkey-seals-biggest-bud get-black-hole-in-u-turn-on-hospitals (accessed on 9 July 2021).

82    Türkiye Cumhuriyeti Cumhurbaşkanlığı Strateji ve Bütçe Başkanlığı, "2020 Yılı Yatırım Programı", Şubat 2020, p. 243. See https://sbb.gov.tr/wp-content/uploads/2020/03/2020 _Yatirim_Programi.pdf (accessed on 9 July 2021).

Third, the exceptional state formed under the AKP government has increasingly managed to bypass legal and institutional checks and balances and enabled the implementation of PPP projects without any delays.

Contrary to liberal-cum-institutionalist accounts that see any PPP as a narrow contractual agreement (and corrupt practice) between the government and the Islamic-influenced Anatolian companies designed in favor of the latter, six showcase case studies illustrated that all fractions of capital (e.g., Islamic-influenced, TÜSİAD-based, and foreign) supported and gained greater profits from PPP projects not just as project companies but also as lenders, engineering-design contractors, input suppliers, and so on.

# CHAPTER 6

# Comparing Alternatives to Privatization

As the previous chapters outlined, privatization in Turkey has not always been that aggressive and comprehensive since its inception in 1984. It has taken sustained political will of the power bloc and dedicated state policies of the AKP government within the favourable context of the post-2001 domestic accumulation regime for privatization process to gain momentum. The privatization program mostly opted for the full divestiture method in the 2000s, and then a mixture of divestiture and PPP methods during the 2010s. The book's central argument is that the acceleration of privatization in Turkey in the post-2001 era has not exclusively provided advantages to (and supported by) favourable capital groups and the AKP elites. On the contrary, the benefits have fallen disproportionately to power bloc with all its fractions – TÜSİAD members, Islamic influenced capital groups, foreign capital groups, and leaders of the AKP – while the costs fall disproportionately onto Turkish popular classes and natural environment of the entire country. As such, Turkey's privatization program served to consolidate the position of *Capital in General* in Turkey.

This implies that an alternative to privatization need to be identified and constructed for the whole society. In this chapter I explore the argument that it is unlikely that we can construct a substantive progressive alternative to privatization without promoting greater democratic (popular) control and a growth in the social-environmental commitment of public assets. I have identified two necessary, if not sufficient, strategies for constructing and defending a substantial alternative program based on democratic control and social-environmental commitment: 1) the building of broad popular political alliances, and 2) conceptalizating the state as a constested space.[1] The construction of democratically controlled and socially-environmentally committed organizations would not only be able to ameliorate the harms of capitalism in the immediate term, but would also strengthen the prospects of the creation of a desirable society beyond capitalism in the future.

I develop this argument by way of three concluding sections. The first section briefly examines the implications of the Turkish privatization experience for the study of political economy of privatization in late developing countries.

---

1  The attempt is not to build a blueprint for an "ideal" roadmap, but rather to offer broad paramaters for what might be considered a substantial alternative to privatization, and what strategies might guide this alternative.

The second section evaluates three potential alternatives to privatization – traditional state ownership and control; corporatization; and democratic control – in several historical settings, including Turkey, the UK, and several Latin American countries. In the third section, I will deal with the questions of strategy to advance our understanding of how we might better construct and defend a future substantive alternative to privatization. This is followed by a brief conclusion.

## 1      Implications of the Turkish Privatization Experience

The alternative approach developed throughout this book contributes to the study of political economy of privatization in late developing countries in different ways.

First, the book demonstrated that privatization is a multi-dimensional process and happens through one or more modes including ownership, management, financing and so on. One should not focus only on SOEs and specifically on divestiture; other forms of privatization processes including outsourcing, transfer of operating rights, and PPPs with different models (BOO, BOT, and BLT) are equally important.

Second, the book showed that privatization processes are variegated and territorially specific, although privatization is a global phenomenon. As was already shown throughout the book, privatization processes occur within particular conditions of national social formation of each country and are historically contingent on domestic capital accumulation patterns, state institutional capacity, relative balance of power between capital and labour, and global pressures. Although hardly new argument, this especially provides a deeper and more detailed alternative explanatory framework than that of overgeneralized (and externally oriented) Marxian explanations of Harvey, Petras and Veltmeyer, which enjoyed the attention of broad audience among scholars of critical international political economy (CIPE).

Third, another important lesson from the study is that privatizations can be complex, involving many issues, a lot of preparation and multiple workstreams. As such, privatizations can also be heavily contested as they are subject to processes of resistance (or support) and are confronted with alternative strategies formulated by different social classes. As Chapter 5 of this book shows, while major business associations and capital groups in Turkey supported PPP projects in the 2010s, the representatives of labour and popular classes such as Gezi protesters, the NFD, the TMMOB and some labour unions launched an organized campaign to block the construction of PPP projects.

Fourth, and very much related with the above point, the book demonstrated that privatization should be seen as a class-based project that attempts to further increase capital accumulation and systematically privileges the interests of capital over those of labouring and popular classes. This is an important point to emphasize as it differs from Weberian-inspired liberal-cum-institutionalist studies of Öniş (2011), Buğra and Savaşkan (2014) and Gürakar (2016) which, as Yalman (2019) succinctly narrated, incline to perceive social class as a rather ineffective unit of analysis, if at all, thus tend to dismiss class analysis, on the grounds that it is unable to explain policy change. These studies that are very popular in Turkey, instead, use "coalitions" and/or "networks" as unit of analysis and explain privatization as a manifestation of "particularism" and "corruption". As such, it is argued that privatizations exclusively privilege the interests of favourable (i.e., loyal, politically connected, and Islamic influenced) business groups that succeeded to establish coalitions with the AKP leadership. According to this perspective, privatization is not considered as a deadly sin of capitalism and capitalist class but is part of corrupt network between a group of favourable business groups and the political leadership.

Fifth, the Marxian-inspired framework adopted in the book has certainly provided some useful insights into investigation of privatization processes in different countries. Four interrelated factors – contemporary capitalism, state, power bloc, domestic capital accumulation – form the framework and can be used to investigate privatization in any specific geographical space. Unlike much of the literature that simply takes either institutions or external dynamics or political struggles as autonomous factors in themselves, this framework may allow researchers to grasp the social reality of privatization process as a dynamic totality.

## 2     What Is a Substantial Alternative to Privatization?[2]

The privatization has been at the forefront of neo-liberal transition for the past four decades. Beginning with the outright divestiture of basic utilities such as water and electricity in the United Kingdom and Chile, privatization has since spread to include virtually every sector imaginable and almost every country in the world (McDonald 2015, 119). The privatization, however, had not yielded positive outcomes for everybody. It is typically low-income and marginalized groups, along with public sector workers, that are most negatively impacted

---

2   A set of normative assessment criteria is summarized in Table 22.

(for example, loss of employment, rising prices, and reduced access to basic services) by these waves of privatization. These negative effects have fuelled anti-privatization movements, as more and more workers, consumers, and citizens have chosen to resist and reverse the implementation of privatizations.

Indeed, in the wake of neoliberal wave, there is a continuing debate about alternatives to privatization. While there is widespread agreement among anti-privatization groups (including labouring and popular classes) that privatization has been marked by dramatic failures and disappointments, alternatives to privatization are as diverse as traditional forms of state ownership, corporatization, and democratic control.

### 2.1    *Traditional State Ownership and Control*

For many opponents of privatization, particularly the labour unions and state bureaucrats, the most obvious alternative to privatization is the traditional forms of state ownership and control. In fact, state-owned and state-operated enterprises dominated the economic scene for much of the 20th century, and the height of state-owned enterprises developing public infrastructure came in the post-Second World War period (McDonald 2015, 120). In different parts of the world, state-owned enterprises not only guaranteed the basic provision of essential goods and services in those areas where markets had failed but were also conditioned by a determination to enhance the prospects of capital accumulation through provision of industrial inputs, infrastructure, and investment capital. As we had seen in Chapter 2, Turkey was one example of those countries which had a weak entrepreneurial capacity for large-scale development projects in the electricity provision, petroleum refining and the ironsteel sector, which resulted in expansion of the state-owned enterprise sector as a precondition for the development of capitalism.

The subsequent rise of neoliberal orthodoxies challenged this growth; it asserted that state-owned and -controlled enterprises were bad for development, an argument that ultimately leads to privatization. Although state-owned and -controlled enterprises are down, they are far from out. Many remain in service today. Indeed, the global financial crisis of 2008, and the ills of privatization have reinvigorated the debate about state ownership as a serious option in development policy (Marois 2013, 2–4). For example, the UK government nationalized three of the UK's largest high street banks such as Northern Rock, HBOS, and the Royal Bank of Scotland in the midst of crisis (Cumbers 2014, 4).

In short, one of the key demands gaining general favor among opponents of privatization, is to keep state-owned and -controlled enterprises just they are (i.e., protection of the status quo). Moreover, these groups go so far as to argue for the nationalization of the other major and economic enterprises, when favourable context emerges.

Those who want to maintain the place of the state-owned enterprises often refer to the potential positive impacts of traditional state ownership and control on national development at multiple levels, including sustainable use of large natural resources, the development marginalized regions, and greater access to essential services for disadvantaged social groups (Chavez and Torres 2014, 18). However, careful investigation shows that traditional state-owned and -controlled enterprises are not that successful at meeting such expectations in our day. With a few exceptions in Latin America (e.g., YPFB in Bolivia and CORPOELEC in Venezuala), traditional state-owned and -controlled enterprises in low- and middle-income countries have experienced bureaucratic efficiency, financial losses, and a failure to extend universal access to public services (Spronk 2010, 156) (See Table 22).

The main cause of these problems has been the fact that traditional state-owned and – controlled enterprises in low- and middle-income countries often tend to suffer from top-down, hierarchical, and undemocratic decion-making. This results in narrow public participation, and little social commitment, which tends to ignore the needs on the ground (Cumbers 2014, 14; Cumbers 2016, 326). Citizens and workers have been able to do little to affect the actual operations or budgetary decisions of traditional state-owned enterprises, except to grumble about their exclusionary and opaque orientation (Albo 1993, 22). In the absence of democratic participation and independent systems of audit (accountability), powerful groups (bureaucratic and capitalist, albeit with differences) in such a country can then capture the state-owned enterprises (Marina-Flores 2015, 154). In that sense, these traditional state-owned enterprises began working for the benefit of the private vested interests of the bureaucratic and capitalist groups, rather than in the interests of any broader conception of the common good, or public interest.

Bureaucratic groups do not often care much about ensuring that the standard rights and services associated with citizenship are met by state-owned enterprises (Albo 1993). This arises from two situations: First, bureaucrats are sometimes subject to a process of capture by the private corporations. This process includes bribery, but also legal donations and other networks of influence that constitute effective state capture (Fine and Hall 2012, 62). Second, bureaucrats sometimes willing to sustain their own power and status within the state by offering employment and other privileges to their electorate and families in the state-owned enterprises they manage.

Capitalist groups, on the other hand, benefit from state-owned enterprises in the form of cheap inputs, special distribution rights, and partnership opportunities, which usually come at the expense of the general population, and/or efficiency targets. An important example is the above mentioned Erdemir in Turkey before its privatization in 2005. Certain capital groups had special agreements to purchase iron and steel inputs from Erdemir at below market price. Some of them enjoyed privileged distribution rights for Erdemir's products on the global market and used these rights to make large profits.[3] In Turkey, and elsewhere, it was the duty loss mechanism – mandated financial losses that are officially assigned to state-owned enterprises and paid from the general state budget – that institutionalized and made such state supports to capitalist groups possible.

Defending these state-owned enterprises, with all their inefficiencies and lack of accountability, does not seem to constitute an acceptable way of developing a substantial alternative to privatization. The solution must lie in not simply defending the traditional form of state-owned enterprises that tend to be subordinated to the economic and political agendas of the various bureaucratic and capitalist groups, but in making them more responsive to the demands of the general population. It seems that the real issue is not more vs. less state, but rather a different kind of state. Before I continue, I want to make it clear that I do not seek to dismiss the importance of state provision. However, if traditional state-owned enterprises want to really exist in the new world, they must move towards more democratic participation and accountability.

### 2.2    *Corporatization*

What of the trend toward corporatization, which is celebrated by its supporters as an effective alternative: to decentralize and depoliticize state-owned enterprises for the sake of ending inefficiencies and unaccountable practices without the need for privatization (see Osborne and Gaebler 1992; Preker and Harding 2003; Shirley, 1999)?

Corporatization refers to a system in which service agencies are owned and operated by the state, but which have a degree of autonomy. They typically have an independent legal status, and are managed by an independent board of directors, with their resources being financially ringfenced from government and other state agency assets and revenues (McDonald 2016, 108). The intent of ring fencing is creation of greater financial transparency, reduction of political interference, and strengthening of managerial accountability within what are relatively autonomous service entities. The practice of corporatization has

---

3    Personal interview with Serdar Koçtürk, Board Member of Kibar Holding, Board Member of the Turkish Exporters Assembly (TIM), Vice Chairman of the Turkish Steel Exporters Association (2008–2012) (February 6, 2013).

COMPARING ALTERNATIVES TO PRIVATIZATION

been extended across a broad range of goods and services, including hospitals, airports, universities, and transport (McDonald 2014, 1–2). The underlying logic behind corporatization is the doctrine of "New Public Management" (NPM), which emerged in the early 1980s, as part of a series of reforms to tackle the perceived deficiencies of the traditional state-owned enterprises (Pollitt, van Thiel and Homburg 2007).

Central to our inquiry is the question of whether corporatization should be seen as a substantial alternative to privatization. The contemporary examples demonstrate that the potential of corporatization as a progressive alternative is often weakened by its actual implementation. This is because the most dominant form of corporatization today is the neoliberal (i.e., commercialized) model (McDonald 2014, 9).[4] Neoliberally corporatized state-owned enterprises run to varying degrees on commercial principles (by managerial or professional groups with little public participation) that often mimic the private sector. They often function using market doctrines, valorizing exchange rate of a service over its actual use value. They also tend to prioritize financial cost-benefit analysis in their decision-making over basic societal objectives, while their employment of private-sector management techniques (such as performance-based salaries and outsourcing) make employees feel insecure and unempowered (McDonald and Ruiters 2012, 4) (See Table 22). For instance, corporatized state-owned enterprises, such as Eskom Electricity and Rand Water in South Africa, have proven themselves to be hyper-commercial entities, cutting off services to millions of low-income households for relatively minor payment infractions, and introducing pre-paid meters that limit access to services (McDonald 2014, 81).

Another striking example of neoliberal corporatization can be seen in an analysis of one of Turkey's state-owned banks, Ziraat Bank. As a result of the post–2001 crisis Banking Sector Restructuring Program, Ziraat Bank began to adhere to private – sector management principles and pursued a commercial outlook in many different parts of Turkey, with the expectation of securing significant profit. To this end, Ziraat Bank began pressuring employees to maximize sales, while also reducing wages and making continuing employment highly precarious. The bank also provided little help in consolidating social

---

4   There are a few exceptions to this trend; one example of non-neoliberal corporatization could be Uruguay's ANTEL. It has managed to provide almost universal coverage of telecommunication services at affordable rates (Cosse, 2014, 172–180). Costa Rica's electricity provider, ICE, could be another example of a non-neoliberal corporatized entity. ICE has extended its services almost universally, and scores well in a wide range of non-monetized performance measures such as affordability (McDonald, 2016, 111).

gains for the benefit of the farmers and rural residents in whose interests it had originally been created.[5]

Given the dominance of neoliberal-oriented commercial imperatives, one should be careful in making calls for the corporatization of state enterprises as a substantial alternative to privatization.[6] Corporatization may be "public" in name, but not necessarily in character. Corporatized state enterprises often do not serve the public common interest – society as a whole and its plurality – as the commercial imperatives seem to override any other concerns (Rooyen and Hall 2007, 6–9).

### 2.3    *Democratic Control*

The analysis so far has suggested that a substantial alternative to privatization cannot be found simply in defense of traditional forms of state ownership, or of corporatization as a mere act of decentralization and depoliticization of state enterprises. Rather, the construction of a substantial alternative to privatization should aim at promoting practices that, through democratic control, enhance community development and the principle of social justice. This would make liberating public assets from the control of narrow state elites and capitalist groups (as happens in traditional state ownership) and cutting commercial profit imperatives (as happens in corporatization) necessary.

There is a wide range of both historical and contemporary examples to be found around the world, and these illustrate that major progress can be made in community development and social justice through introduction of diverse models of democratic control. In these examples, democratic control has proven to be a potent tool in making public assets more responsive to the needs of the general populace.

The first important example is the "re-municipalization" of local services following earlier, unpopular, privatizations. This has been most prevalent in the water and sanitation sectors, where, since 2000, 235 towns and cities across the world have taken their services and assets back into local forms of public ownership and control (Cumbers 2016, 327). Re-municipalization has offered important opportunities to promote universal access to water by building democratic governance around municipalities and other local authorities. It has also enhanced the environmental sustainability and effectiveness of

---

5    "Bankalarda bir seyler oluyor" [Something is happening in the banks], Birgün, April 23, 2016; "Hedef baskısı kamu bankasında" [Sales target pressure in public banks], Yenicağ, July 20, 2015.

6    For a comprehensive analysis of the neoliberalization of public universities, see Peter Fleming's (2021) recent book, 'Dark Academia: How Universities Die', London: Pluto Press.

public water operations (Lobina 2016, 5). There is strong evidence that re-municipalization has resulted in greater accountability and increased real investment in water systems, and has produced higher levels of transparency (Kishimito, Lobina and Petitjean 2015, 115). Yet re-municipalization is not perfect. If the newly established democratic governance mechanism (or capacity) is weak, then it runs the known risk of capture by elite groups (i.e., village heads, local notables, politicians), particularly at the level of city governance (Cumbers 2014, 24), which may ultimately lead to disappointing financial management (Chowns 2015).

The second significant example of democratic control is in the realm of worker control. Workers' control generally refers to organizational arrangements whereby ordinary employees are allowed to exert control over decision-making in various aspects of their work. The variants of worker control initiatives stretch from the lower range – an extension of the scope of collective bargaining, and an erosion of managerial prerogatives – to the higher range, with wide-scale participation of workers in actual decision-making (Bayat 1991, 3–4). Worker control initiatives are common in countries like Costa Rica, India, Venezuela, Bangladesh, and others. In the Bangladeshi capital, Dhaka, for example, the water supply in parts of the city is co-managed by a workers cooperative, which has achieved substantial efficiency improvements, not only in customer services, billing, and collections, but also in improving water access for slum dwellers (TNI 2004, 14). In Costa Rica, Banco Popular is a bank that is worker-owned and -controlled. The bank's collective "Assembly of Workers of the Popular Bank and Communal Development" governs its operations and ensures that the bank's mission to protect the economic welfare of its workers, and betterment of the working environment are met (Marois 2013, 13). However, the worker control initiatives may sometimes be less effective in securing broader societal objectives such as ensuring environmental sustainability (Cumbers 2014, 24).

A third example of democratic management is user cooperatives. User cooperatives can be defined as enterprises owned by their customers and managed democratically for their benefit. User cooperatives are oriented toward service quality, accessibility, and accountability, rather than pecuniary profit. As such, incentives are structured towards cost minimization for a given service quality, rather than profit maximization for a given level of cost minimization (Kay, Ramsay and Hernat 1996). The user cooperative SAGUAPAC (Cooperativa de Servicios Publicos Santa Cruz Ltd.), for example, has proved successful in delivering clean water in the Bolivian city of Santa Cruz since 1979 (TNI 2004, 14). All the 96,000 customers living in the nine water districts of Santa Cruz are members of the cooperative and have the right to vote in the cooperative's

General Assembly of Delegates. The assembly elects part of the administrative board and the supervisory board. The assembly is also vested with power to appoint and fire a general manager (Lobina and Hall 2000, 50). As part of its social commitment, the cooperative charges a subsidized rate for the first 15 cubic meters of water consumed by a household each month, and those customers who fail to pay are not disconnected (TNI 2004, 15). Despite successes in many criteria, user cooperatives may suffer from unwillingness to undertake costly long-term investments, and cost minimization may sometimes come at the cost of working conditions, wages, and other worker's benefits (e.g., the quality of the workplace) (Bakker 2008, 242–243).

Our final example of democratic control is the hybrid organizations that include local communities, workers' and sometimes users' cooperatives in the ownership and management mix. For example, the municipality of Cape Town, in South Africa, has extended proper water services to the previously neglected black townships through the implementation of a participatory restructuring exercise, which has included vital inputs from user groups and the local trade unions (Lobina and Hall 2000, 51). In another interesting case, the municipality of Ovacık, in Turkey, has established a hybrid organization in league with local farmers and beekepers. This engages in not only agricultural production, but also marketing activities such as product development and distribution. The local communal assembly takes most of the decisions regarding the venture and a local community commission informs the community of the organization's income and expenses. The body provides jobs for 50 families in the local areas, and all the profits are used to fund grants to students in hardship.[7] The main difficulty for hybrid organizations lies in ensuring the sustainability of solidarity among the various stakeholders.

Table 22 outlines a set of normative criteria for evaluating the substantiality of alternatives to privatization. No single example excels in all the criteria listed above, and what may be seen as crucial in one case, may be less crucial in another (McDonald 2015, 128). Nevertheless, whatever example is chosen (we have seen that there are many different combinations), the aspiration should favour institutionalizing democratic control mechanisms in which the capacity of local communities, workers and users is enhanced, and should involve decision-making and management that is expanded for the fulfilment of the

---

7   "Fatih Maçoğlu: İstanbul'da Komünist bal satışına başladık" [Fatih Maçoğlu: We started selling communist honey in Istanbul], *Evrensel,* 15 October 2017; "Tunceli'nin Ovacık İlçesinde Komünist Partili Belediye'nin Organik Ürünleri Türkiye Pazarında" [Organic products from the Communisty Party's municipality of Ovacık are on the Turkish market], *Haberler.Com,* 19 October 2017.

TABLE 22    Normative criteria for evaluating the substantive nature of alternatives to privatization

| | |
|---|---|
| Participation | – Is the depth and scope of participation adequate (i.e., what is open to participation, and is it sufficient for policy making, budget decisions, day-to-day operations, etc.)? |
| | – Is participation equitable in terms of gender, race, and income? |
| Access | – Is physical service delivery accessible for the different social groups (e.g., location, gender, class)? |
| | – Is the quality of service equitable for the different social groups? |
| | – Are the pricing systems (e.g., tariff structures) fair? |
| Efficiency | – Is the service delivered in a financially efficient manner? |
| | – Do efficiency gains undermine other potentially positive outcomes (e.g., affordability, working conditions)? |
| | – Is adequate investment being made in long-term maintenance? |
| Sustainability | – Are there adequate financial resources available to ensure a successful continuity of the service? |
| | – Is there sufficient political support for the service entity at the different levels of government? |
| | – Is the service using natural resources in a sustainable way? |
| Social commitment | Does the service involve a commitment to "societal objectives", including democracy and community development? |
| Accountability | – Are the service providers accountable to the end-users? |
| | – Are the service providers responsive to, and dealing with, the concerns and comments of the end-users? |
| Transparency | – Does the public understand the operational mandates of the service provider? |
| | – Does the public have regular access to data about policy decisions and the capital-operating budgets of the service deliverer? |
| Quality of the workplace | – Do front-line workers participate in the management or policymaking of the service? |
| | – Do workers receive a fair salary and benefits? |
| | – Do workers feel 'empowered'? |
| Solidarity | – Does the service help build solidarity between different sectors of society workers, community, and end-users? |

SOURCE: MCDONALD (2015).

general social needs of the populace (Cumbers 2014, 20). Democratic control and social commitment lie at the core (or are interconnected with) of all the criteria listed above, and thus are the basis for substantive progressive alternatives to privatization. For example, the criteria for participation, accountability, transparency, quality of the workplace and solidarity include elements of democratic control in different tones and degrees.

It is difficult to generalize and replicate these democratic examples in every low- and middle-income country because local conditions and demands vary so greatly. Historical specificity, ideological superstructure, institutional framework, and state capacities are some of the factors that can enable, or prevent, the success of democratic alternative in each context (McDonald 2015, 128). Geographically, the largest number of successful examples of the democratic alternatives mentioned in this article comes from Latin America. This should come as no surprise, since the region has been subject to a wider range of experimentation with socialism, active social citizenship, and greater state capacity to deliver, as well as institutional resilience (Grugel and Riggirozzi 2012, 16). If one wonders why Costa Rica is so good at nurturing successful alternatives, one must take into account the deeprooted social democratic nature of Costa Rican society, in combination with the ingrained principles of equity and social justice that guide the functioning governmental agencies. These are ideals that have been consistently defended by broad sectors of Costa Rican society (Chavez 2013, 5–6).

In formulating and defending these democratic alternatives, we should also be aware of the huge challenges that lie before them. As Ben Fine and David Hall remind us, the systemic grip of the capitalist market poses a serious challenge to any democratic alternatives (2012, 45). The capitalist market applies great pressure on nascent democratic alternatives to force them to compete and be profit oriented. For example, the Mondragon Cooperative, and a number of contemporary examples of commons initiatives and fair-exchange movements, have been unable to resist such pressures from the capitalist market, and so have lost most of their original democratic ideals over time (Errasti, Bretos and Nunez 2017).

Maintaining democratic ideals in alternative experiments under these conditions requires high levels of political commitment from activits and active reliance on broad popular movements (Hahnel 2016; Poulantzas 1978). Democratic alternatives might also do well to reject the concept of "partial citizenship", which many residents of developing countries experience daily, and which reproduces the inequitable power relations and resource allocation that exist within these communities (Bakker 2008, 246). For instance, they are sometimes unfriendly to member of specific ethnic groups or immigrants

(New Politics Research Project 2016, 21). One possible way of dealing with this is to shift attention from identity to class politics.


## 3      The Question of Strategy: How to Construct and Defend a Substantial Alternative?

A democratic and socially committed alternative to privatization is possible. Indeed, given the failures in privatizations and serious problems with at least two other alternatives to privatization (traditional state ownership and corporatization), construction of a democratic and socially committed alternative to privatization is an urgent necessity. Given that the systemic grip of capitalism favours the private over the public sector (Fine and Hall 2012, 46, 61), the construction and defense of a democratic and socially committed alternative to privatization can probably only be achieved by means of a strategic and long-term vision. This requires insistence on the primary of politics – rather than waiting for economic crises and failures of privatization – alongside intermediate objectives and conjunctural tactics and proposals (Albo 2012b, 21). In what follows, I will now elaborate two concrete strategies aimed at creating a democratic and socially committed alternative to privatization.[8]


### 3.1      *Building Alliances*
The starting point in constructing and defending a democratic and socially committed alternative to privatization is what Marta Harnecker refers to as "the creation of an alternate social bloc" (2016a, 23). To do this, it is fundamental that we build alliances and fronts among all those with an interest and belief in democratic and socially committed public assets: labour unions, public enterprise workers, the new working class, users of the services, and local community representatives. Each actor needs to frame the struggle against privatization, and everyone's issue must become key to resistance: workers defending jobs and working conditions, users of service seeking to improve the level and quality of service provision, and local community representatives seeking to make services available to different social groups in a sustainable way (Albo 2012b, 20). However, the process of convergence is likely to be messy, since there are conflicting demands being made by diverse actors. This

---

8    In doing this, I am inspired by Poulantzas' account of a strategy towards democratic socialism which is based on the articulation of forces within and outside of the state (Poulantzas 1978, 251–265).

necessarily entails a certain degree of compromise on the part of the actors, which will result in concessions made by each.

For a start, labour unions must agree to develop a wider societal dimension to sustain solidarity with the new working class of informal workers, migrant workers, the rural poor, and dispossessed people (Chang 2015, 190). These divergent elements of the new working class are important because they have been active participants in struggles for alternatives in different parts of the world (Spronk 2007, 8). TEKEL – the Turkish state monopoly of tobacco and alcohol – witnessed worker resistance to privatization in the early months of 2010, which can be seen, in this sense, as an important example showing that articulating differing labour practices in a common struggle is possible and effective when done properly (Ercan and Oğuz 2015, 130). The site of TEKEL workers' resistance, a "tent city", became, in a short time, the hub for solidarity among organized, unorganized, collective, and individual initiatives generated in every part of Turkey (Özuğurlu 2011, 181).[9]

It has become increasingly clear that the unions, which are based on the concept of a solid/fixed/coherent working class, can no longer act on their own within the context of the fragmented labour relations and employment conditions prevalent in these neoliberal times (Chang 2015, 190). If the unions were to act in opposition to privatization in the cause of defending the rights of their members in full and secure employment, without finding ways to work in parallel with the new working class, then advocates of privatization would only defeat them more easily.

The workers – both unionized and non-unionized new working class – could then break out of the traditional terrain of industrial conflict to deepen cooperation with the wider community (Herman et.al. 2012, 156). There are actual examples of this worker-community alliance. In the case of Turkish Telecom, two sectoral labour unions cooperated with KİGEM (the Center for the Development of Public Management) to legally challenge Turkish Telecom's privatization.[10] In another interesting case, Valle del Cauca (Colombia), two public sector unions, and the members of a community-run aqueduct project built a worker-local community alliance to strengthen autonomous community water management in the area (Dumontier, Spronk and Murray 2016, 23–24).

---

9    Although the TEKEL resistance was an important example, it shouldn't be generalized. Organized labor in Turkey is far from establishing alliances with the non-unionized new working class. First, the unions still fail to develop a wider societal dimension. Second, the AKP government's charitable distributions and populist social aid networks have recruited much support from the new working class.

10   "Telekom'da kirli oyun" [Dirty game in Turk Telekom], *Evrensel,* June 28, 2001.

The process of building alliances cannot be completed without inclusion of the users of the services. To include users, the workers and local community organizations should choose to develop specific methods to enable them to collaborate with users, in the formulation of strategies opposing privatization or in the construction of public services that can be managed in a democratic and truly common way (Wainwright 2013, 6). For example, workers could choose to contest the privatization of public assets via strikes, but these stop-pages often have negative effects on service users and thus transform the latter into avid supporters of privatization. Rather, workers could choose to contest privatization via new and innovative strategies that combine worker and user interests. The new forms of service disruption in public hospitals are possible models. For example, the opening of "free clinics", rather than "occupied clin-ics", could ensure that there are no division of interest between the unions and service users.[11]

Despite a history of tension between workers and service users, when they work together effectively the results can be influential. One important exam-ple is the cooperation between workers in the health sector and users of the services in Malaysia. The Malaysia Citizens' Health Initative (CHI), which is comprised of NGOs, consumer organizations, and several key health trade unions, played an important role in the campaign to stop hospital privatiza-tions and to promote greater community involvement in matters of health pol-icy (Lethbridge 2004, 234–238).

At this point you might think that building alliances among workers, users, and a local community to construct and defend a substantial alternative to pri-vatization seems to be a rather difficult and time-consuming process, as allince members (with varying background and interests) have to agree on a common platform, and then develop some level of mutual trust (Herman et.al. 2012, 159). Yet, building these alliances is not impossible. One must look at how different actors (e.g., IFIs, the USA, the EU, the neoliberal state elites, national capi-tal, internationalized capital, inward-oriented companies, outward-oriented companies, small-scale producers, and large-scale producers) developed their capacity to compromise, and to establish global and national alliances to pro-moting privatization.

The Turkish privatization experience is more than illustrative in this respect. Although privatization has been on Turkey's policy agenda since 1984, it only became the case after more than 15 contested years and much political

---

11    "The Privatisation and Internationalisation of Public Services in a Time of Austerity," andresbieler.blogspot.com, March 15, 2013.

posturing. It was only when the competing interests of the various fractions of capital (domestic vs. national capital; Anatolian vs. Istanbul-based; small and medium-sized enterprises vs. the holding groups) and state elites (neoliberal state elites vs. national interest-oriented state elites) were aligned in the post-2001 crisis era that privatization was launched in Turkey. Given how difficult it was to promote and achieve privatization, the construction and defense of substantial alternative to privatization will require a combination of factors on a similar scale of power and influence. Only a direct and combined political confrontation by the worker-user-local community alliance will lead to formation of a substantial democratic alternative, in a manner like what the divided proponents of privatization managed to achieve.

### 3.2    *Making the State an Operationally Contested Space/Process*

While building the worker-user-local community alliance is vital, it does not guarantee that the democratic and socially committed alternative will emerge solely in a bottom-up way. This is because the conditions necessary to construct and defend a democratic and socially committed alternative involve heavy doses of state policy and intervention, in combination with applicable regulations and laws (Cumbers 2016, 328). Construction of a democratic and socially committed alternative thus requires the alliance to act within the state, and to develop an influence that promotes their interests, identities, and values, and weakens the proponents of privatization.

As argued elsewhere, despite its origins and evolution, the state needs not be treated as the exclusive instrument of capital, nor as a neutral stakeholder that acts above society in its commitment to the common good. Instead, a Poulantzian understanding of the state may be described, which sees the state as a condensation of social class relations (Poulantzas 1978, 123). Poulantzas reminds us that capitalist states are relational formations, and, as such, they comprise and constitute historically specific material condensation and institutionalizion of politico-ideological relations that are malleable but also momentarily fixed and formative (Poulantzas 1978, 129).

The state is the heart of the exercise of political power, structured in a particular way, where different social and political forces struggle (Poulantzas 1978, 258). Yet the capitalist state is not neutral. Rather, it constitutes a strategic terrain that is equipped with structural selectivity and unequal representation, which is why different social forces have different degrees of access to it (Brand and Heigl 2011, 248). The dominant forces (e.g., the capitalist class) by and large structurally and strategically dominate the state, albeit not completely. For this reason, subaltern forces and actors are also found within the state, but in an asymmetrical relationship (Brand 2013, 108).

Based on this conception, a worker-user-local community alliance is not seen as being simply "against", or "outside", the state, since it is internal to social class relations and therefore is mediated by the state, which is itself a specific field of power and struggle (New Politics Research Project 2016, 16). Indeed, the strategic guide for the alliance could be the operational use of the state, up to certain extent, as a contested space through which engagement in efforts countering privatization and promoting democratic alternatives should be directed. It is important to note that at some point "creating more space to act within the state" must give way to "a ruptural change", as a result of which the popular masses transform state power and achieve political hegemony within the strategic terrain of the state (Poulantzas 1978). Below are some concrete strategies, which were mainly collected from Turkish situations, for worker-user-local community alliance to operate within their state apparatuses.

First, it is possible for an alliance to use existing state capacities to block privatization and construct a democratic alternative. For example, an alliance could seekt to oppose privatization and avert the threat of privatization-induced job losses by recourse to labor laws and judicial institutions (Brand and Heigl 2011, 257). A popular alliance may also refer to the universal nature of the welfare state, notions of public interest, and the progressive potential of state-led redistributive strategies in defence of SOEs, while at the same time fostering democratic advance (New Politics Research Project 2016, 7; Bakker 2008, 248; Albo 1993, 32). An important instance of this was the legal battle mounted by the Petrol-İş, to prevent privatization of Tüpraş (See Chapter 4). As Petrol-İş Central Committee Member, İbrahim Doğangül, stated in a personal interview, the union was well aware of the fact that the Turkish judiciary, at that time, still reflected the logic of accumulation, based on notions of public and national interest that could potentially be used against the market logic of privatization.[12]

There is also a space for electoral politics to be used as part of a strategy of co-opting existing state capacities. In this respect, popular consultation and/or plebiscites can be very interesting spaces allowing a worker-user-local community alliance to mobilize behind the single concrete task of convincing many people, who previously may not have known how to contribute to building a better world. A significant example of this was the referendum held in Uruguay in 2003 over whether to repeal or ratify a law paving the way for privatization of the state oil company, ANCAP. The vote to reject prevailed by a wide margin -62.02% of the vote (Harnecker 2016a, 23).

---

12    Interview with Ibrahim Doğangül, Petrol-İş Central Committee Member, October 12, 2012.

Second, in addition to using the state's extant capacities, there is the possibility of working towards a multi-level strategy of state transformation by building effective interconnetions between the state apparatus and the worker-user-local community alliance. This is a political strategy designed to make the state more public and thus better able to defend the public interest. Such an action would: 1) institutionalize and expand the networks of resistance (i.e., specific branches of the state in which the masses may attain relevant positions) within the institutional framework of the state; 2) establish innovative ways of integrating the resistance to privatization and foster the development of coherent democratic alternatives using political parties.

Let me go into greater detail. Worker-user-local community representatives are often present in the state and may exist in its institutional structure in specific roles, so forming "centers of resistance" (Poulantzas 1978, 141–142). However, there is divergent structural selectiveness in different sectors of the state, which is why, historically speaking, it has been easier for dominated classes' alliances to better access some of the apparatuses (e.g., schools, the army, the elected institutions), than others (e.g., the police, the judiciary, the economic administration). The popular alliance not only has to better institutionalize its vision, interests, and presence in those apparatuses to which it already has access; it has also to try and expand the "centers of resistance" within the state so as to influence as many apparatuses as possible (Brand and Heigl 2011, 251). This is difficult, but not impossible. If an alliance formulates and propagates alternative projects (which are possible, already existing, or under construction) that support welfare spending and development planning, while changing the concepts and practices of state institutions so that they embody public and national interest, it would be possible to establish connections with, and within, the state authorities and apparatuses, which also exhibit an opacity and resistance of their own to privatization.

One actual example of this is the case of KİGEM – the Center for the Development of Public Management – in Turkey. KİGEM was established in 1994 through the cooperation of labour unions, leftist academics, and retired state bureaucrats (especially from judiciary), in effort to institutionalize the capacities of the anti-privatization camp and to stop privatizations.[13] KİGEM built its opposition to privatization on the protection of public interest, and on preservation of Parliament's ultimate authority vis-à-vis the executive. It

---

13    Personal interview with İzzettin Önder, Professor of Economics at İstanbul University,
       İstanbul Representative of KİGEM, February 5, 2013.

opposed privatization through the judiciary by establishing links with those judges on the benches of the Constitutional Court that tended to oppose neo-liberalism and privatization, and who seemed to base their rulings on public interest and unity of the state (Oğuz 2008, 176). Thanks to the efforts of KİGEM, the Constitutional Court emerged as the key institution voicing the concerns of the Turkish anti-privatization camp – i.e., the Constitutional Court turned into a "center of resistance". In just one example, following the appeal by KİGEM, the Constitutional Court blocked Türk Telekom's privatization several times between 1993 and 2000.

Worker-user-local community alliances also need to come up with innovative ways of integrating the resistance to privatization and the development of coherent democratic alternatives into political parties. It is true that there have been some cases in which specific political parties have supported campaigns against privatization. These include the fact that in the 1990s nearly every successful struggle against privatization in Turkey involved some elements of the opposition parties. For example, the DSP (Democratic Left Party), RP (Welfare Party) and MHP (Nationalist Action Party) exhibited strong resistance to the Türk Telekom privatization on the floor of the Turkish Grand National Assembly between 1994 and 2001 (Zaifer 2018). Moreover, the campaign against energy privatization in Australia was constructed explicitly around the alternative policies of the then opposition Australian Labor Party (Hall, Lobina and Motte 2005, 294).

However, there are cases in which campaigns have been unable to work with a political party from which support would logically have been expected (Albo 2012b, 5). Many social democratic parties and traditional labor parties have long since ceased to have a strong connection with the masses, and they all too often accept privatizations and marketizations – if not openly, then through negotiations behind closed doors (Herman et.al., 2012, 165). In Turkey, for example, the main opposition, the CHP (Republican People's Party), has been heavily influenced by the discourse of privatization, and consequently did little to stop the momentum of privatization that emerged during 2000s.[14] In South Africa, the governing African National Congress (ANC) has been instrumental in water privatizations (Hall, Lobina and Motte 2005).

These negative outcomes have led to a tendency within the popular alliances to dismiss political parties, an attitude that has not helped to overcome the weakness of such alliances (Harnecker 2016a, 16). However, the

---

14    Personal interview with Oğuz Oyan, CHP Parliamentarian, 2002–2015.

parties – especially when they are part of the government – are important actors in potentially exercising specific powers, including those redistributing finance, demanding higher public spending, making commitments to welfare, and defending public services. These are powers that could support the capacities of worker-user-community alliances in resisting privatization and transforming the management of public assets in a democratic and accountable direction (Wainwright 2012, 152). For these reasons, a new relationship between an alliance and progressive political parties would be useful. A progressive political party is one that respects principles of non-exploitation and has political independence vis-à-vis the politics of the dominant classes (Das 2017, 550–555).

The writings of Marta Harnecker (2016a; 2016b) and Hilary Wainwright (2012) offer important insights into the establishment of these new relationships. First, the relationship between a worker-user-community alliance and a progressive political party would be one of mutual collaboration, which in time leads to a profound transformation of the party into an instrument capable for cohering the many expressions of the different actors in the anti-privatization resistance and struggle (Harnecker 2016b). Second, a new kind of party would effectively serve within a framework of commitment (shared values and goals) that has been developed with the participation of wider network of anti-privatization struggles and movements, which also include worker-user-community alliances. The forms of accountability and transparency laid out for their representatives in implementing the framework of such a commitment would also be central to the organizational character of the party. There must be a structure in which the people are always connected to the party, even if they are not members of the party, and this must enable criticism of the party and open it to new experiences (Wainwright 2012, 155–156). Third, a new kind of party would require specific organizationl forms (e.g., mechanisms that involve elected representatives not as leaders, but as fellow citizens) countering pressures that normally draw delegates into the flytrap of parliamentary politics, with all its tendencies to create a separate, elite, political class (Wainwright 2012, 155–156). This would enable the party to continue open up the state to anti-privatization struggles and strengthen organized links to society. In short, even after the disappointment of the Syriza experiment in Greece (and to some extent Labour Party experience in the UK), I believe that dismissing the idea of working with political parties is not the way forward. Relatively little has still been done in finding innovative ways to transform political parties such that it would be possible to integrate them into the anti-privatization struggles.

## 4    Conclusion

The Turkish case had critical implications for privatization processes in other late developing countries. One important implication of this case is that privatization is multi-dimensional, variegated, territorially specific, and class-based project that involves many issues, a lot of preparation and multiple work-streams. As such, privatization cannot be simply explained by taking either institutions or external pressure or political struggles as autonomous factors in themselves. Privatization must be studied as a dynamic totality – a logical construct that refers to the way the whole is present through internal relations in each of its parts (i.e., contemporary capitalism, state, power bloc, domestic capital accumulation) (Ollman 1993). Another implication of Turkish case is that the costs of privatization (both in the form of divestiture and PPP) fall disproportionately onto popular and labouring classes as well as the natural environment of the entire country.

State ownership, corporatization, and democratic control constitute three potential alternatives to the privatization. Through the study of these alternatives in several historical settings, including Turkey, the UK, and several Latin American countries, it is unlikely that we can construct a substantive progressive alternative to privatization without promoting greater democratic control and a growth in social-environmental commitment of public assets. Working squarely within the view that the experience of contesting capitalist power within capitalist societies is crucial for building the capacity to transcend capitalism as such, the chapter calls for a sophisticated, non-binary approach to combining various arenas (inside the state; outside the state) in which democratic control may be built. The construction of a substantial alternative to privatization based on democratic control would therefore promote the welfare and development of the popular and laboring classes.

# TÜSİAD-based Conglomerates

| Conglomerate | Revenue (2002–2018) | Input supplier and lender role: Indicators | Direct involvement in privatization |
|---|---|---|---|
| *Koç Holding*<br>Founded in 1926 by Vehbi Koç. Known as the largest industrial and services group in Turkey in terms of revenues, exports, and number of employees. Focuses on four main industries as energy (Tüpraş), finance (Yapı Kredi), consumer durables, and automotive.<br><br>Vehbi Koç is one of the twelve founders of TÜSİAD. Mustafa Koç served as the chairman for the High Advisory Council of TÜSİAD. | 2002: $9bn<br>2009: $29bn<br>2018: $30bn | Asphalt/Bitumen Sales of Tüpraş:<br>2009: 1.99mn tons<br>2018: 2.93mn tons<br>Jet Fuel Domestic Sales of Tüpraş:<br>2009: 2.66mn tons<br>2018: 4.86mn tons<br>Loans of Yapı Kredi Bank:<br>2009: $26bn<br>2018: $58bn | 1  Secured the tender for Tüpraş privatization in 2005 for a price of $4.1 billion.<br>2  Established a joint venture with THY to operate in the field of fuel storage and refueling of aircrafts in 2009, which significantly increased Tüpraş's fuel sales.<br>3  Provided (Yapı Kredi Bank) $800 million debt finance for Gebze–Orhangazi–İzmir Motorway PPP Project in 2013.<br>4  Was awarded a 30-year concession to operate Fenerbahçe and Kalamış marinas for the sum of $664 million in 2014.<br>5  Took over Menzelet and Kılavuzlu (178-MW) Hydro Electric Power Plants (HEPPs) from privatization portfolio in 2017 with a price of $357 million.<br>6  Provided (Yapı Kredi) $115 million debt finance for Dardanelles Bridge PPP Project in 2018. |

| Conglomerate | Revenue (2002–2018) | Input supplier and lender role: Indicators | Direct involvement in privatization |
| --- | --- | --- | --- |
| *Sabancı Holding* Established in the late 1920s by Sabancı family as a cotton trading company. Known to be the second largest conglomerate in Turkey. Primary activities are in financial services (Akbank), energy (Enerjisa), cement (Akçansa, Çimsa), retail and industrial sectors. Sakıp Sabancı is one of the twelve founders of TÜSİAD. Ömer Sabancı elected as the chairman of the TÜSİAD (2004–2007). | 2003: $7.2bn 2009: $12.1bn 2018: $16bn | Cement and Clinker Sales of Akçansa: 2009: 6.5mn tons 2018: 7.1mn tons Cement and Clinker Sales of Çimsa: 2009: 5.8mn tons 2018: 6.3mn tons Loans of Akbank: 2009: $29bn 2018: $56bn | 1 Won Başkent Electricity Distribution (ED) privatization tender with $1.2bn in 2008. 2 Completed Dağ Pazarı (39-MW) and Bares (142-MW) Wind Power Plants (WPPs) with BOO method in 2012. 3 Constructed Menge (89-MW) HEP with BOT method in 2012. 4 Won Istanbul Anatolian Side ED ($1.22bn) and Toroslar Electricity ED ($1.72bn) privatization tenders in 2013. 5 Put Tufanbeyli (450-MW) Thermal Power Plant (TPP) into operation with BOO method in 2016. 6 Succeeded in the wind power capacity auctions held by TEİAŞ with the Erciyes WPP project (65-MW) in 2017. 7 Provided concrete and cement for the Dardanelles Bridge and Northern Marmara PPP Projects between 2013 and 2018. 8 Provided $800 million loan for Gebze–Orhangazi–İzmir Motorway PPP Project in 2013. |

| Conglomerate | Revenue (2002–2018) | Input supplier and lender role: Indicators | Direct involvement in privatization |
|---|---|---|---|
| *Borusan Holding* Began in 1944 as a trading firm involved in iron-steel trade and exportation of agricultural products. Later expanded into steel production, (Borçelik, Borusan Mannesmann), distributorship (Borusan Caterpillar) logistics and energy (Borusan EnBW). Today with nearly 11,000 employees, Borusan operates in 12 countries over 3 continents. The founder and honorary chairperson, Asım Kocabıyık, worked on the TÜSİAD Board for 15 years. | 2002: $1.0bn 2009: $3.0bn 2018: $4.8bn | Pipe Sales of Bor. Mannesmann: 2009: 546k tons 2018: 833k tons Flat Steel Sales of Borçelik: 2009: 1.0mn tons 2018: 2.1mn tons Machinery and Power System Sales of Borusan Caterpillar: 2009: $406mn 2018: $964mn Installed Capacity of Bor. EnBW: 2009: 0 MW 2018: 505 MW | 1 Steel production companies of the holding – Mannesmann and Borçelik – played key roles in the supply chains of infrastructure, energy and health PPPs projects. 2 Won a tender for $420mn natural gas pipeline project, which consists of supplying 30% of the pipes for the 1,900km TANAP in 2014. 3 Sold nearly 200 heavy machines in Northern Marmara Highway PPP project in 2016. 4 Won the tender to supply 400 machines and after-sales service for the 3rd Airport PPP in 2017. 5 Supplied power systems and emergency generators to PPP-based city hospitals (e.g., Adana City Hospital, Yozgat City Hospital) in 2017 and 2018. 6 Became the second highest winner (395-MW) of the wind power capacity auctions held by TEİAS in June and December 2017. |

| Conglomerate | Revenue (2002–2018) | Input supplier and lender role: Indicators | Direct involvement in privatization |
|---|---|---|---|
| *Tekfen Holding* Founded in 1956 by Feyyaz Berker, Nihat Gökyiğit and Necati Akçağlılar as an engineering consulting and construction company. Its first assignment was the stabilization of roadway shoulders at 9 NATO airports built in various places around Turkey. Today conducts its operations through 40 companies, 12 subsidiaries and 19,180 employees in three main areas: contracting, agriindustry, and real estate development. Feyyaz Berker is one of the twelve founders of TÜSİAD. | 2003: $820mn 2009: $1.5bn 2018: $2.3bn | | 1  Acquired Samsun Fertilizer Plant (which controls 11% of Turkey's annual installed fertilizer production capacity) from privatization portfolio in 2005 ($44mn), which made Tekfen as Turkey's largest fertilizer producer. 2  Undertook the repair and enhancement of the 1,071km stretch of the Baku-Tbilisi-Ceyhan crude oil pipeline that falls within Turkey's borders between 2013 and 2016. The project brought $136mn. 3  Won the tender for the construction of the Afyonkarahisar-Uşak Section of the Ankara-İzmir Rapid Train project for TL879mn. 4  Secured a TL165 million contract with its foreign partner (American Parsons) to provide engineering and construction support for Dardanelles Bridge and Kınalı-Balıkesir Motorway PPP project in 2017. |

| Conglomerate | Revenue (2002–2018) | Input supplier and lender role: Indicators | Direct involvement in privatization |
|---|---|---|---|
| *Enka Holding*<br>Founded in 1957 by Şarık Tara as a contracting company. Entered the industrial market in 1973 with the establishment of Çimtaş Steel. Then expanded its contracting activities in Middle East and Russia. Today operates in engineering and construction, power generation, real estate investment and management as well as trading sectors with over 40,000 employees.<br>Şarık Tara is an old member of TÜSIAD. Current Chairman of the Board, Sinan Tara, is also a member. | 2004: $3.1bn<br>2009: $5.1bn<br>2018: $2.9bn[a] | Production Output (e.g., pressure vessels, structural steel, steel wind towers, tanks, generators, piping systems) of Çimtaş Steel:<br>2009: 35k tons<br>2019: 70k tons | 1 Selected as the subcontractor of IHI Japan on the İzmit Bay Crossing Suspension Bridge (Osmangazi Bridge) PPP Project in 2013. Çimtaş's scope covers 18k tons of tower blocks and 34k tons of suspended girder panels.<br>2 Fabricated and delivered 7,000 tons of wind towers for wind turbine manufacturers Nordex and Enercon in 2013, which supplied the winners of YEKA renewable energy auctions.<br>3 Performed the construction of Shoring Systems for TBM Launch and Receiving Structures of Eurasia Tunnel PPP Project between 2014 and 2016.<br>4 Awarded a contract for the fabrication and delivery of steel components for the 1915 Çanakkale Bridge PPP Project in 2018. The total weight of the components to be fabricated by Çimtaş is over 100k tons. |

| Conglomerate | Revenue (2002–2018) | Input supplier and lender role: Indicators | Direct involvement in privatization |
|---|---|---|---|
| *Anadolu Holding* Originally established in 1950 by the Yazıcı and Özilhan families. Principal business lines include beer (Efes) and soft drink (Coca-Cola), retail, automotive (Isuzu) and energy. Tuncay Özilhan, Chairman of Anadolu Holding, served as the Chairman of TÜSİAD from 2001 and 2003 and he is currently Chairman of its High Advisory Council. | 2003: $1.0bn 2009: $4.7bn 2018: $7.9bn | Automotive Sales of Anadolu Holding: 2009: $354mn 2018: $730mn[b] | 1 Constructed Aslancık Dam & Hydroelectric Power Plant (120-MW) in 2014. All generated electricity sold under Turkey's Renewable Energy Source Support Mechanism (YEKDEM). |
| *Eczacıbaşı Holding* Founded in 1942 by Nejat Eczacıbaşı as a pharmaceutical laboratory. Became a prominent Turkish industrial group with 44 companies and over 11,400 employees. Core sectors are building products (Vitra), consumer products (Selpak) and healthcare (Eczacıbaşı Pharmaceuticals Marketing). Nejat Eczacıbaşı is one of the founders of the TÜSİAD. | 2003: $1.7bn 2009: $2.5bn 2018: $3.0bn | The construction of healthcare campuses with PPP model and the increasing expansion of Turkish healthcare sector had positive impact on holding's growth in healthcare division. | Not interested in privatization opportunities in Turkey. International revenues made a critical contribution to holding's performance. In 2018, international revenues contributed 56 percent of holding's total revenue. |

| Conglomerate | Revenue (2002–2018) | Input supplier and lender role: Indicators | Direct involvement in privatization |
|---|---|---|---|
| *Akkök Holding*<br>Founded in 1952 by Raif Dinçkök as an industrial company, Akkök Holding ranks among the most well-established industrial groups in Turkey. The Group conducts operations in the fields of textiles, chemicals (Aksa, DowAksa), energy (Akenerji), and real estate, with 19 enterprises. Known to be Turkey's leading group in the chemicals industry. Ali Dinçkök, Ayça Dinçkök, Ömer Dinçkök and Raif Dinçkök are TÜSIAD members. | 2005: $1.0bn<br>2009: $2.1bn<br>2018: $2.8bn | Acyclic Fiber Sales of Aksa:<br>2009: $585mn<br>2018: $732mn<br>Installed Capacity of Akenerji:<br>2009: 496MW<br>2018: 1,224MW | 1  Publicly announced that it is willing to put particular emphasis on upcoming privatization opportunities in 2006.<br>2  AKCEZ, a consortium formed by Akkök, Akenerji, and CEZ Group, a Czech energy conglomerate wins the privatization tender of Sakarya Electricity Distribution with $600mn bid in 2008. This single procurement increased the Holding's combined net sales by 33% (from $1.25bn in 2008 to $2.1bn in 2009). |
| *Zorlu Holding*<br>Founded in 1953 by Mehmet Zorlu as a textile company in Denizli. Later expanded into energy and electronics businesses in 1990s. Today Zorlu Holding is a major conglomerate with over 60 companies in textiles, consumer electronics (Vestel), energy (Zorlu Energy), real estate, and mining sectors. | 2002: $2.3bn<br>2009: $4.2bn<br>2018: $5.3bn | Installed Capacity of Zorlu Energy Group:<br>2009: 660 MW<br>2018: 1,303 MW<br>Total Sales Revenue of Vestel:<br>2009: $3.0bn<br>2018: $3.3bn | 1  Obtained natural gas distribution license tenders and begins providing natural gas distribution services in Gaziantep and Trakya regions in 2006.<br>2  Purchased the state land in İstanbul (Zincirlikuyu) from privatization portfolio with a bid of $800 million in 2008. Zorlu Centre, which has built on this purchased land, became the main project of Zorlu Real Estate Group. |

| Conglomerate | Revenue (2002–2018) | Input supplier and lender role: Indicators | Direct involvement in privatization |
|---|---|---|---|
| Ahmet Nazif Zorlu, Olgun Zorlu, Şule Zorlu and Mehmet Emre Zorlu are TÜSİAD members. | | | 3 Won the privatization tender for ADÜAŞ, which includes nine power plants with a total installed capacity of 141-MW, with a bid of $510 million in 2008. |
| | | | 4 Took over the Osmangazi Electricity Distribution Region (that is bought in 2010 by Turkey's Yıldızlar Holding from privatization portfolio) for $360 million and entered electricity distribution business in 2017. |
| *Akfen Holding* Established in 1976 as an industrial goods producing company. Upon establishment of Akfen Construction in 1986, became one of the most important infrastructure holdings in Turkey. Public construction tenders, BOT contracts, and privatization tenders constitute a major part of holding's activities. Honorary President of Akfen Holding, Hamdi Akın, is active TÜSİAD member. Pelin Akın, Nuri Akın and Selim Akın are also TÜSİAD members. | 2006: $425mn 2009: $686mn 2018: $1.3bn | Installed Capacity of Akfen Energy Group: 2010: 6 MW 2018: 302 MW | 1 Won the BOT tender for the İstanbul Atatürk Airport Int. Terminal ($305mn) with an operation period of 7 years in 1997. 2 Won the tender for the privatization of vehicle inspection stations with a bid of $613mn in 2005. 3 Won the privatization tender of Mersin Port with a bid of $755mn in 2005. 4 Won the BOT tender for İzmir Adnan Menderes Airport Int. Terminal with an investment value of $1.29bn in 2005. 5 Won the lease contract for İstanbul Atatürk Airport International Terminal with a price of $2.5bn in 2005. |

| Conglomerate | Revenue (2002–2018) | Input supplier and lender role: Indicators | Direct involvement in privatization |
|---|---|---|---|
| | | | 6 Won the tender for the privatization of Istanbul Sea Ferries with a bid of $86mn in 2011. |
| | | | 7 Purchased a plot of land in Mersin from privatization portfolio for a price of TL40 million in 2011. |
| | | | 8 Won the tender for Isparta City Hospital PPP project with $264mn in 2013. |
| | | | 9 Won the tender for Tekirdağ ($252mn) and Eskişehir ($461mn) City Hospital PPP projects in 2014. |
| *GAMA Holding* Founded in 1959 by three engineering graduates (e.g., Erol Üçer) as a construction company. With its multiple shareholder structure, holding later entered industry, infrastructure (mostly BOT), and energy sectors. Erol Üçer elected as the TÜSİAD member of supervisory board in 2003. Hakan Özman, Vice Chairman of GAMA, is also a member of TÜSİAD. | 2002: $400mn 2009: $1.3bn 2018: $2.0bn | | 1 Won 672-MW Birecik HEPP BOT tender with its foreign partners (Philipp Holzmann of Germany, Strabag of Austria) in 1995. The project cost nearly $1bn. |
| | | | 2 Completed İzmit Water Supply Project ($89mn) with BOT model in 1999. |
| | | | 3 Won the tender for İzmir Bayraklı City Hospital PPP project ($614mn) with its partners (Türkerler Holding and General Electric) in 2014. |
| | | | 4 Won the tender for Kocaeli City Hospital PPP project ($396mn) with its partners (Türkerler Holding and General Electric) in 2014. |

| Conglomerate | Revenue (2002–2018) | Input supplier and lender role: Indicators | Direct involvement in privatization |
| --- | --- | --- | --- |
| *Rönesans Holding* Founded by Erman Ilıcaklı in Russia in 1993. Launched its first project in Turkey in 2004 and expanded significantly within a short period of time. Currently operating in construction, real estate development, energy, and healthcare sectors. Erman Ilıcaklı was the TÜSİAD vice president between 2012 and 2014. İpek Ilıcaklı Kayaalp is also a member of TÜSİAD. | 2005: $300mn 2009: $1bn 2018: $5bn | Installed Capacity of Rönesans Energy: 2009: 16MW 2018: 166MW | 5 Won the tender for the privatization of Karacaören 1 and Karacaören 2 HEPPs (36-MW) with a bid of $178mn in 2016. 1 Won Adana City Hospital PPP project tender with $683mn bid in 2013. 2 Won Elazığ Fethi Sekin City Hospital PPP project tender with $390mn bid in 2014. 3 Won Bursa City Hospital PPP project tender with $399mn bid in 2015. 4 Won Yozgat City Hospital PPP project tender with $184mn bid in 2015. 5 Won Başakşehir Çam & Sakura City Hospital PPP project tender with $1.55bn bid in 2016 6 Purchased 51-MW Şanlıurfa HEPP from privatization portfolio for a price of TL247mn in 2016. |

| Conglomerate | Revenue (2002–2018) | Input supplier and lender role: Indicators | Direct involvement in privatization |
|---|---|---|---|
| *STFA Group*<br>Established by two young civil engineers, Sezai Türkeş and Feyzi Akkaya, in 1938 as a construction company. Then entered construction equipment and energy sectors. Won several foreign construction tenders in Libya, Saudi Arabia, Egypt and Qatar since 1972. Currently, it operates in construction (STFA Construction), construction equipment (JCB), and energy (Enerya) sectors. Adnan Nas, Chairman of the Board of STFA Group, is an active member of TÜSİAD. | 2009: $700mn<br>2018: $1.3bn | As the largest construction equipment dealer in Turkey and the sole trader for JCB for Turkey since 1974, it benefited enormously from construction boom and accompanying PPP projects in Turkey during 2010s. | 1 Acquired (Enerya Enerji) gas distribution licence for 30 years in 2009. As of today, it is the second biggest natural gas distributor of Turkey with more than 1.2 million subscribers in a total of 11 cities.<br>2 Worked as the subcontractor for the Gebze-Orhangazi-İzmir Motorway (incl. Osmangazi Bridge) PPP project between 2012 and 2016. |
| *Alarko Holding*<br>Founded in 1954 by İshak Alaton and Üzeyir Garih as a limited company to operate in the fields of heating, air-conditioning, and cooling. | 2003: $180mn<br>2009: $800mn<br>2018: $913mn | Total Installed Capacity of Alarko Energy Group: 2009: 115MW | 1 Constructed Hasanlar (10MW) and Berdan (10MW) HEPPs with BOT model in 1991. Operated these plants for 20 years until 2011.<br>2 Constructed Tohma (12.5MW) HEPP with BOT model in 1998. Operated that plant for 20 years until 2018. |

| Conglomerate | Revenue (2002–2018) | Input supplier and lender role: Indicators | Direct involvement in privatization |
|---|---|---|---|
| Today, the company is one of the leading industrial enterprises with operations in 5 different fields of activity: contracting, energy (Altek), industry (Alarko Carrier), tourism, and real estate. Leyla Alaton is a member of TÜSİAD. | 2018: 1,539MW | Alarko Carrier benefited from the growing heating, ventilating and air conditioning (HVAC) market in Turkey in the mid- and late 2010s especially with the implementation of PPP Hospital Projects. | 3  Acquired Meram Electricity Distribution from a privatization tender (with Cengiz Holding) in 2009 by paying $440mn. 4  Provided Alarko Carrier liquid chillers, air-cooled chillers and cooling towers to several city hospital PPP projects (including Ankara Bilkent and Isparta City Hospitals) between 2012 and 2018. 5  Acquired Gönen HEP (10MW) from a privatization tender in 2018 by paying TL65mn. |

a  That reduction largely stems from the decreasing construction works in Enka's operating regions abroad – Middle East and Russia.
b  It is positively affected by the implementation of PPP projects in road transportation network.

# Islamic-Influenced and/or Anatolian Companies Having Close Relations with AKP-Erdoğan

| Conglomerate | Revenue (2002–2018) | Input supplier and lender role: Indicators | Direct involvement in privatization |
|---|---|---|---|
| *Cengiz Holding* Founded in 1987 as a construction company. Entered energy and mining sectors in 2000s through privatization tenders and PPP projects. Listed among world's 10 most privatization and PPP winning companies during 2010s. Today conducts its operations through 35 companies and 15,000 employees in three main areas: construction, energy, and mining, | 2012: $3bn 2018: $5bn | Installed Capacity of Cengiz Holding: 2018: 3,446MW | 1 Purchased Eti Bakır copper mine from privatization ($22mn) in 2004. 2 Secured the tender for Eti Aluminium plant privatization ($305mn) in 2005. 3 Won Meram Electricity Distribution (ED) privatization tender (with Alarko) with $440mn bid in 2009. 4 Won Çamlıbel ED privatization (with Kolin-Limak) with $258.5mn bid in 2010. 5 Won Uludağ ED privatization (with Kolin-Limak) with $940mn bid in 2010. 6 Won Akdeniz ED privatization (with Kolin-Limak) with $546mn bid in 2013. 7 Won Boğaziçi (İstanbul European Side) ED privatization tender (with Kolin and Limak) with $1.96bn bid in 2013. |

| Conglomerate | Revenue (2002–2018) | Input supplier and lender role: Indicators | Direct involvement in privatization |
|---|---|---|---|
| Mehmet Cengiz, Chairman of the Board of Directors, originates from the hometown of Tayyip Erdoğan. Known with his close relations to Erdoğan's government. | | | 8 Won Istanbul's Third Airport BOT tender (with Limak, Kolin, Mapa and Kalyon) in 2013. Each holds 20% of the shares of the consortium.<br><br>9 Won the tender for Kınalı-Odayeri and Kurtköy-Akyazı sections of Northern Marmara BOT tender (with Limak, Kolin, Kalyon) in 2016. |
| *Çalık Holding*<br>Established in 1981 by Ahmet Çalık as a textile company. Currently operates in energy, construction, mining, textile and media sectors across 22 countries.<br><br>Ahmet Çalık is one of the closest friends of Erdoğan. Newspaper, Sabah, and the channel, ATV, had been allies of Erdoğan since Çalık | 2003: $804mn<br>2009: $1.5bn<br>2018: 2.1bn | | 1 Won the privatization tender of Bursa Gas Distribution company for a price of $120mn in 2004.<br><br>2 Participated Türk Telekom and Tüpraş privatization tenders in 2005 but failed to win them.<br><br>3 Acquired Yeşilırmak ED from privatization portfolio with $44mn bid in 2010.<br><br>4 Purchased Aras ED (with Kiler Holding) from privatization portfolio with $128mn bid in 2013. |

| Conglomerate | Revenue (2002–2018) | Input supplier and lender role: Indicators | Direct involvement in privatization |
|---|---|---|---|
| Holding purchased them in 2008. Erdoğan's son in law, Berat Albayrak, was CEO of Çalık Holding until late 2013. Holding is also a founding member of MÜSİAD. | | | |
| *Limak Holding* Founded in 1976 in Ankara by Nihat Özdemir and Sezai Bacaksız as a construction company. Entered energy sector in the late 1990s and cement sector in the early 2000s. Heavily involved in privatizations and PPP-based infrastructure projects in the 2010s (one of the world's top 10 private sponsors of privatization-PPP projects). Currently operates in a wide range of sectors from construction to tourism, cement to infrastructure and energy. | 2005: $350mn 2009: $1bn 2018: $4.2bn | Installed Capacity of Limak Energy: 2012: 435Mw 2018: 3,000MW Cement Group Production of Limak: 2012: 7.0mn tons 2018: 9.2mn tons | 1 Bought alcoholic drink arm of Tekel in 2003 in privatization tender ($292mn). 2 Participated Erdemir and Petkim privatization tenders in 2005 and 2008 respectively but failed to win them. 3 Won Uludağ EDC and Çamlıbel EDC privatization tenders (with Kolin and Cengiz) for a total price of $1.2bn in 2010. 4 Acquired 36-years' operating rights of İskenderun Port from Turkish State Railways with a payment of $327mn in 2012. 5 Won Akdeniz EDC and Istanbul European Side EDC privatization tenders (with Cengiz and Kolin) for a total price of $2.5bn in 2013. 6 Purchased Hamitabat Power Plant in a privatization tender ($105mn) in 2013. |

| Conglomerate | Revenue (2002–2018) | Input supplier and lender role: Indicators | Direct involvement in privatization |
|---|---|---|---|
| Although Nihat Özdemir and Ebru Özdemir are members of TÜSİAD, they tend to stay away from upper echelons of the organization. However, they have long-standing and close personal ties to Erdoğan. | | | 7 Won Istanbul's Third Airport BOT tender (with Limak, Kolin, Mapa and Kalyon) in 2013. Each holds 20% of the shares of the consortium.<br>8 Acquired Yeniköy (420-MW) and Kemerköy (630-MW) TPPs (with İç İçtaş Holding) with a total price of $2.6bn in 2014.<br>9 Won the tender for Kurtköy-Akyazı sections of Northern Marmara BOT contract (with Cengiz) in 2016.<br>10 Won Dardanelles Bridge and Kınalı-Balıkesir Motorway BOT contract with SK Engineering, Daelim and Yapı Merkezi in 2017. |
| *İç İçtaş Holding*<br>Established in 1969 by İbrahim Çeçen as a construction company in Ağrı (then moved to Ankara). Carried out various construction projects in Turkey and abroad (mainly Middle East and Central Asia). Ankara-based holding | 2005: $250mn<br>2009: $500mn<br>2018: $2.2bn | Installed Capacity of İç İçtaş Holding:<br>2009: 274MW<br>2018: 1,450MW | 1 Purchased Tekel Bomonti land ($42mn) from the privatization portfolio and constructed one of the Europe's biggest hotels on it.<br>2 Won Trakya EDC privatization tender with $575mn in 2011.<br>3 Constructed Zafer Airport under $60mn PPP-based BOT contract in 2012.<br>4 Won the BOT contract for 114-km section of Northern Marmara Motorway that includes the Third Bosporus Bridge with an investment amount of $3.89bn in 2012 (with an Italian construction company Astaldi). |

| Conglomerate | Revenue (2002–2018) | Input supplier and lender role: Indicators | Direct involvement in privatization |
|---|---|---|---|
| entered energy, tourism and infrastructure sectors with privatization and PPP projects. Ibrahim Çeçen is a close friend of Erdogan. Holding is considered as one of the richest members of the Islamic-influenced capital in Turkey. | | | 5  Acquired Yeniköy (420-MW) and Kemerköy (630-MW) TPPs in a privatization tender (with Limak Holding) at a cost of $2.6bn in 2014. <br> 6  Won a tender to privatize Kadıncık 1 (70-MW) and Kadıncık 2 (56-MW) HEPPs at a cost of $300mn in 2016. <br> 7  Won the BOT contract for construction and operation of Menemen-Aliağa-Çandarlı Motorway (€392mn) in partnership with Astaldi in 2017. |
| *Kolin Group* Founded in 1977 by Koloğlu family as a construction company in Elazığ (then moved Ankara). Since 2003 the Group has done significant work in the energy, port management, mining, and tourism sectors (mostly through privatizations and PPPs) | 2005: $204mn <br> 2009: $707mn <br> 2018: $2.6bn | Installed Capacity: <br> 2009: 105MW <br> 2018: 1,100MW | 1  Purchased ESGAZ, a natural gas distribution company when it was privatized in 2003 ($43mn). <br> 2  Built Çanakkale Kolin Hotel with BOT model (and obtained operating licence for 49 years) in 2003. <br> 2  Acquired Dikili Port using 30-year BOT model in 2004. <br> 3  Acquired with a 29-year BOT to construct Çanakkale Kepez Port in 2004. <br> 4  Acquired Malatya Hekimhan Iron Mine from privatization in 2007. <br> 5  Acquired Sigacik Marina as a 23-year BOT model in 2007. |

| Conglomerate | Revenue (2002–2018) | Input supplier and lender role: Indicators | Direct involvement in privatization |
| --- | --- | --- | --- |
| Celal Kologlu, Board Member of Kolin Group, is the President of the Turkish Employers Association of Construction Industries. Turkey's former Ministry of Transport (2002–2016), former PM (2016–2018) and loyal Erdoğan supporter, Binali Yıldırım, is closely connected to the Sefine Shipyard of Kolin Group. | | | 6  3-Won Uludağ EDC and Çamlıbel EDC privatization tenders (with Limak and Cengiz) for a total price of $1.2bn in 2010.<br>7  Won Akdeniz EDC and Istanbul European Side EDC privatization tenders (with Cengiz and Limak) for a total price of $2.5bn in 2013.<br>8  Won Istanbul's Third Airport BOT tender (with Limak, Cengiz, Mapa and Kalyon) in 2013. Each holds 20% of the shares of the consortium.<br>9  Won the tender for Kınalı-Odayeri and Kurtköy-Akyazı sections of Northern Marmara BOT tender (with Limak, Cengiz, Kalyon) in 2016. |
| *Nurol Holding*<br>Founded in 1966 by Çarmıklı family as a construction company. Today Ankara-based company is highly active in building, public works, energy and tourism, and a pioneer in the field of Turkish defence sector. | 2006: $536mn<br>2009: $590mn<br>2018: $1.2bn | | 1  Constructed Bosporus Tube Tunnel Crossing (with its partners) for Ministry of Transport between 2004 and 2013 at a cost of $1.3bn.<br>2  Acquired operating rights of Göksu HEPP with installed capacity of 11MW through privatization for 49 years in 2013 with a price of $57.5mn. |

| Conglomerate | Revenue (2002–2018) | Input supplier and lender role: Indicators | Direct involvement in privatization |
|---|---|---|---|
| Its arms business focuses on armoured vehicles and includes a joint venture with British arms company BAE Systems. The company is still a TÜSİAD member. Çarmıklı family also formed personal connections with the key AKP officials, as evidenced in 2012 by the presence of the then Minister of Economy and the Mayor of Ankara at the wedding of the son of Erol Çarmıklı. | | | 3  Won Gebze-Orhangazi-İzmir Motorway (including Osmangazi Bridge) BOT tender (with Makyol Holding, Özaltın Construction, Göçay Construction, Yüksel Holding, and Astaldi Construction) in 2009. The Turkish-Italian consortium was awarded a 22-year and 4-month BOT contract. |
| *Kalyon Holding* Founded in 1974 in Gaziantep by brothers Hasan Kalyoncu and Cemal Kalyoncu as a construction company. Today operates in construction, energy and infrastructure sectors. | 2010: $106mn 2013: $139mn 2018: $500mn | | 1  Won Istanbul's Third Airport BOT tender (with Limak, Cengiz, Mapa and Kolin) in 2013. Each holds 20% of the shares of the consortium. 2  Won the tender for Kınalı-Odayeri and Kurtköy-Akyazı sections of Northern Marmara BOT tender (with Limak Holding, Kolin Group, Cengiz Holding) in 2016. |

| Conglomerate | Revenue (2002–2018) | Input supplier and lender role: Indicators | Direct involvement in privatization |
|---|---|---|---|
| Group had close relations with the National Vision Movement of the Erbakan's Islamic Welfare Party in the 1990s. Currently it has close ties with the governing AKP and President Erdoğan. In 2004, then Prime Minister Erdoğan was a witness in Ömer Faruk Kalyoncu's wedding. Former AKP ministers Abdullah Gül, Recep Akdağ and Cemil Çiçek were also among guests in the wedding. In 2019, Erdoğan and his wife Emine Erdoğan were the marriage witnesses of Haluk Kalyoncu, who is the vice Chairman of the group. | | | 3  Won the first solar energy YEKA tender with its partner (China Electronics Technology Group Corporation — CETC) in 2017 for the construction of the 1GW capacity plant in Karapınar (south of Ankara) at a cost of 6.99 cents per kilowatt-hour. The total investment is worth $1bn. |

# Divestitures in Turkey between 2010 and 2018

The divestiture of electricity distribution companies and the beneficiary firms between 2010 and 2013

| Company | Winner firm | Year | Price ($ million) |
|---|---|---|---|
| Osmangazi | Yıldızlar sss | 2010 | 485.0 |
| Uludağ | Cengiz-Kolin-Limak | 2010 | 940.0 |
| Çamlıbel | Cengiz-Kolin-Limak | 2010 | 258.5 |
| Çoruh | Aksa | 2010 | 227.0 |
| Yeşilırmak | Çalık | 2010 | 441.5 |
| Fırat | Aksa | 2010 | 230.2 |
| Trakya | İçtaş | 2011 | 575.0 |
| Akdeniz | Cengiz-Kolin-Limak | 2013 | 546.0 |
| Boğaziçi (İstanbul Europe) | Cengiz-Kolin-Limak | 2013 | 1960.0 |
| Gediz | Elsan-Tümaş-Karaçay | 2013 | 1231.0 |
| Aras | Kiler-Çalık | 2013 | 128.5 |
| Dicle | İşkaya | 2013 | 387.0 |
| Ayedaş (İstanbul Anatolia) | Sabancı (Enerjisa) | 2013 | 1227.0 |
| Van Gölü | Türkerler | 2013 | 118.0 |
| Toroslar | Sabancı (Enerjisa) | 2013 | 1725.0 |

Selected divestitures of the small river-type hydroelectric power plants and the beneficiary firms between 2010 and 2014

| Plants | Winner firm | Year | Price ($ million) |
|---|---|---|---|
| Bayburt, Çemişgezek, Girlevik | Boydak Holding | 2011 | 29.0 |
| Bünyan, Çamardı, Pınarbaşı, Sızır | Kayseri ve Civari Enerji A.Ş. | 2011 | 69.7 |
| Çağ, Otluca, Uludere | Nas Enerji A.Ş. | 2011 | 40.8 |
| Kovada I, Kovada II | Batı Anadolu Group | 2011 | 56.0 |
| Hasanlar | Batı Anadolu Group | 2013 | 30.8 |

| Plants | Winner firm | Year | Price ($ million) |
|---|---|---|---|
| Göksu | Nurol Holding | 2013 | 57.5 |
| Berdan | Tayfurlar Enerji A.Ş. | 2013 | 47.0 |
| Kısık | Kılıç Enerji A.Ş. | 2013 | 27.1 |
| Kayaköy | Veysi Madencilik İnşaat Ltd. | 2014 | 10.3 |

Divestitures of the TPPs and the beneficiary firms between 2013 and 2016

| Plants | Installed capacity (MW) | Winner firm | Year | Price ($ million) |
|---|---|---|---|---|
| Seyitömer | 600 | Çelikler Holding | 2013 | 2248.0 |
| Kangal | 457 | Konya Şeker Enerji | 2013 | 985.0 |
| Hamitabat | 1156 | Limak Holding | 2013 | 105.0 |
| Yatağan | 630 | Bereket Enerji | 2014 | 1091.0 |
| Çatalağzı | 300 | Bereket Enerji | 2014 | 350.0 |
| Kemerköy and Yeniköy | 1050 | İç İçtaş-Limak | 2014 | 2671.0 |
| Orhaneli and Tunçbilek | 575 | Çelikler Holding | 2015 | 521.0 |
| Soma-B | 990 | Konya Şeker Enerji | 2015 | 685.5 |
| Hopa | 50 | Cengiz Holding | 2016 | 76.0 |

Selected divestitures of hydroelectric plants and the beneficiary firms between 2016 and 2018

| Plants | Winner firm | Year | Price ($ million) |
|---|---|---|---|
| Karacaören I, Karacaören II | Gama Holding | 2016 | 177.6 |
| Manavgat | Kibar Holding | 2016 | 131.2 |
| Fethiye | Cengiz Holding | 2016 | 44.8 |
| Kadıncık I, Kadıncık II | İç İçtaş Holding | 2016 | 299.8 |
| Doğankent, Kürtün, Torul | Kolin Holding | 2016 | 435.2 |
| Şanlıurfa | Rönesans Holding | 2017 | 68.6 |

| Plants | Winner firm | Year | Price ($ million) |
|---|---|---|---|
| Adıgüzel, Kemer | Bereket Enerji | 2017 | 91.4 |
| Almus, Köklüce | Gülsan Holding | 2017 | 212.6 |
| Menzelet, Kılavuzlu | Koç Holding | 2018 | 335.0 |
| Gönen | Alarko Holding | 2018 | 12.3 |

Divestitures of sugar factories and the beneficiary firms in 2018

| Sugar factory | Acquirer | Price ($ million) |
|---|---|---|
| Afyon | Doğuş Yiyecek ve İçecek Üretim | 161 |
| Turhal | Kayseri Şeker | 126 |
| Çorum | Safi Katı Yakıt | 117 |
| Bor | Doğuş Yiyecek ve İçecek Üretim | 75 |
| Kırşehir | Tutgu Gıda Türizm | 73 |
| Elbistan | Mutlucan Tuz Madencilik | 66 |
| Muş | MBD İnşaat & Öz Er-Ka İnşaat | 51 |
| Alpullu | Binbirgıda Tarım Ürünleri | 33 |
| Ercincan | Albayrak Group | 32 |
| Erzurum | Albayrak Group | 32 |

# References

Adaman et al. (2014) "Hitting the Wall: Erdogan's construction-based, finance-led growth regime", *The Middle East in London,* 10: 3, 7–8.

ADB, EBRD, IDB, IsDB and WBG (2016) The APMG Public-Private Partnership (PPP) Certification Guide. (available online: https://ppp-certification.com/pppguide/download).

Ahmad, F. (1993) The Making of Modern Turkey. London: Routledge.

Akça, İ. (2014) "AKP, Hegemonya Projesi ve Kriz Dinamikleri", *Başlangıç,* 1 (1), pp. 11–30.

Akçay, Ü. (2021) "Authoritarian consolidation dynamics in Turkey", *Contemporary Politics,* 27 (1), pp. 79–104.

Akdemir, E., Basci, E. and Togan, S. (2007) "Telecommunications Policy Reform in Turkey", *World Economy,* 30: 7, 1114–1138.

Akkaya, Y. 2002. The working class and unionism in Turkey under the shackles of the system and developmentalism. In *The Ravages of Neoliberalism: Economy, Society and Gender in Turkey,* eds. S. Savran and N. Balkan, 129–44. New York: Nova Science.

Albo, Greg. 1993. "Democratic Citizenship and the Future of Public Management." in G. Albo, D. Langille and L. Panitch, eds., *A Different Kind of State? Popular Power and Democratic Administration.* Toronto, Canada: Oxford University Press.

Albo, G. 2005. Contesting the new capitalism. In *Varieties of Capitalism, Varieties of Approaches,* ed. D. Coates, 63–82. New York: Palgrave Macmillan.

Albo, G. (2009) "The New Economy and Capitalism Today", in N. Pupo, M. Thomas (eds), *Interrogating the New Economy,* Toronto: University of Toronto Press.

Albo, G., S. Gindin, and L. Panitch. 2010. *In and Out of Crisis: The Global Financial Meltdown and Left Alternatives.* Oakland: PM Press.

Albo, G. (2012a) "Contemporary Capitalism", in B. Fine and A. Saad-Filho (eds) *Elgar Companion to Marxist Economics,* London: Elgar.

Albo, G. (2012b) "The Crisis and Economic Alternatives." In L. Panitch, G. Albo and V. Chibber, eds., *Socialist Register 2013: The Question of Strategy.* Pontypool, Wales: Merlin Press.

Alchian, A. and Demsetz, H. (1972) "Production, Information Costs, and Economic Organization", *The American Economic Review,* 62: 5, 777–795.

Almeida, P. (2010) "Movement Partyism: Collective Action and Oppositional Political Parties", in Nella Van Dyke and Holly J. McCammon (eds) Strategic Alliances: Coalition Building and Social Movements. Minneapolis, London: University of Minnesota Press.

Angın, M., and P. Bedirhanoğlu. 2012. Privatization processes as ideological moments: The Block sales of large-scale state enterprises in Turkey in the 2000s. *New Perspectives on Turkey* 47 (1): 139–67.

Angın, M. And Bedirhanoğlu, P. (2013) AKP Dööönüşümü [Large-scale privatizations and state transformation in Turkey in the AKP period]. *Praksis* 30–31 (1): 77–98.

Ataay, F. (2003) "Enerji Sektöründe Özelleştirme: Rekabetçi Bir Piyasada Yönetişim mi?", Praksis, 9: 1, pp. 221–246.

Atasoy, Y. (2007), "The Islamic Ethic and the Spirit of Turkish Capitalism Today", in L. Panitch and C. Leys (eds) *Socialist Register 2008: Global Flashpoints, Reactions to Imperialism and Neoliberalism*, Halifax: Fernwood Publishing.

Atiyas, İ. 2009. Recent privatization experience of Turkey: A reappraisal. In *Turkey and the Global Economy: Neoliberal Restructuring and Integration in The Post-Crisis Era*, ed. Z. Önişş.

Atiyas, İ., Bakış, O. and Gürakar E. Ç. (2019) Anatolian Tigers and the Emergence of the Devout Bourgeoisie in the Turkish Manufacturing Industry. *In Crony Capitalism in the Middle East: Business and Politics from Liberalization to the Arab Spring*, ed. I. Diwan, A. Malik and İ. Atiyas, London: Oxford University Press.

Aykut, E. 2015. Türkiye, Körfez sermayesi'nin yeni yatırım alanı. *Birgün* 24: 1–3.

Bakker, K. (2008) "The Ambiguity of Community: Debating Alternatives to Private – Sector Provision of Urban Water Supply." *Water Alternatives*, 1:2, 236–252.

Barth, R. and Hemphill, W. (2000) Financial Programming and Policy: The Case of Turkey. Washington D.C: IMF Institute.

Başkaya, F. 2012. *Paradigmanın İflası* [The Bankruptcy of Paradigm]. İstanbul: Maki Basın Yayın.

Bayat, A. (1991) *Work, Politics and Power: An International Perspective on Workers' Control and Self-Management*. New York: Monthly Review Press.

Bayliss, K., and B. Fine. 2008. *Privatization and Alternative Public Sector Reform in Sub-Saharan Africa: Delivering on Electricity and Water*. Basingstoke: Palgrave Macmillan.

Bedirhanoglu, P. and Yalman, G. (2010) "State, Class and the Discourse: Reflections on the Neoliberal Transformation in Turkey", in Saad-Filho A. and Yalman, G. (eds) *Economic Transition to Neoliberalism in Middle-Income Countries*, London: Routledge.

Bedirhanoğlu, P. (2020) "Social constitution of the AKP's strong state through financialization: state in crisis, or crisis state?", in Bedirhanoğlu (eds) Turkey's New State in the Making. London: ZED Books.

Bekmen, A. (2013) "State and Capital in Turkey During the Neoliberal Era" in Ismet Akca, Ahmet Bekmen and Baris Alp Ozden (eds) Turkey Reframed: Constituting Neoliberal Hegemony. London: Pluto Press.

Belke, A. et.al. (2007) "The Different Extent of Privatization Proceeds in OECD Countries: A Preliminary Explanation Using a Public-Choice Approach", *FinanzArchiv / Public Finance Analysis,* 63: 2, 211–243.

Bernstein, H. (2010) "Globalization, neoliberalism, labour, with reference to South Africa" in Saad-Filho and Yalman (eds) Economic Transitions to Neoliberalism in

Middle-Income Countries: Policy dilemmas, economic crises, forms of resistance. London and New York: Routledge.

Bilim, Sanayi ve Teknoloji Bakanlığı (2011) Beyaz Eşya Sanayi Sektörü Raporu, Ankara: Sanayi Genel Müdürlüğü.

Birtek, F. 1985. The rise and fall of Etatism in Turkey, 1932–1950: The uncertain road in the restructuring of a semiperipherial economy. *Review* 8 (3): 407–38.

Blind, P. 2008. *Democratic Institutions of Undemocratic Individuals: Privatization, Labour and Democracy in Turkey and Argentina.* New York: Palgrave Macmillan.

Boardman, A. and Vining, A. (1989) "Ownership and Performance in Competitive Environments: A Comparison of the Performance of Private, Mixed and State-Owned Enterprises", *Journal of Law and Economics,* 32: 1, 1–33.

Boito, L. A. (2010) "Social Class and Politics in Brazil: From Cardoso to Lula" in Saad-Filho and Yalman (eds) Economic Transitions to Neoliberalism in Middle-Income Countries: Policy dilemmas, economic crises, forms of resistance. London and New York: Routledge.

Boratav, K. 1974. *100 Soruda Türkiye'de Devletçilik* [Etatism in Turkey in 100 Questions]. İstanbul: Gerçek Yayınevi.

Boratav K (2010) ÜÜ*Türk Mühendis ve Mimar Odaları Birliği, Türkiye'de Özelleştirme Gerçeği Sempozyumu III.* Ankara.

Boratav, K. 2011. *Türkiye İktisat Tarihi: 1908–2009* [The Economic History of Turkey: 1908–2009]. Ankara: İmge Kitapevi.

Borsa İstanbul (2000a) *Özelleştirme İdaresi Başkanlığı'nööneminin Sonuçları Hakkında Kamuoyunu Bilgilendirmes*i, 30 Mart 2000, Borsa Başkanlığı Duyurusu, available online: www.kap.gov.tr.

Borsa İstanbul (2000b) *Tüpraş'in Hisse Senetlerinin Halka Arzı,* 10 Nisan 2000, Borsa Baskanlığı Duyurusu, available online: www.kap.gov.tr.

Bortolotti, B., Fantini, M. and Siniscalco, D. (2003) "Privatisation around the world: evidence from panel data", *Journal of Public Economics,* 88: 1, 305–332.

Bortolotti, B., and M. Faccio. 2009. Government Control of Privatized Firms. *The Review of Financial Studies* 22 (8): 2907–2939.

Boubakri et al. (2008a) "Privatization in Developing Countries: Performance and Ownership Effects", *Development Policy Review,* 26: 3, 275–308.

Boubakri et al. (2008b) "Politically connected newly privatized firms", *International Journal of Corporate Finance,* 14 (1), pp. 654–673.

Boycko, M., Shleifer, A. and Vishny, R. (1996) Privatizing Russia, Cambridge: MIT Press.

Brand, U., and M. Heigl. 2011. Inside and outside: The state, movements and radical transformation in the work of Nicos Poulantzas. In *Reading Poulantzas*, ed. A. Gallas, L. Bretthauer, J. Kannankulam, and I. Stutzle, 246–61. Exeter: Merlin Press.

Brand, U. 2013. "The Role of the State and Public Policies in Processes of Transformation." In M. Lang and D. Mokrani, eds., *Beyond Development.* Amsterdam: TNI.

Brenner, N., J. Peck, and N. Theodore. 2010. Variegated neoliberalization: Geographies, modalities, path-ways. *Global Networks* 10 (2): 182–222.

Buchanan, J. (1975) The Limits of Liberty: Between Anarchy and Leviathan. Chicago: The University of Chicago Press.

Buğra, A. 1994. *State and Business in Modern Turkey: A Comparative Study*. Albany: State University of New York Press.

Buğra, A., and O. Savaşkan. 2014. *New Capitalism in Turkey*. Cheltenham: Edward Elgar.

Burnham, P. (1997) "Globalization: States, markets and class relations", *Historical Materialism*, 1:1, 150–160.

Callinicos, A. (2016) Marxism and the Very Idea of Critical Political Economy. In *The Palgrave Handbook of Critical International Political Economy* (eds). A. Cafruny, L. Talani and G. Martin, pp. 49–65. London: Palgrave Macmillan.

Cammack, P. (2020) "Reproduction Versus Transformation: The Case of the Asian Infrastructure Investment Bank", *Global Society*, 34 (3), pp. 409–423.

Castel, R. (2003) From Manual Workers to Wage Laborers: Transformation of the Social Question. New Brunswick, London: Transaction Publishers.

Cebeci, A. (2012) Bilmediğimiz Kapitalizm: Gizli Elin Kurumsallaşması, İstanbul: Sav Yayınları.

Celasun, O. (1999) "The 1994 Currency Crisis in Turkey". Policy Research Working Papers no. 1913. Washington: World Bank.

Chang, D. (2015) "The Rise of East Asia: A Slippery Floor for the Left", in Pradella, L. and Marois, T. (eds) *Polarising Development: Alternatives to Neoliberalism and the Crisis*, London: Pluto Press.

Chavez, Daniel. 2013. "The Costa Rican Electricity Institute (ICE): An Exceptional Public Enterprise in an Atypical Social Democracy." *Transnational Institute*, 1:7 (available online).

Chavez, Daniel, and Sebastian Torres. 2014. "Introduction: Public Enterprises and Development in Latin America and the World." In D. Chavez and S. Torres, eds., *Reorienting Development: State-Owned Enterprises in Latin America and the World*. Amsterdam: Transnational Institute.

Chong, R. and Lopez-de-Silanes (2003) Privatization in Latin America: Myths and Reality, Stanford: Stanford University Press.

Chowns, Ellie. 2015. "Is Community Management an Efficient and Effective Model of Public Service Delivery? Lessons from the Rural Water Supply Sector in Malawi." *Public Administration and Development*, 35:1, 263–276.

Cömert, H. And Yeldan, E. (2018) "A Tale of Three Crises Made in Turkey: 1994, 2001 and 2008–09" in Yalman, Marois and Gungen (eds) The Political Economy of Financial Transformation in Turkey. London: Routledge.

Cosse, Carolina. 2014. "ANTEL: A Socially Committed Public Enterprise at the Fore – front of Technological Innovation." In D. Chavez and S. Torres, eds., *Reorienting*

*Development: State-Owned Enterprises in Latin America and the World.* Amsterdam: Transnational Institute.

Crabtree, D. Thirlwall, P. (1993) Keynes and the Role of the State: The Tenth Keynes Seminar held at the University of Kent at Cantenbury, 1991. London: MacMillan Press.

Crew, A. and Parker, D. (2008) Developments in the Economics of Privatization and Regulation, London: Edward Elgar.

Cumbers, Andrew. 2014. *Renewing Public Ownership: Constructing a Democratic Economy in the Twenty-First Century.* London: Centre for Labour and Social Studies.

Cumbers, A. 2016. "Economic Democracy: Reclaiming Public Ownership as the Pragmatic Left Alternative." *Juncture,* 22:4, 324–328.

Çakal, R. (1996) "Doğal Tekellerde Özelleştirme ve Regulasyon", *DPT Uzmanlık Tezi,* Ankara: DPT.

Çavdar, A. 2014. Reached for the state, got capital instead. *Perspectives: Political Analysis and Commentary* 8 (1): 8–13.

Çelik, A. (2015) "Turkey's New Labour Regime Under the Justice and Development Party in the First Decade of the Twenty First Century: Authoritarian Flexibilization", *Middle Eastern Studies,* 51: 4, pp. 618–635.

Çokgezen, M. 2000. New fragmentations and new cooperations in the Turkish bourgeoisie. *Environment and Planning C: Government and Policy* 18 (1): 525–44.

Das, Raju. 2017. *Marxist Class Theory for a Skeptical World.* Leiden, The Netherlands: Brill.

Dinler, D. 2012. *Trade Unions in Turkey.* Berlin: Friedrich Ebert Stiftung.

Doğan, N. 2012. *Rakamlarla Özelleştirme: Türkiye'de ve Dünyada Özelleştirme Uygulamaları* [Privatization with Numbers: Privatization Implementations in Turkey and the World]. Ankara: Özelleştirme İdaresi.

Dorlach, T., and O. Savaşkan. 2018. The Political Economy of Economic and Social Policy in Turkey: An Introduction to the Special Issue. *Journal of Balkan and Near Eastern Studies* 20 (4): 311–317.

DPT (1990) Altıncı Beş Yıllık Kalkınma Planı, Ankara: DPT.

DPT (2000a) Sekizinci Beş Yıllık Kalkınma Planı. Ankara: DPT.

DPT (2000b) Sekizinci Beş Yıllık Kalkınma Planı: Demir-Çelik Sanayii Özel Ihtisas Komisyonu Raporu, Ankara: DPT.

Drahokoupil, J. (2009) Globalization and the State in Central and Eastern Europe: The Politics of Foreign Direct Investment. London: Routledge.

Dumontier, Belanger, Susan Spronk, and Adrian Murray. 2016. "Work of the Ants: Labour and Community Reinventing Public Water in Colombia." In David McDonald, ed., *Making Public in a Privatized World: The Struggle for Essential Services.* London: Zed Books.

Emek, U. (2015) "Turkish Experience with public private partnerships in infrastructure: Opportunities and challenges", *Utilities Policy,* 37 (1), pp. 120–129.

Emek, U. (2017) "Public-Private Partnerships in the Turkish Healthcare Sector: Policy, Procedure and Practice". In: Nikolai Mouraviev, Nada Kakabadse (eds) Public-Private Partnerships in Transitional Nations: Policy, Governance and Praxis. UK: Cambridge Scholars Publishing.

Enka (2004) Annual Report (can be accessed: www.enka.com).

EPEC (2015) Market Updated: Review of the European PPP Market in 2015. European Investment Bank: available online: https://www.eib.org/attachments/epec/epec _market_update_2015_en.pdf.

EPEC (2019) Market Update: Review of the European PPP Market in 2018. Luxembourg: European PPP Expertise Centre.

Ercan, F. 2012. Fuat Ercan ile Söyleşi. Yarın Gazetesi 8: 1–11.

Ercan, F., and Ş. Oğuz. 2006. Resclaing as a class relationship and process: The case of public procurement law in Turkey. Political Geography 25 (1): 641–56.

Ercan, F. and Oğuz, Ş. (2015) From Gezi resistance to soma massacre: Capital accumulation and class struggle in Turkey. Socialist Register 51 (1): 114–35.

Ercan, F. and Oğuz, Ş. (2020) "Understanding the rcent rise of authoritarianism in Turkey in terms of the structural contradictions of the process of accumulation", in Bedirhanoğlu (eds) Turkey's New State in the Making. London: ZED Books.

Erol, M. E. (2018) "State and Labour under AKP Rule in Turkey: An Appraisal", Jorunal of Balkan and Near Eastern Studies.

Errasti, Anjel, Ignacio Bretos, and Aitziber Nunez. 2017. "The Viability of Cooperatives: The Fall of the Mondragon Cooperative Fagor." Review of Radical Political Economics, 49:2, 181–197.

Ertuna, Ö. 1998. Constraints of privatization: The Turkish case. Paper presented at the Mediterranean development forum, Marrakech, September 3–6.

Esen, B., and S. Gümüşçü. 2018. Building a Comparative Authoritarian Regime: State-Business Relations in the AKP's Turkey. Journal of Balkan and Near Eastern Studies 20 (4): 349–372.

FESSUD (2013) Comparative Perspective on Financial System in the EU: Country Report on Turkey. Leeds: FESSUD.

Fıçıcı, A. 2001. Political Economy of Turkish Privatization: A Critical Assessment (Working paper). New Hampshire College.

Fine, B. 1997. Privatisation: Theory and lessons from the UK and South Africa. Seoul Journal of Economics 10 (4): 373–414.

Fine, B., and D. Hall. 2012. Terrains of neoliberalism: Constraints and opportunities for alternative models of service delivery. In Alternatives to Privatization: Public Options for Essential Services in the Global South, ed. D. McDonald and G. Ruiters, 45–70. London: Routledge.

Fine, B. and Saad-Filho, A. (2017) "Thirteen Things You Need to Know About Neoliberalism", Critical Sociology, 43: 4–5, 685–706.

Fleming, P. (2021) Dark Academia: How Universities Die. London: Pluto Press.

Gereffi, G. and M. Korzeniewicz (1994) Commodity Chains and Global Capitalism. Westport, Connecticut, London: Praeger.

Grugel, Jean, and Pia Riggirozzi. 2012. "Post-Neoliberalism in Latin America: Rebuilding and Reclaiming the State After Crisis." *Development and Change*, 43:1, 1–21.

Gupta, A. (2000) Beyond Privatization. London: MacMillan Books.

Gülalp, H. (2001) "Globalization and Political Islam: The Social Bases of Turkey's Welfare Party", *International Journal of Middle East Studies*, 33:1, 433–448.

Gültekin-Karakaş, D. 2009. *Global Integration of Turkish Finance Capital: State, Capital and Banking in Turkey*. Saarbrucken: VDM Verlag.

Gültekin-Karakaş, D., and F. Ercan. 2013. Is financialization a form of dependency or a strategy for the external financing need of productive capital? Presentation delivered at IIPPE, the Fourth Annual Conference in Political Economy, July 9–11, Hague, Netherlands.

Güngen, A. R. (2020) "Turkey's Financial Slide: Discipline By Credit in the Last Decade of the AKP's Rule" in Bedirhanoğlu et al. (eds) Turkey's New State in the Making: Transformations in Legality, Economy and Coercion. London: Zed Books.

Gürakar, E. 2016. *Politics of Favoritism in Public Procurement in Turkey*. New York: Palgrave Macmillan.

Güran, M. 2011. The political economy of privatization in Turkey. In *The Political Economy of Regulation in Turkey*, ed. T. Çetin, 23–51. Oxford: Springer.

Gürcan, E., and C. Peker. 2015. A class analytic approach to the Gezi park events: Challenging the middle class myth. *Capital & Class* 39 (2): 321–43.

Gürcan, E. F., and B. Mete (2017) *Neoliberalism and the Changing Face of Unionism: The Combined and Uneven Development of Class Capacities in Turkey*. Cham: Palgrave Macmillan.

Hahnel, Robin. 2016. "Breaking with Capitalism." In Robin Hahnel and Erik Olin Wright, *Alternatives to Capitalism*. London: Verso.

Hale, W. (1981) The Political and Economic Development of Modern Turkey. London: Croom Helm.

Hall, David, Emanuele Lobina, and Robin Motte. 2005. "Public Resistance to Privatization in Water and Energy." *Development in Practice*, 15:3–4, 286–301.

Hall, D. (2008) "Protecting workers in PPPs", *Public Services International Research Unit*, available online: https://www.epsu.org/sites/default/files/article/files/PPPs1-barg -d4-finalLAYOUT-2.pdf (accessed on 7 August 2021).

Hall, D. (2015) Why Public-Private Partnerships Don't Work: The many advantages of the public alternative. Public Services International Research Unit, University of Greenwich, UK.

Harnecker, Marta. 2016a. "Ideas for the Struggle." (http://oldandnewproject.net/Ess ays/Harnecker_Ideas.pdf).

Harnecker, M. 2016b. "Social Movements and Progressive Governments: Building a New Relationship in Latin America." *Monthly Review,* 67:8.

Harris L (2013) Variable histories and geographies of marketization and privatisation. In: Harris L, Goldin J and Sneddon C (eds) *Contemporary Water Governance in the Global South.* London: Routledge, 118–130.

Harvey, D. 2003. *The New Imperialism.* Oxford: Oxford University Press.

Harvey D (2007) Neoliberalism as creative destruction. *Annals of the American Academy of Political and Social Science* 610(1): 22–44.

Harvey, D. (2011) The Enigma of Capital and the Crises of Capitalism. London: Profile Books.

Hentz, J. (2000) "The Two Faces of Privatization: Political and Economic Logics in Transitional South Africa", *The Journal of Modern African Studies,* 38 (2), pp. 203–223.

Heper, M. 1985. *The State Tradition in Turkey.* Walkington: The Eothen Press.

Herman, Chris, *et al.* 2012. "The Struggle for Public Services." In Christoph Herman and Jorg Flecker, eds., *Privatisation of Public Services: Impacts for Employment, Working Conditions and Service Quality in Europe.* Routledge: London.

Hodge, G. and Greve, C. (2009) "PPPs: The Passage of Time Permits A Sober Reflection", *Economic Affairs,* 29 (1), pp. 33–39.

Hodge, G., Greve, C. and Boardman, A. (2012) "Introduction: the PPP phenomenon and its evaluation" in Hodge, Greve and Boardman (eds) International Handbook on Public-Private Partnerships. London: Edward Elgar.

Hoşgör, E. (2011) "Islamic Capital/Anatolian Tigers: Past and Present", *Middle Eastern Studies,* 47: 2, 343–360.

IBRD (1972) Appraisal of the Erdemir Steel Plant Expansion Project. IBRD: Industrial Projects Department.

IMF (1997) 'IMF Concludes Article IV Consultation with Turkey', *Public Information Notice,* No. 97/17, 5 August 1997, Washington, DC: IMF: available online: https://www .imf.org/en/News/Articles/2015/09/28/04/53/pn9717 (accessed on 14 July 2020).

IMF (1998) *Turkey: Memorandum of Economic Policies,* 26 June 1998, Washington, DC: IMF.

International Monetary Fund. 2000. *Report on the Observance of Standards and Codes (ROSC) Turkey: Fiscal Transparency.* Washington, DC: IMF.

IMF (2001) IMF Approves Augmentation of Turkey's Stand-By Credit to US$19 Billion, 15 May 2001, Washington, DC: IMF.

IMF (2004) Turkey – Letter of Intent, 2 April 2004, Washington, DC: IMF: available online: https://www.imf.org/external/np/loi/2004/tur/01/index.htm (accessed on 14 August 2020).

Inan, A. 1972. *Devletçilik İlkesi ve Türkiye Cumhuriyetinin Birinci Sanayi Planı* [Principle of Etatism and the First Industrialization Plan of the Turkish Republic].

Insel, A. 1995. *Türkiye Toplumunun Bunalımı* [The Crisis of the Turkish Society]. Istanbul: Birikim Yayınları.

Investment Support and Promotion Agency of Turkey (2014) Healthcare Industry in Turkey: available online: www.invest.gov.tr.

Kalkınma Bakanlığı (2014) Kamu Özel İşbirliği: Özel İhtisas Komisyonu Raporu. Ankara (Yayın No: KB: 2875 – ÖİK: 725).

Kalkınma Bakanlığı (2016) Dünyada ve Türkiye'de Kamu Özel İşbirliği Uygulamalarına İlişkin Gelişmeler 2015. Ankara (available online: https://www.sbb.gov.tr/kamu -ozel-isbirliginde-gelismeler-yayinlar/).

Kalkınma Bakanlığı (2018) Kamu Özel İşbirliği Uygulamalarında Etkin Yönetim: Özel İhtisas Komisyonu Raporu. Ankara (Yayın No: KB: 2983 – ÖİK: 765).

Kay, Neil, Harvie Ramsay, and Jean Francois Hernat. 1996. "Industrial Collaboration and the European Internal Market." *Journal of Common Market Studies*, 34:3, 465–475.

Kepenek, Y. 1990. *Türkiye'de Kamu İktisadi Teşebbüsleri* [State Economic Enterprises in Turkey]. Ankara: Gerçek Yayınevi.

Keyder, Ç. 1987. *State and Class in Turkey: A Study in Capitalist Development*. London and New York: Verso.

Kılcı, M. (1994) Başlangıcından Bugüne Türkiye'de Özelleştirme Uygulamaları: 1984– 1994, Ankara: DPT.

Kıraç, İ. (2006) Ömrümden Uzun İdeallerim Var. İstanbul: Suna ve İnan Kıraç Vakfı.

Kishimoto, S. and Petitjean, O. (2017) Reclaiming Public Services: How cities and citizens are turning back privatisation. Amsterdam, Paris: Transnational Institute.

Kıyan, Z. and Yüksel, H. (2011) "The GATS and the Globalizing Public Services: The Case of Turkey and Türk Telekom", *TODAEI's Review of Public Administration*, 5: 1, 35–68.

Kjellstrom, S. 1990. *Privatization in Turkey* (Policy, Research, and External Affairs Working Papers). Washington, DC: The World Bank.

Koç, V. 1983. *Hayat Hikayem*. İstanbul: Celtut Matbaacılık.

Koç, V. 1987. *Hatıralarım, Görüşlerim, Öğütlerim*. İstanbul: Hürriyet Ofset.

Kraan, D., D. Bergvall, and I. Hawkesworth. 2007. Budgeting in Turkey. *OECD Journal on Budgeting* 7 (2): 7–58.

Krueger, A. (1990) "Government Failures in Development", *NBER Working Paper Series*, 3340: 1, 1–26.

Kutlay, M. (2015) The Turkish Economy at a Crosroads: Unpacking Turkey's Current Account Challenge. Global Turkey in Europe, Working Paper 10.

Kutun, M. (2020) "The AKP's move from depoliticization to repoliticization in economic management" in Bedirhanoğlu et.al. (eds) Turkey's New State in the Making: Transformations in Legality, Economy and Coercion. London: ZED Books.

Lapavitsas, C. (2005) "Mainstream Economics in the Neoliberal Era" in Saad-Filho, A. and Johnston, D. (ed) *Neoliberalism: A Critical Reader*, London: Pluto Press.

Lethbridge, Jane. 2004. "Combining Worker and User Interests in the Health Sector: Trade Unions and NGOs." *Development in Practice*, 14:1–2, 234–247.

Lobina, Emanuele. 2016. "Water Remunicipalisation as a Global Trend: Calling for Progressive Policies." *Conference paper presented at Encuentro de Ciudades por el Agua Publica,* City of Madrid (November 3–4).

Lobina, Emanuele and David Hall. 2000. "Public Sector Alternatives to Water Supply and Sewerage Privatization: Case Studies." *International Journal of Water Resources Development,* 16:1, 35–55.

Magnus, R. and Ekin, I. (2013) "Road PPPs in Turkey", *Infrastructure Journal.*

Mansfield, B. 2008. *Privatization: Property and Remaking of Nature and Society Relations.* London: Blackwell Publishing.

Marina-Flores, Abelardo. 2015. "Beyond Neoliberalism and New Developmentalism in Latin America: Towards an Anti-Capitalist Agenda." In L. Pradella and T. Marois, eds., *Polarising Development: Alternatives to Neoliberalism and the Crisis.* London: Pluto Press.

Marois, T. 2012. *States, Banks and Crisis.* Cheltenham: Edward Elgar.

Marois, Thomas. 2013. *State-Owned Banks and Development: Dispelling Mainstream Myths.* London: Municipal Services Project.

Marois, T. (2015) "Banking on Alternatives to Neoliberal Development". In: Pradella, Lucia and Marois, Thomas, (eds.), *Polarizing Development: Alternatives to Neoliberalism and the Crisis.* London: Pluto Press.

Marois, T., and A. Güngen. 2016. Credibility and class in the evolution of public banks: The case of Turkey. *Journal of Peasant Studies* 43 (6): 1285–309.

Marois, T. 2019. The Transformation of the State Financial Apparatus in Turkey since 2001. In *The Political Economy of Financial Transformation in Turkey*, eds. G. Yalman, T. Marois and A. Güngen. Abingdon, Oxon, UK: Routledge.

McDonald D and Ruiters G (2012) *Alternatives to Privatisation: Public Options for Essential Services in the Global South.* London: Routledge.

McDonald, D. (2014) "Public Ambiguity and the Multiple Meanings of Corporatization", in McDonald, D. (eds) *Rethinking Corporatization and Public Services in the Global South,* London: Zed Books.

McDonald, D. (2015) "Defend, Militate and Alternate: Public Options in a Privatized World." In L. Pradella and T. Marois, eds., *Polarising Development: Alternatives to Neoliberalism and the Crisis.* London: Pluto Press.

McDonald, D. (2016) "To Corporatize or Not to Corporatize (And If So, How?)." *Utilities Policy,* 40:1, 107–114.

Megginson, W. and Netter, J. (2001) "From State to Market: A Survey of Empirical Studies on Privatization", *Journal of Economic Literature*, 39: 2, 321–389.

New Politics Research Project. 2016. The New Politics Research Agenda Workshop Report, Amsterdam (February 13–14).

Neyzi, N. (1963) Türkiye Petrol Sanayii. İstanbul: Sermet Matbaası.

North Anatolian Development Agency (2016) Özel Hastane Ön Fizibilite Raporu. See
    https://www.kuzka.gov.tr/paylasim/yayinlar/rapor_analiz/2016-RP-9-105_ozel_h
    astane_(on_fizibilite)_raporu.pdf (accessed on 7 July 2021).

Ocaklı, F. 2018. Reconfiguring State-Business Relations in Turkey: Housing and
    Hydroelectric Energy Sectors in Comparative Perspective. *Journal of Balkan and
    Near Eastern Studies* 20 (4): 373–387.

Oğuz, Ş. 2008. Globalization and the contradictions of state restructuring in Turkey
    (Ph.D. thesis, York University, Toronto).

Oğuz, Ş. 2016. Yeni Türkiye'nin Siyasal Rejimi. In *Yeni Türkiye? Kapitalizm, Devlet,
    Sınıflar,* ed. T. Tören and M. Kutun, 81–127. İstanbul: Sosyal Araştırmalar Vakfı.

Osborne, David and Ted Gaebler. 1992. *Reinventing Government: How the Entrepreneurial
    Spirit Is Transforming the Public Sector.* Reading, Massachusetts: Addison-Wesley.

Ollman, Bertell (1993), Dialectical Investigations, New York: Routledge.

Öniş, Z. 2011. Power, interests and coalitions: The political economy of mass privatiza-
    tion in Turkey. *Third World Quarterly* 32 (4): 707–724.

Oxford Business Group (2007) The Report: Turkey 2007. Oxford Business Group.

Özcan, G., and U. Gündüz. 2015. Energy Privatisations, Business-Politics Connections
    and Governance Under Political Islam. *Environment and Planning C: Government
    and Policy* 33 (1): 1714–1737.

Özcan, İ. Ç. (2018) "The privatization of roads: An overview of the Turkish case", *Case
    Studies on Transport Policy.*

Öztürk, Ö. 2010. *Türkiye'de Büyük Sermaye Grupları: Finans Kapitalin Oluşumu ve
    Gelişimi* [Big Capital Groups in Turkey: The Formation and Development of
    Financial Capital]. İstanbul: Sav Yayınları.

Öztürk, Ö. (2015) "The Islamist Big Bourgeoisie in Turkey" in Balkan, Balkan and Öncü
    (eds) The Neoliberal Landscape and the Rise of Islamist Capital in Turkey. New York,
    Oxford: Berghahn.

Özuğurlu, M. 2011. "The Tekel Resistance Movement: Reminiscences on Class Struggle."
    *Capital & Class,* 35:2, 179–187.

Özveri, M. (2005) SEKA'da Neler Oldu SEKA'lı Neler Söyledi, *Türk Tabipler Birliği
    Mesleki Sağlık ve Güvenlik Dergisi,* pp. 17–21, https://dergipark.org.tr/en/download/
    article-file/823140.

Pala, K. (2018) "Sunuş" in Kayıhan Pala (eds) Türkiye'de Sağlıkta Kamu-Özel
    Ortaklığı: Şehir Hastaneleri. İstanbul: İletişim.

Papadopoulos, T. (2015) Privatized Companies, Golden Shares and Property Ownership
    in the Euro Crisis Era: A Discussion After Commission v. Greece.

Parker, D. and Saal, D. (2003) "Introduction", in Parker, D. and Saal, D. (eds) *International
    Handbook on Privatization,* Cheltenham: Elgar.

Petras J and Veltmeyer H (2001) *Globalization Unmasked: Imperialism in the 21st
    Century.* Halifax: Fernwood.

Petras J and Veltmeyer H (2004) World development: Globalization or imperialism? In: Veltmeyer H (ed.) *Globalization and Anti-Globalization: Dynamics of Change in the New World Order*. Aldershot: Ashgate.

Petras, J. and Veltmeyer, H. (2007) Multinationals on Trial. Aldershoot: Ashgate.

Petrol-İş. 2005. *Tüpraş Gerçeği* [Reality of Tüpraş]. Ankara: Petrol-İş Yayını.

Pollitt, Christopher, Sandra van Thiel, and Vincent Homburg. 2007. *The New Public Management in Europe: Adaptations and Alternatives*. Houndmills, England: Palgrave Macmillan.

Poulantzas, N. [1968] 1978. *Political Power and Social Classes*. London: Verso.

Poulantzas, N. [1970] 1979. *Fascism and Dictatorship*. London: Verso.

Poulantzas, N. [1974] 1978. *Classes in Contemporary Capitalism*. London: Verso.

Poulantzas, N. [1978] 2000. *State, Power and Socialism*. London: Verso.

Preker, Alexander, and April Harding. 2003. *Innovations in Health Service Delivery: The Corporatization of Public Hospitals*. Washington, DC: World Bank.

Presidency of the Republic of Turkey Investment Office (2019) Investing in Infrastructure & Public Private Partnership (PPP) in Turkey: available online: https://www.invest .gov.tr/en/library/publications/lists/investpublications/infrastructure-industry.pdf (accessed on 15 January 2021).

Privatization Barometer. 2015. *The PB Report 2014/2015: The Wave Builds*. www.privati zationbarometer.net.

PWC (2017) Capital Projects and Infrastructure Spending in Turkey: available online: https://www.pwc.com.tr/tr/advisory/capital-project-and-infrastructure-spe ndingin-turkey-pwc.pdf.

Ramamurti, R. 2000. Why are Developing Countries Privatizing? *Journal of International Business Studies* 23 (2): 225–249.

Reich, R. (2015) Saving Capitalism: For the Many, Not the Few. New York: Alfred A. Knopf.

Rooyen, Carina, and David Hall. 2007. *The Confused Case of Rand Water in South Africa*. London: Municipal Services Project.

Rowthorn, B. and Chang, H. (1993) "Public Ownership and the Theory of the State", in Clarke, Pitelis (eds) *The Political Economy of Privatization*, London: Routledge.

Roy, A. (2001) Power Politics, Cambridge: South End Press.

Saad-Filho, A. (1998) "Redefining the Role of the Bourgeoisie in Dependent Capitalist Development", *Latin American Perspectives*, 25 (1), pp. 192–197.

Saad-Filho, A. 2003. New dawn or false start in Brazil? The political economy of Lula's election. *Historical Materialism* 11 (1): 3–21.

Saad-Fiho, A. 2008. Marxian and Keynesian critiques of neoliberalism. In *Socialist Register 2008*, ed. L. Panitch, C. Leys, and G. Albo, 337–45. Nova Scotia: Fernwood Publishing.

Samson, C. (1994) "The Three Faces of Privatization", *Sociology*, 28 (1), pp. 79–97.

Savran, S. 2011. *Türkiye'de Sınıf Mücadeleleri: 1908–1980* [The Class Struggle in Turkey: 1908–1980]. İstanbul: Yordam Kitap.

Saygılı, S. and Taymaz, E. (2001) "Privatization, Ownership and Technical Efficiency: A Study of the Turkish Cement Industry", *Annals of Public and Cooperative Economics*, 72: 4, 581–605.

Selwyn, B. (2016) "Theory and practice of labour-centred deveopment", *Third World Quarterly*, 37: 6, pp . 1035–1052.

Shirley, M. 1983. *Managing State-Owned Enterprises*. World Bank Staff Working Paper No. 577. Washington: World Bank.

Shirley, Mary. 1999. "Bureaucrats in Business: The Roles of Privatization Versus Corporatization in State-Owned Enterprise Reform." *World Development*, 27:1, 115–136.

Shleifer, A. and Vishny, R. (1998) The Grabbing Hand: Government Pathologies and Their Cures, Cambridge: Harvard University Press.

Shonfield, D. (1965) Modern Capitalism: The Changing Balance of Public and Private Power. New York: Oxford University Press.

Silverman, R. 2014. Dogan versus Erdogan: Business and politics in AKP-era Turkey. *Mediterranean Quarterly* 25 (2): 131–51.

Sönmez, M. (1978) Kapitalist Devlet İşletmeleri ve Türkiye. Ankara: Şafak Matbaası.

Sönmez, M. 1987. *Türkiye'de Holdingler* [Holdings in Turkey]. Istanbul: Gözlem Yayıncılık.

Soysal, M. 2005. *Özelleştirmeler ve Hukuksal Savaşım* [Privatizations and My Legal War]. Ankara: TMMOB. http://docplayer.biz.tr/6605169-20-yilinda-turkiye-de-ozell estirme-gercegi-sempozyumu.html.

Spronk, S. (2007) "Roots of Resistance to Urban Water Privatization in Bolivia: The "New Working Class", the Crisis of Neoliberalism, and Public Services", *International Labour and Working-Class History*, 71: 1, 8–28.

Spronk, S. (2010) "Water and Sanitation Utilities in the Global South: Re-Centering the Debate on Efficiency." *Review of Radical Political Economics*, 42:2, 156–174.

Spronk, S and Webber, JR (2007) Struggles against accumulation by dispossession in Bolivia: The politi-cal economy of natural resource contention. *Latin American Perspectives* 34(2): 31–47.

Standing, G. (1997) "Globalization, Labour Flexibility and Insecurity: The Era of Market Regulation", *European Journal of Industrial Relations*, 3 (7), pp. 7–37.

Sturup, S. (2013) "A Foucault perspective on public-private partnership mega-projects" in Greve and Hodge (eds) Rethinking Public-Private Partnerships: Strategies for turbulent times. London and New York: Routledge.

Szyliowicz, J. (1991) Politics, Technology and Development: Decision Making in the Turkish Iron and Steel Industry. London: Macmillan Press.

Şahin, S. 2010. Privatization as a hegemonic process in Turkey. *Journal of Contemporary European Studies* 18 (4): 483–98.

Şenalp, G. 2012. *Ulusöö*[The Formation of Transnational Capital: Turkey and Koç Holding Example]. İstanbul: Sosyal Araştırmalar Vakfı.

Şeni, N. 1978. *Emperyalist Sistemde Kontrol Sanayii ve Ereğli Demir Çelik* [The Control Industry and the Ereğli Iron and Steel within the Imperialist System]. İstanbul: Birikim Yayınları.

Tansel, C. B. (2019) "Reproducing authoritarian neoliberalism in Turkey: urban governance and state restructuring in the shadow of executive centralization", *Globalizations,* 16 (3), pp. 320–335.

Tanyılmaz, K. (2015) The Deep Fracture in the Big Bourgeoisie of Turkey. In *The Neoliberal Landscape and The Rise of Islamist Capital in Turkey,* ed. N. Balkan, E. Balkan and A. Öncü, 89–117. New York, Oxford: Berghahn.

Taylan, T. 1984. Capital and the state in contemporary Turkey. *Khamsin: Journal of Revolutionary Socialists of the Middle East* 11 (1): 5–47.

Taymaz, E., and E. Voyvoda. 2009. Industrial restructuring and technological capabilities in Turkey. In *Turkey and the Global Economy,* ed. Z. Önişş.

T.C. Cumhurbaşkanlığı Strateji ve Bütçe Başkanlığı (2019) Kamu-Özel İşbirliği Raporu 2018. Ankara: Sektörler ve Kamu Yatırımları Genel Müdürlüğü.

Tecer, M. (1992) "Privatization in Turkey", Cashiers d'etudes sur la Medirranee orientale et le monde turco-iranien (CEMCO), 14:1, 133–145.

Tekfen (2017) Annual Report (can be accessed: https://www.tekfen.com.tr/en/annual -reports-4-26).

Tezel, Y. 1999. Sanayide Devlet Kapitalizminin Ortaya Çıkışı [The Emergence of State Capitalism in Industry]. In *75 Yılda Çarklardan Çhip'lere,* ed. O. Baydar. İstanbul: Tarih Vakfı Yayınları.

The Trade Union of Public Employees in Health and Social Services (2021) 2021 Yılı Sağlık Bakanlığı Bütçesinin Değerlendirilmesi. See https://ses.org.tr/wp-content/ uploads/2020/11/SES-Genel-Merkez-2021-Sağlık-Bakanlığı-Bütçe-Değerlendirme -Raporu-1.pdf (accessed on 8 July 2021).

Therborn, G. (1976) Science, Class and Society, London: Verso.

Tittenbrun, J. (1996) Private Versus Public Enterprises: In Search of the Economic Rationale for Privatization. London: Janus.

TNI. 2004. "Reclaiming Public Water: Participatory Alternatives to Privatization." Amsterdam: TNI Briefing Series.

TOBB (1993) Özelleştirme: Özel İhtisas Komisyonu Raporu, Ankara: TOBB Yayınları.

Transparency International Turkey (2017) Obstacles Against Good Governance: A Case By Case Summary, Energy and Construction Sectors, http://www.seffaflik.org/wp-content/uplo ads/2019/05/Obstacles-Against-Good-Governance.pdf (accessed on 16 September 2021).

Türk, Y. (2011). Türkiye'de Özellestirme Uygulamalarının Analizi, Ankara: DPT.

Türkiye Kömür İşletmeleri Kurumu (2019) Türkiye Kömür İşletmeleri Kurumu: 2018 Faaliyet Raporu. Ankara.

TÜSİAD (1986) Özelleştirme: KİT'lerin Halka Satışında Başarı Koşulları. TÜSIAD.

TÜSİAD (1992) Türkiye'de Özelleştirme Uygulamaları. TÜSİAD.

TÜSİAD. 1995. *Optimal Devlet* [The Optimal State]. http://tusiad.org/tr/tum/item/1798 -optimal-devlet.

TÜSİAD (1998) "Rekabet Hukuku'nda Anlaşma, Uyumlu Eylem ve Kararlar", *TÜSİAD Rekabet Stratejileri Dizisi 4*, no. TÜSİAD-T/98, 12/244.

TÜSİAD (1999) "Beyaz Eşya Yan Sanayiinde Rekabet Stratejileri ve İş Mükemmelliği" (Yayın No. TÜSİAD-T/99, 6-263), *TÜSİAD Rekabet Stratejileri Dizisi 5*, available online: www.tusiad.org.tr.

TÜSİAD (2003) "Türkiye, yabancı sermaye girişi sağlamak için hukuksal ve kurumsal altyapısını tamamlamalıdır", *TÜSİAD Basın Bülteni*, 21 Nisan 2003, available online: www.tusiad.org.tr.

TÜSİAD (2005) "TÜSİAD Yönetim Kurulu Başkanı Ömer Sabancı'nın YASED'in Düzenlediği 'Yabancı Yatırımcıların Gözdesi: Fırsatlar Ülkesi Türkiye' Konulu Konferans Konuşması", *TÜSİAD Konuşmalar*, 9 Kasım 2005, available online: www .tusiad.org.tr.

TÜSİAD (2009) "The Making of a Regional Power", *Private View*, 14 (1), pp. 1–100.

Uğurhan, F. (2018) "Orda Bir Hastane Var Uzakta: Mersin Şehir Hastanesi" in Kayıhan Pala (eds) Türkiye'de Sağlıkta Kamu-Özel Ortaklığı: Şehir Hastaneleri. İstanbul: İletişim.

Veblen, T. (1957) The Theory of the Leisure Class: An Economic Study of Institutions. London: Unwin LTD.

Vickers, J. and Yarrow, G. (1988) Privatization: An Economic Analysis. London: MIT Press.

Wainwright, Hilary. 2012. "Transformative Power: Political Organization in Transition." In L. Panitch, G. Albo and V. Chibber, eds., *Socialist Register 2013: The Question of Strategy*. Pontypool, Wales: Merlin Press.

Wainwright, H. 2013. "Participatory Alternatives to Privatization." Speech given to social movements in Greece (February).

Weiker, W. (1981) The Modernization of Turkey: From Ataturk to the Present Day. London: Holmes and Meier Publishers.

Weizsacker et al. (2005) *Limits to Privatization: How to Avoid too Much of a Good Thing*. London: Earthscan.

Wojewnik-Filipkoswska, A. and Wegrzyn, J. (2019) "Understanding of Public-Private Partnership Stakeholders as a Condition of Sustainable Development", *Sustainability*, 11 (1), pp. 1–16.

Wolcott, P. and Cagiltay, K. (2001) "Telecommunications, Liberalization and the Growth of the Internet in Turkey", *The Information Society*, 17: 1, 133–141.

World Bank (1992) Turkey: Towards an Information-Based Economy. Washington: World Bank (Report No. 10759-TU).

World Bank. 1993. *Turkey: State-Owned Enterprises Sector Review*. Report No. 10014-TU. Washington: World Bank.

World Bank (2015) Sources of Financing for Public-Private Partnership Investments in 2015, can be accessed on https://ppi.worldbank.org/content/dam/PPI/resources/ppi_resources/topic/2015-PPP-Investments-Sources.pdf.

World Bank. 2017. *PPP Reference Guide 3.0*. Washington: World Bank Publications.

World Bank Group (2017) Benchmarking PPP Procurement 2017 in Turkey, can be accessed on https://www.procurementinet.org/wp-content/uploads/2017/02/Turkey.pdf.

World Bank (2019) Private Participation in Infrastructure: 2019 Annual Report, can be accessed on www.worldbank.org/ppp.

World Development Indicators (1980) can be accessed (https://databank.worldbank.org/source/world-development-indicators).

Yalman, G. 2002. The Turkish State and Bourgeoisie in Historical Perspective: A Relativist Paradigm or a Panoply of Hegemonic Strategies? In *The Politics of Permanent Crisis: Class, Ideology and State in Turkey*, eds. N. Balkan and S. Savran. New York: Nova Science Publishers.

Yalman, G. 2009. *Transition to Neoliberalism: The Case of Turkey in the 1980s*. İstanbul: Bilgi University Press.

Yalman, G. (2016) "Crises as Driving Forces of Neoliberal Transformismo: The Contours of the Turkish Political Economy since the 2000s", in Cafruny, Talani and Martin (eds) *The Palgrave Handbook of Critical International Political Economy*. London: Palgrave Macmillan.

Yalman, G. (2019) "Putting the Turkish Financial System into Historical Perspective" in Yalman, Marois and Güngen (eds) *The Political Economy of Financial Transformation in Turkey*. London and New York: Routledge.

Yalman G and Topal A (2017) Labour containment strategies and working class struggles in the neoliberal era: The case of TEKEL workers in Turkey. *Critical Sociology*. Epub ahead of print 22 August 2017.

Yarrow, G. (1989) "Privatization and Economic Performance in Britain", *Rochester Conference Series on Public Policy*, 31: 1, 303–344.

Yeldan, E. (2005) "Assessing the Privatization Experience in Turkey: Implementation, Politics and Performance Results", *Report Submitted to Economic Policy Institute, 1–32*.

Yescombe, E. R. (2007) Public-Private Partnerships: Principles of Policy and Finance. Oxford: Elsevier and BH.

Yücesan-Özdemir, G., and A. Özdemir. 2007. Trade unionism in Turkey. In *Trade Union Revitalisation: Trends and Prospects in 34 Countries*, ed. C. Phelan, 461–75. London: Peter Lang.

Zaifer, A (2018) The acceleration of privatisation: Understanding state, power bloc and capital accu-mulation in Turkey. *Review of Radical Political Economics*. Epub ahead of print 4 July 2018. DOI: 10.1177/0486613417740698.

Zaifer, A. 2020. Variegated Privatisation: Class, Capital Accumulation and State in Turkey's Privatisation Process in the 1980s and 1990s. *Critical Sociology* 46 (1): 141–56.

# Index

www.ingramcontent.com/pod-product-compliance
Lightning Source LLC
Chambersburg PA
CBHW062107040426

42336CB00042B/2528